HOPE IN HARD TIMES

HOPE IN HARD TIMES

Norvelt and the Struggle for Community During the Great Depression

Timothy Kelly | Margaret Power | Michael Cary

THE PENNSYLVANIA STATE UNIVERSITY PRESS
UNIVERSITY PARK, PENNSYLVANIA

Library of Congress
Cataloging-in-Publication Data

Names: Kelly, Timothy, 1960– , author. | Power, Margaret, 1953– , author. | Cary, Michael D., 1950– , author.
Title: Hope in hard times : Norvelt and the struggle for community during the Great Depression / Timothy Kelly, Margaret Power, Michael Cary.
Description: University Park, Pennsylvania : The Pennsylvania State University Press, [2016] | Includes bibliographical references and index.
Identifiers: LCCN 2015050848 | ISBN 9780271074665 (cloth : alk. paper) | ISBN 9780271074672 (pbk. : alk. paper)
Subjects: LCSH: Norvelt (Pa.)—History. | Norvelt (Pa.)—Social conditions—History. | Planned communities—Pennsylvania—Norvelt—History. | New Deal, 1933–1939—Pennsylvania—Norvelt. | Depressions—1929—Pennsylvania—Westmoreland County.
Classification: LCC F159.N88 K45 2016 | DDC 974.8/81—dc23
LC record available at http://lccn.loc.gov/2015050848

Printed in the United States of America
Published by
The Pennsylvania State University Press,
University Park, PA 16802-1003
The Pennsylvania State University Press is a member of the Association of American University Presses.

It is the policy of The Pennsylvania State University Press to use acid-free paper. Publications on uncoated stock satisfy the minimum requirements of American National Standard for Information Sciences—Permanence of Paper for Printed Library Material, ANSI Z39.48–1992.

Frontispiece: Lois and Jean Schlingman, painting their house, ca. 1942. Photo: Lois Weyandt personal collection.

CONTENTS

ILLUSTRATIONS

Figures

Maps

Tables

ACKNOWLEDGMENTS

Many people assisted in the research and writing of this book, and we want to recognize many of them individually.

Many former and current Norvelt residents shared their memories of living in the New Deal community, and we list them in the bibliography. They provided vital insights into the lived experience of the homesteads, and were unfailingly generous with their time and memories. We would especially like to thank Earl Saville and Lois Weyandt for their unfailing generosity, for sharing their memories of life in Norvelt, and for opening their archives to us. We are very sorry that Earl died before this book was published.

The librarians at our home institutions offered guidance and support throughout the project that proved vital to our progress. At Saint Vincent College, Br. David Kelly, OSB, Denise Hegemann, and the rest of the library staff guided digital searches, lent materials from the stacks, and in many other ways helped with our research. Marlo Verrilla's interlibrary loan wizardry made resources available almost instantly. At Seton Hill, Eileen Moffa worked to acquire interlibrary loan items quickly and cheerfully.

The staff of the National Archives and Record Administration in College Park, Maryland, was efficient and professional, and allowed us to gather critical documents and architectural drawings. In Chicago, at the Great Lakes Region branch of the National Archives, Glenn Longacre proved to be especially supportive of our research. Donald Davis at the archives of the American Friends Service Committee in Philadelphia guided us expertly through materials in their possession. Harrison Wick, archivist at the Indiana University of Pennsylvania Archives, graciously remained after normal hours to locate materials and provide digital image copies, and the friendly staff at the University of Pittsburgh Library were also very helpful. Elaine de Frank at the Coal and Coke Heritage Center, Penn State University Fayette, generously opened the center's rich archives on mining, miners, and the patch communities to us. We are especially grateful for the numerous interviews with miners and their families she made available to us.

At Saint Vincent College, we want to acknowledge the crucial role that Fr. Rene Kollar, OSB, played in supporting the work at every stage. He opened the monastery guest house for Margaret Power's visits to the region to work on research and writing and underwrote Tim Kelly's expenses for critical research trips to Washington, D.C., and Philadelphia, as well as for conference presentations to share the work at important stages. The Faculty Development Committee awarded support on two separate occasions that expedited research and writing.

Saint Vincent College history majors offered key assistance to us at various stages in the project. Regina Brinza provided critical research assistance in the summer of 2011 in various archives and digital media. She unearthed important documents and accompanied two of the authors on a tour of Arthurdale, West Virginia. Stevie Kiesel, Bethanne Dishler, Zara Wallace, Johnny Sigg, and Casey Wertz worked diligently to transcribe oral interviews from recordings that we provided to them.

We want to offer special thanks to the editors at Penn State University Press. Patrick Alexander showed early interest in the book and offered a contract that provided a welcome boost. Kendra Boileau participated in a very productive meeting in January 2012 that helped to set the direction for the next few years of work. Most important to this project was Kathryn Yahner's consistent support and extraordinary patience as we worked through the early drafting process, many revisions, and final editing.

This work was collaborative throughout, and we worked through all of the rewarding and stress-inducing experiences that inevitably arise among those working together on a project to produce such a volume. We know that our collaboration produced a stronger and richer work than any one of us could have produced alone. But the project also makes demands on those not directly engaged in the research and writing, such as family and friends. It is important to note the sacrifices that they have made throughout this project's long germination.

Tim: I would like to acknowledge the material and emotional support that my children, Caitlin, Erin, and Eamon, have offered consistently. Though they did not participate directly in the book's production, they endured long discussions of its contents, and their patience and encouragement were vital throughout. They have come into adulthood during these Norvelt years. Kim has extended even greater patience and support, enduring endless discussions of details too minute even to make it into this volume. She has been gracious enough to remain interested in the project through many years, and has allowed it to roam around in our lives for far longer than either of us imagined when it began.

Margaret: I would like to thank Arthur, Joanne (deceased), John, Patrick, and Sheri Boyle for the hours of conversation about Westmoreland County and the unstinting hospitality they offered me as I conducted research for this book. I would also like to thank Joan Chandler for her suggestion for the book title. I am also grateful to David Montgomery, who shared his deep knowledge and insights into the U.S. labor movement with me. Had it not been for my mother, Flora Margaret Power, I would not have participated in this project. After falling and breaking her hip, she was hospitalized in Westmoreland County Hospital. The other patient in the room, with whom I briefly spoke, was from Norvelt. My conversation with her and the certainty that I would be making frequent visits to the area to take care of my mom, led me to undertake this project. I am very sorry my mom is not alive to witness the publication of the book; she would have been so thrilled by it! Melinda, my sister, was a great source of support during the writing. She kindly accompanied me to Saint Vincent College when I conducted research for the book and when Tim, Mike, and I met to chart it out.

Michael: I am grateful to my family for their support, including Erin, who read chapter drafts and offered critical commentary, and especially Eloise, for her assistance and forbearance during the hours and years when this project demanded much attention.

Introduction

By the spring of 1933, Anthony Wolk had been out of work for four straight years. For at least ten years before that, he had burrowed into the earth in various coal mines throughout Westmoreland County, in southwestern Pennsylvania, to dig out the carbon that fueled the United States' industrial revolution. Everyone and every business needed coal, from the largest steel mills that lined the Monongahela, Allegheny, and Ohio Rivers near Pittsburgh to the smallest row houses that housed many of the families who sent their fathers and sons into those mills. So too did the railroads, which carried the steel used to build the taller and taller skyscrapers that created the distinctive skylines that characterized every U.S. city. Once completed, those buildings relied on coal to produce the steam to stay warm in the winter. Coal mining in Westmoreland County ought to have been the most secure occupation in the United States. The Connellsville coal seams that ran through the county were the richest known energy deposits in the world and created fabulous wealth for a handful of the nation's shrewdest and most ruthless businessmen.

But Anthony Wolk did not get rich mining coal. He never even got comfortable enough to provide the kinds of things to which middle-class American families had grown accustomed: indoor plumbing, hot water on demand, electricity to run a host of new appliances aimed at easing domestic work. In the flush times, he could provide food for his family, clothes for the growing children, and a roof over their heads. But these were not flush times, not even close. The bottom fell out of the coal industry, and the Wolks fell through the abyss. Much of the rest of the nation had endured for the past four years what coal miners had lived for more than a decade—intermittent work, decreased wages, lost savings, hungry children. More than half a million American coal miners lost their jobs, and economists expected that three hundred thousand of them would never work again. Wolk had no good reason to believe that he would be one of the "lucky" two hundred thousand who might get back into the mines, even part time. And yet he had no good alternative. Where would an ex-miner find work in the United States during the Depression? How would he feed his family? Where might they live? So when David Day, a Quaker who worked with the federal Division of Subsistence Homesteads, came to Greensburg, Pennsylvania, with plans to build a new community in

Westmoreland County with beautiful houses, acres of land, a factory for jobs—all for the unemployed—Wolk jumped at the chance to sign on.

So too did Sara Kelley and her husband, John. Sara was a joiner who valued family and community and participated enthusiastically in social events. John had labored in the H. C. Frick Company coal mines for twenty years, and then for five more with the Jamison Coal and Coke Company. But the mines closed and he found himself out of work. Sara's dream of owning her own home seemed gone forever when a neighbor told her that the government was building new homes near Mount Pleasant. John went to the Greensburg courthouse to sign up for the program, and the family ended up in a six-room house on 2.9 acres in the new community, known as Westmoreland Homesteads. John started working for the Works Progress Administration, and Sara immersed herself in the life of the community.[1]

Westmoreland Homesteads offered Sara many opportunities to delve into community life. She became the first female member of the Activities Council, then its treasurer. Soon after, she started working in the Westmoreland Homesteads pants factory, where she rose from the sewing machines to an inspector's position. She joined the women in the cannery in 1934, when the houses were first under construction, and filled jars with the fruits and vegetables grown in the community's gardens. Each family earned canned fruits and vegetables commensurate with the time they labored in the garden and cannery. Sara worked a lot, so she remembers getting ninety-two cans of corn delivered to her home, along with beets, beans, tomatoes, and even chickens. Her neighbors recall that she "could be counted upon to volunteer for committees, to press for action, to unite neighbors, to encourage cooperation whether it was for promoting art classes, drama groups, baby clinics, the Mothers' Club or just community get togethers."[2] In fact, Sara emerged in the pages of the community newsletter as she organized a Well Baby Clinic, chaired the PTA Program Committee, was a pioneering member of the Health Committee, and helped form the Westmoreland Enterprises organization to try to entice a factory to the community. She also hosted Eleanor Roosevelt on the first lady's only visit to the community that would later bear her name.

Anthony Wolk and Sara Kelley were not alone. Nearly two thousand couples applied for one of the two hundred and fifty homes that made up Westmoreland Homes, soon to be renamed Norvelt, after EleaNOR RooseVELT.[3] Most people who have not lived in or near Norvelt have probably never heard of it. But it was one of the United States' most innovative and humane responses to the suffering that suffused the nation. A New Deal community that has not only survived but thrived since its founding in 1934, it offers tangible proof that federal intervention, when combined with a receptive, eager, and hardworking population, can succeed. Seen in this light, this study of Norvelt provides more than just a new historical perspective on the New Deal and the Roosevelt administration. It also suggests a possible model for subsequent economic crises.

Norvelt's story is compelling on a number of levels, and merits attention for anyone interested in the human struggle against forces too large to surmount individually. It is the story of ordinary people joining in a common effort to survive, and even thrive, in the face of the worst economic depression in our nation's history. What the federal government made possible for the people of Norvelt to accomplish eight decades ago has attained mythic status among those few who know its history—mostly the homesteader generation and their descendants.[4] It deserves a wider audience.

It deserves a wider audience in part because it is instructive for us today. We live in a time when Americans have lost faith in government's capacity to work positively in people's lives—to improve their health, raise their standard of living, allow them to pursue happiness more abundantly. Norvelt reminds us that an ambitious and innovative federal government once aspired to lofty goals and largely succeeded.

The people of Norvelt and the federal government succeeded not only in creating a community in which members became more physically comfortable than before—warmer in winter, well fed, freer from unsanitary conditions—but also more civically engaged, more robustly ambitious. Not only did homesteaders not lose their ambition for productive work when their homes became more comfortable, their children more thoroughly educated, their physical well-being secured, but they went on to extraordinary accomplishments. They share readily with visitors the number of college graduates, doctors, and lawyers that their community has produced. Their experience puts the lie to the notion, long prevalent among some in U.S. culture, that this kind of security erodes character, demeans human productivity, and weakens society.

Norvelt's experiences in the 1930s offer a clear insight into the contours of U.S. working-class and middle-class lives as one community began the powerful transition from the former to the latter. Its members all hailed from what Jacob Riis a generation earlier called the "other half." The men toiled hard in the mines and factories of western Pennsylvania to provide just enough for their families to endure. The women labored long hours bearing and raising children, attending to boarders, trying to create a home that insulated their families from deprivation's gnawing reminders of life's harsh realities—hunger, cold, illness, anxiety, and ever-present messages that their lives mattered little to the economic and political powers that shaped U.S. society. The children went without—without enough food, health care, clothing, school, opportunity. Their lives in coal-patch communities across southwestern Pennsylvania offer a good insight into working-class life in the early twentieth-century United States.

Once they arrived in Norvelt, homesteaders seized the opportunity to create the kind of middle-class lives that had seemed so elusive in the years before. Their new expectations, activities, and practices help us to understand what it meant to be middle class in the United States. One thing that middle-class life entailed was membership in local communities that worked to build and sustain economic

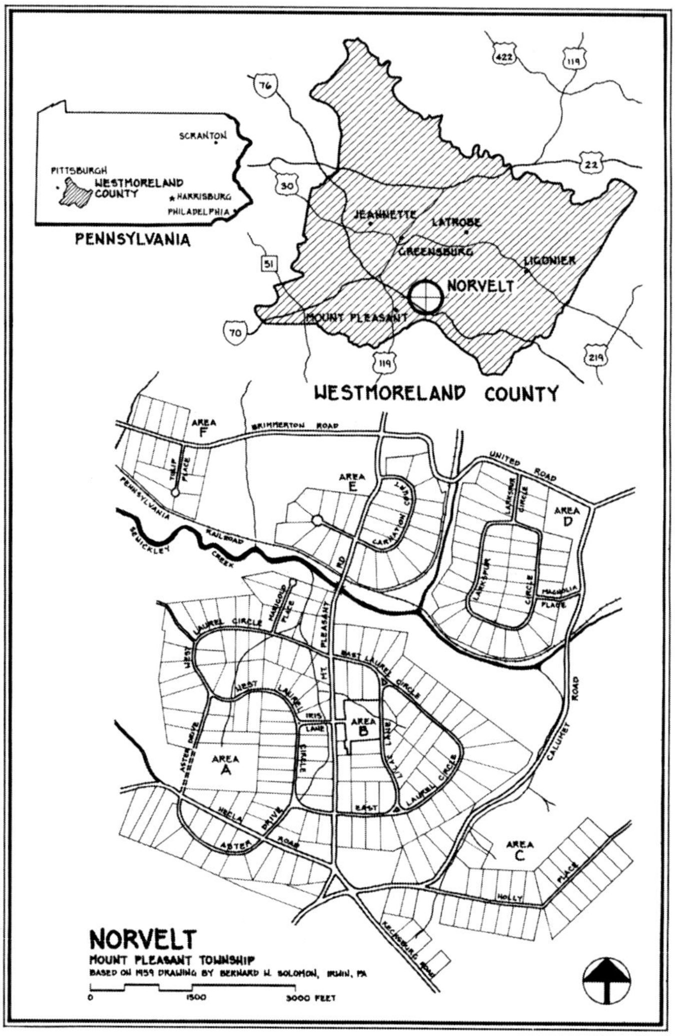

MAP 1
Norvelt, Westmoreland County, and Pennsylvania. Norvelt is located in Westmoreland County, in the heart of the coal-mining region just east of Pittsburgh, Pennsylvania. Mulrooney, *A Legacy of Coal.*

and social well-being. Much of Norvelt's story inevitably involves homesteaders' efforts, mostly successful, to join together to lift each other up physically, culturally, socially, and economically.

Community creation necessarily requires people to establish bonds between each other to create networks of social, physical, and cultural support. These bonds allow members to make special claims upon each other that those outside the networks cannot tap. Homesteaders worked hard at this. They created clubs and societies and joined together to can vegetables and fruits, to run a cooperative store, to establish a volunteer fire department. They worked self-consciously at cooperation across ethnic and religious divides that split other towns and cities.

But building community almost inevitably entails creating boundaries as well, erecting walls between members and nonmembers. Sometimes communities do this to acknowledge the limits of their reach, such as how far a volunteer fire department will travel to fight a fire, or from how far away children may come to school. Limited resources dictate that local communities make reasonable assessments about whom to include in their ethic of care and whom to exclude. But at other times, communities set boundaries to guard against threats, real and imagined. In Norvelt, one of the perceived dangers was racial integration. Like many white Americans, homesteaders saw their own security and well-being as dependent on the exclusion of African Americans from their midst. White homesteaders acted from the outset to prevent blacks from moving into Norvelt, and only one black family ever lived in the community. Norvelt residents never conquered this prejudice, and in this discrimination they have embodied one white, middle-class characteristic that still haunts their story and our nation today.

Norvelt also helps us to understand middle-class life through its domestic architecture—the shape, size, and uses of its homes. This much was clear from the outset, when Roosevelt administration officials debated whether to include indoor plumbing and central heat in homes for working-class families. Though these had become standard elements in middle-class homes, some in the administration, by one account including even Franklin Roosevelt himself, saw them as too generous for mining families. Providing homes with these amenities pushed homesteaders firmly across the class divide into the middle class.

Architect Paul Bartholomew drew up Cape Cod–style houses for the community. The style had become very popular across the country in the 1920s in emerging middle-class suburban communities. He included separate bedrooms for parents and children, boys and girls, and afforded levels of privacy not attainable in coal-patch communities. In doing so, he elevated the tension between individualism and community that poverty necessarily erased for many working-class families. Privacy, once a luxury, became a reasonable expectation.

This tension played out on a different level in the gardens as well. The design called for individual family gardens rather than a common, cooperative produce farm. Though homesteaders joined together to learn to preserve their gardens' output, sometimes even participating in group canning, and families often shared their gardens' produce with neighbors, each family minded its own garden. The cooperative agriculture that did exist—a dairy farm, hog operation, and poultry house—depended on hired labor rather than resident volunteer efforts. The gardens joined individual families in common food-production efforts, but divided each family from its neighbors.

Norvelt provides a clear window through which to view the emerging twentieth-century U.S. middle class. Elevated through the conscious efforts of Americans using their federal government to advance the public welfare, housed in modest and attractive homes equipped with modern amenities, bound to each other through commitments of mutual care balanced against the ideals of individualism, trapped in racial prejudices that compromised their commitment to fairness and equality, the homesteaders in Norvelt represented the essential characteristics of twentieth-century U.S. middle-class life.

But Norvelt's early history is a quintessentially Depression story, and as such fits into the United States' broader narrative of both suffering and redemption at that peculiar moment in the nation's history. Americans have told that narrative differently across time, and a brief review of that changing story helps to situate our contribution.

The Great Depression and the New Deal in Historical Perspective

Americans have debated the New Deal since its inception, and historians too have been divided. Once enough time had passed to gain perspective, historians presented the New Deal as a positive and dramatic response to the Great Depression. Two decades after the New Deal's peak, Arthur Schlesinger Jr. traced the crisis and response in great detail in his three-volume work on the age of Roosevelt. He concluded his work by contrasting Roosevelt's pragmatic experimentation to end the Depression and preserve democracy and Europe's slide into ideologically driven totalitarianism. Schlesinger saw the New Deal as a successful reformation of society dedicated to responsive, pragmatic government.[5] William Leuchtenburg's 1963 *Franklin D. Roosevelt and the New Deal* extended Schlesinger's basic interpretation in a more manageable single volume that brought the story up to the outbreak of World War II. He argued that the New Deal did not pull the United States all of the way out of the Great Depression, but did provide needed economic stimulation in the early 1930s to offer significant recovery. Perhaps more importantly, it for the first time committed the federal government to the welfare of its citizens and "marked a greater upheaval in American institutions than in any similar period in our history, save perhaps for the impact on the South of the Civil War." He referred to the period as the "Roosevelt Revolution."[6]

New Left historians challenged that notion in a number of interpretive articles published in the 1960s and 1970s, such as Barton J. Bernstein's "The New Deal: The Conservative Achievements of Liberal Reform." These authors argued for the New Deal's essentially conservative achievements. At a moment when the Depression profoundly challenged capitalism's viability and therefore placed progress toward economic democracy and racial equality within reach, the New Deal made it possible for old patterns to persevere. It did not so much constitute a revolution as avert one. A number of state and local histories confirmed that little that justly could be labeled revolutionary occurred. Economic elites still dominated, New Deal programs excluded or segregated African Americans, capitalism survived.[7]

David Kennedy's 1999 prize-winning volume on the period in the Oxford History of the United States returned to the Leuchtenburg story, in both broad strokes and many of its particulars.[8] He saw the Great Depression as a crisis that shook "the American way of life to its foundations." The New Deal did not fully resolve this crisis, in Kennedy's narrative. However beneficial it may have been for individual families or unemployed workers who gained a source of income, and however long lasting the commitment of the federal government to citizens' welfare, it took the mammoth scale of federal spending on World War II to bring the nation fully out of the Great Depression. Historians have generally adopted this perspective.[9]

The conservative revolution that swept the U.S. political and economic realms beginning in the 1980s eventually found its way into historical interpretations of the Great Depression and the New Deal. By the turn of the twenty-first century, the strong belief in market infallibility spurred new interpretations that turned the received orthodoxy on its head. According to these interpretations, the New Deal did not ameliorate or help to turn back the Great Depression, but rather extended and deepened it. These presentations did not typically come from academic historians, who still upheld the Leuchtenburg-Kennedy consensus, but from conservative think tanks such as the Council on Foreign Relations, the Cato Institute, and the Liberty Fund, and even from economists in academia, for whom market adulation had become orthodoxy.[10]

The economic collapse of 2008 came just as this new interpretation was gaining traction, and undermined the power of these works to challenge the Leuchtenburg-Kennedy narrative in favor of one that highlighted the dangers of government regulation and intervention. Few could miss the irony of the free market's greatest champions clamoring for the federal government to bail out the banks and brokerage houses—those very financial institutions that had prospered under "burdensome" New Deal–era regulations and then foundered when set free. Academic economists rediscovered John Maynard Keynes and saw again the virtues of an aggressive macroeconomic policy aimed at offsetting the collapse the unfettered free market had brought about.[11]

Reaction against this new interpretation often stressed the economic virtues of New Deal building projects. Felix Rohatyn celebrated the work of the Rural Electrification Administration to extend electricity to American farmers, and the Reconstruction Finance Corporation's work to finance relief and building projects throughout the nation.[12] Michael Hiltzik explored the construction of the Hoover Dam approvingly and determined that the largest federal building project to date helped to transform the United States "from a society that glorified individualism into one that cherished shared enterprise and communal social support."[13] His later "modern" history of the New Deal extended that interpretation to Roosevelt's broad program of projects.[14] John Stuart admired the dramatic improvement in South Florida's landscape that New Deal building projects accomplished.[15] Nick Taylor extolled the Works Progress Administration not only for the jobs that it provided to those out of work, but also for building roads, bridges, and schools.[16] Robert D. Leighninger Jr. surveyed the vast building projects constructed under the auspices of a dozen New Deal programs and concluded that any assessment of the New Deal must include recognition of these projects and the activities that they made possible for travelers, communities, and families.[17] Jason Scott Smith asked if the

New Deal construction projects were "successful in laying the structural foundations for postwar economic development and prosperity," and he answered with a resounding yes.[18] Alexander J. Field asked essentially the same question about federal spending on infrastructure projects throughout the 1930s and determined that the post–World War II prosperity rested significantly on this expansion of transportation capacity.[19] Michael Lind saw government-sponsored infrastructure projects as central to U.S. prosperity and growth not only in the New Deal era, but throughout U.S. history.[20]

Most New Deal building projects involved public works structures that aimed to serve a broad public good. The Hoover Dam generated hydroelectric power that served residents in Arizona, California, Nevada, and New Mexico. The Rural Electrification Administration brought electricity to millions of farmers and their families. The trails that the Civilian Conservation Corps created and maintained in American forests served all who visited. The roads, bridges, tunnels, and highways that the federal government built benefited all commercial and recreational travelers. Thousands of people flocked to events in San Francisco's Cow Palace, hundreds of thousands of fans packed Miami's Orange Bowl over the years, and millions of people took off from and landed at LaGuardia Airport in the decades since the New Deal built it.

One project of considerably smaller scale once garnered significant national scrutiny and played a central role in defining the New Deal's reach and direction. This federal program sought to build residential communities for working-class and farming families that strained under the weight of unemployment, hunger, and a range of other deprivations. It combined modest housing with small-scale subsistence farming in an effort to provide physical relief, basic human dignity, and an alternative to the competitive culture that seemed content to allow, or perhaps even force, these families to suffer so greatly. This project, called the subsistence homestead program, eventually established thirty-four communities in eighteen different states, captured the sustained attention of the nation's first lady, and therefore remained on the mind of the president himself for the length of the New Deal.

Historians have been divided over the program's success. Paul Conkin's comprehensive review of New Deal community-building programs, including the subsistence homesteads and greenbelt communities, appeared in 1959 and remains the definitive work on the subject. He noted that the program's broad social and cultural aim of reorienting values away from competition and toward cooperation largely failed. Too many in Congress opposed this aim and so subverted key elements of the program at critical moments, and residents themselves never embraced this new way of approaching their lives—as opposed to the security and stability that the communities offered, which residents did embrace enthusiastically. Nonetheless, in the end, Conkin noted, "for each dollar expended, the communities represented more tangible, enduring achievements than most other relief expenditures."[21] In 1946, C. Harvey Grattan saw the communities as good models for semirural housing developments, but found that "[t]he government's experiments with 'subsistence farms' show quite clearly that except in rare and exceptional instances that prove little (like the Granger Homesteads in Iowa, sponsored and fostered by Monsignor Ligutti of the National Catholic Rural Life Conference) the effect on the incomes and security of the participants was decidedly trivial."[22] T. Swann Harding studied the communities a decade after they started and noted that residents resented any sense that they benefited from government largesse, and they abandoned the farming aspects of the communities when war-preparation work provided enough income to buy food at stores. But he also concluded that "very valuable scientific experiments have been performed and much has been learned that will enable us to go ahead more wisely in the postwar world if we but heed. Moreover, some of the homesteads were very successful."[23]

Historians and contemporary commentators interested in the subsistence homestead projects have focused disproportionately on Arthurdale, West Virginia, the first homestead undertaken and Eleanor Roosevelt's clear favorite. They tend to use Arthurdale as representative of the entire program and reach conclusions about Arthurdale that they project broadly onto the rest of the communities and the program as a whole. Most of them conclude that Arthurdale was a failure because it drained resources far out of proportion to the families that it benefited directly. William Leuchtenburg, for example, wrote, "Arthurdale proved an expensive failure." Further, he concluded, "Ostensibly experimental and utopian, the subsistence homesteads movement soon seemed rather a quest for an ark of refuge, an indication of the despair of the early thirties." Such historians find the program to have been economically inefficient and ideologically ineffective. They tend to accentuate the problems, exaggerate the costs, and ignore the successes, especially the long-term successes, in Arthurdale, and they generally neglect the other projects.[24]

Architectural historian Diane Ghirardo's New Left critique found the program wanting for very different reasons. She drew parallels between the New Deal communities and similar projects undertaken in Fascist Italy around the same time. Both shared a high degree of government control and supervision of the settlers, manifested through a careful selection process and disciplined by the threat of eviction. Community housing efforts in both Italy and the United States avoided land expropriation or intervention in the private housing industry, built far fewer low-cost housing units than were needed, reinforced traditional social patterns with respect to gender and race relations, and overall sought to preserve the position of capitalism.[25]

A growing literature presents a more nuanced and, in many cases, favorable assessment of the program. As historians turned their attention to specific homestead communities, they found much to admire. Robert Carriker examined subsistence homestead programs in the far west states of Arizona, California, and Washington and concluded that "the tendency to blanket the [Division of Subsistence Homesteads] and its projects with condemnation fails to appreciate the good that came from some of the individual homestead communities, particularly those of the Far West."[26] Timothy J. Garvey examined homesteads in Duluth, Minnesota, and determined that they constituted a "successful experiment in community housing."[27] Evelyn Hargis concluded largely the same thing about the Cumberland Homesteads community near Crossville, Tennessee. She wrote,

> This community of subsistence farms as envisioned by the Roosevelt administration, is often called the most successful of all those established under the original plan. Jobs were generated, skilled workers emerged, productive farms and pastures were created, families built and had homes during those hard years. Ties of neighborly love and kinship were forged that have lasted to the present time. The homesteaders dealt with a hard life, a shortage of conveniences, and little money with an enthusiasm and willingness because they knew they were building a community where they would live, work, and raise their families.[28]

Blanche Wiesen Cook reached similarly positive conclusions about Arthurdale itself, the homestead community most often identified as representative of the failed program. She observed, "For sixty years, pundits and politicians judged Arthurdale a failure. But the homesteaders' descendants are still living on the land; their children and their children's children still enjoy the bright pleasant homes that have withstood all those bitter mountain winters, with temperatures twenty, thirty, forty degrees below zero, in warmth and comfort. For the people, Arthurdale was marvelous, and they called it 'utopia.'" Moreover, Cook wrote, "From the point of view of the people of the community, everything about it worked: The school and sense of community endured, the residents flourished, and they continued to believe their own experiences might be, should be, put to future use."[29]

Our study of Norvelt, Pennsylvania, has led us to similarly positive conclusions. There seems little room to debate whether the homesteaders' lives improved in every measureable way. They lived far more comfortably than they did before coming to Norvelt. Moreover, they exercised more autonomy and agency in this centrally planned government-supported community than they had in the company-owned coal-patch towns that dotted the region. They exhibited a loyalty to the community that those in nearby Hunker, Mammoth, and Kecksburg never manifested. We reach these conclusions by tracing their stories and analyzing their lives across eight chapters.

Chapter 1 explores the background of many of the original Norvelt homesteaders. It focuses on the mines and coke ovens where many of the men worked and the patch (mining and coke) communities where they and their families lived before they moved to Westmoreland Homesteads. Most of the miners and their families were recent Catholic immigrants from eastern and southern Europe, people whom mine and coke owners—and much of U.S. society—categorized as racialized others. Forced to work for low pay in difficult conditions and to live in isolated and impoverished patches, they looked to each other, their churches, and the United Mine Workers for support and community. This chapter explores the conditions in which they lived and their efforts, largely unsuccessful in Westmoreland County, to leverage better lives in persistently difficult circumstances.

Chapter 2 addresses the developments that made working-class lives even more difficult in the twentieth century's third and fourth decades. The Great Depression, which hit the United States so powerfully as the 1920s came to a close, reached Pennsylvania mining families even earlier. The end of World War I also brought an end to flush times for the coal industry, and mining families faced hard times throughout most of the same decade in which much of the rest of the nation was "roaring." The chapter addresses the broad economic depression that plagued the United States overall, and then narrows its focus to the specific struggles that southwestern Pennsylvanians faced.

Chapter 3 explores the response to the economic crisis, as first Herbert Hoover and then Franklin Roosevelt sought to devise ways to weather and then reverse the Great Depression. It examines key characteristics of Roosevelt's New Deal manifested in the subsistence homestead program that created Norvelt. This chapter introduces the ideological foundations for the program and key policy makers and administrators who made it a reality: Joseph Bankhead, M. L. Wilson, Clarence Pickett, and Eleanor Roosevelt.

Chapter 4 tells the story of Norvelt itself. Norvelt began as Westmoreland Homesteads, one of four subsistence homestead communities administered for the federal government by the Quakers. This chapter traces its origins as a federal New Deal program in 1934 and explores the economic programs and social organizations the community developed to organize and sustain itself. It follows the residents' struggles and successes, and the tensions that emerged among the residents between the cooperative ideal and pulls of individualism.

Chapter 5 addresses the challenges that Norvelt faced from without and within, as the local newspapers' ideological opposition and persistent economic hardship generated opposition to community initiatives. Increasing federal concerns about efficiency constrained opportunities, while a local group of residents arose to demand more federal support. The opposition cost some community managers their positions, and the steady drumbeat of criticism made the community's difficult undertaking more treacherous still. But the homestead families persisted throughout.

Chapter 6 continues the story of Norvelt. The chapter begins with a description of Eleanor Roosevelt's 1937 visit to the community. It then explores the establishment of the pants factory and the labor disputes that ensued. Next, it discusses how the garden project evoked both the cooperative ethos and the tendency to individualism. The chapter ends with the sale of the houses to residents following World War II and Norvelt's eventual transformation into a successful middle-class community.

Chapter 7 follows the story of Norvelt with a close examination of its homes, the community's most prominent and frequently noted physical characteristic. The homes included not only the houses, but also grape arbors, garages, and chicken coops. This chapter examines the ways that homesteaders shaped their experiences within the constraints that the homes imposed. It explores the tension between community and individualism embodied in Norvelt's architecture, a tension that homesteaders did not resolve fully by the time the federal government sold the homes to their residents in 1946.

Chapter 8 examines how Norvelt has evolved in the last seventy years and the political changes that have occurred in it since it began. It explores why Norvelt, a solidly Democratic New Deal community in the 1930s and 1940s, became a Republican stronghold by the second decade of the twenty-first century. To answer this question, it discusses how people in Norvelt understand and use their past to explain their own successes and to distance themselves from the poor of today. It also considers how ideas about race have affected this white community's sense of itself, its political affiliations, and its notion of who is and who is not entitled to government support.

The book ends with a short conclusion.

A Brief Commentary on Sources

One of the authors' strongest regrets is that we started this project after the last of the original adult homesteaders had died. As a result, we were not able to speak with them about their lives before they moved to Westmoreland Homesteads or during the many decades they lived in what became Norvelt. However, we have had the pleasure of meeting and talking with the children of the homesteaders and their grandchildren, many of whom still inhabit Norvelt. They have been among our best and most informative sources into their past and the history of Norvelt.

Norvelters exhibit understandable pride in their community today and grateful recognition of the hard work that their parents and grandparents expended to build it. When asked to talk about the past, the generation of Norvelters who were children in the 1930s and 1940s joyfully shared their memories of what sounds like an idyllic childhood growing up in the New Deal community. A sharp contrast emerges between life in the patch communities, with all the deprivations and indignities that it entailed, and conditions in Westmoreland Homesteads. This contrast comes out strongly in the stories their parents told them and, in some cases, their own remembrances of their earliest years. What stands out in all the stories is the important role that family and community played in shaping the contours of people's lives and ameliorating the abysmal conditions in which the miners and their families subsisted.

Our interviews with Norvelters offered us important insights into what life was like in Norvelt from the 1930s through the present. Given the lack of memoirs, letters, or diaries from the period, our conversations with residents of Norvelt have deepened our understanding of how individual residents experienced and remembered what growing up in Norvelt was like.[30]

Several themes emerged from our conversations with the people of Norvelt. The common element that runs through all the interviews is how much they love Norvelt and are grateful to be associated with it. The people we interviewed were thrilled to talk about their community and its past and present because it embodies what they consider to be a model community, the most successful New Deal community.

Many Norvelters, particularly those who came from the patch (mining) communities, contrasted their parents or grandparents' lives in Norvelt with their previous conditions. They spoke about how tough their lives or those of their families had been prior to moving to Westmoreland Homesteads. They routinely expressed gratitude to the Roosevelt administration, and most particularly to Eleanor Roosevelt, for offering them not just a home, but also the opportunity to leave behind the misery in which they had been living and join a thriving community. One other value that many interviewees stressed was the work ethic.[31] The community succeeded because everyone in it worked. Men, and some women, had jobs; children had chores; and everyone had and fulfilled their responsibilities to their families and to the community.

People's memories of social relations reflected a similar idealization of the past. Most people recall growing up in Norvelt, their family life, their time at school, the various activities they engaged in, the groups they belonged to, and their friendships as harmonious. By and large, interviewees were either reluctant to share or no longer remembered the conflicts and discord that inevitably plague most, if not all, communities.

Many of the people we interviewed discussed events and situations that had occurred more than sixty or seventy years ago. They lived in Norvelt as young children, during the first two critical decades of its existence (the 1930s and '40s). The interviews, like all interviews, necessarily reflect an individual's memory of the past, not an objective snapshot of it. While we have every reason to believe people's stories that growing up in Norvelt was wonderful, we also recognize that the interviewees shared "the pervasive American tendency to romanticize the child and childhood." They remember the past, their own and that of others, through their present. In other words, they understood their past through "adult, learned categories."[32] By emphasizing the happiness of their youth, they also affirm who they are in the present, honor the memory of their parents, and valorize the community of which they are such proud members.

Although each person we spoke to had his or her own individual memories, we also noticed that many people shared what we term a collective memory and what historian David Thelan refers to as "social memory." Thelan argues, "People develop a shared identity by identifying, exploring, and agreeing on memories."[33] Many of the people we interviewed have lived practically their entire lives in or close to Norvelt. One person is the fourth generation of his family to reside in what is a very small community. The fact that they have lived in close proximity to each other in a geographically compact and demographically homogenous area argues for the intermingling of people's memories and the development of shared recollections of the community's past. Norvelters' highly positive view of Norvelt reflects each person's individual experiences and thoughts as well as the community's perspective on itself as a whole.

The overwhelmingly positive descriptions of life in Norvelt in the 1930s and '40s obscure the fact that there were, inevitably, conflicts. When prodded, several of the interviewees remembered that one's religion, either Protestant or Catholic, represented a key marker of difference among the inhabitants. Catholic and Protestant parents discouraged their girls and boys from dating each other. As Carol Davis recalled, "I was never allowed to date any Catholic boys, and my Catholic girlfriends were not allowed to date Protestant boys." However, she added,

> there was never any problem in Norvelt about any families getting along. The people that lived across the street from us were Catholic; they spoke Hungarian in their home. They're like my second family. We were back and forth constantly. We just weren't allowed to date. They just didn't want us marrying into another religion, I think because the Catholics were so adamant that if you married you had to convert. [So] the Protestants just sort of said, the heck with that then, if we aren't good enough then you aren't good enough for us. It was more of a reaction.[34]

Racial differences and the discrimination that ensued were more contentious than religion and, in general, denied. As we will see in chapter 5, the board at Westmoreland Homesteads voted to reject any black families who applied to obtain a home. Nevertheless, Helen White, the mother of the White family, which was black, persisted in her effort to obtain admission to Norvelt. She succeeded in winning the intervention of the Roosevelt administration on her behalf, and the White family moved in.

In addition to the interviews, one particularly valuable source was the community newspaper, the *Homestead Informer*, which the administration and the people of Norvelt published from 1935 to 1937.[35] It offers a window onto the activities, interests, and thinking of members of the Norvelt community. It also shows a community that increased in self-confidence as members of Norvelt, especially women, took over the reporting and writing of the publication.

The U.S. censuses allowed us to trace the racial composition of Norvelt from 1940 to 2010. Until 2010 most of the censuses did not list Norvelt as an independent entity. Instead, they combined it with Calumet, the small former mining community that borders Norvelt. As a result, we could not establish the precise population of Norvelt. However, since both communities were practically 100 percent white from the 1940s to 2010, we could determine the racial composition of Norvelt.

A specific problem emerged with the 1940 census. In 2012, the Census Bureau released copies of the original population schedules that provide detailed information about the populations of cities, towns, and local communities broken down into enumeration districts (EDs).[36] The population schedules list the names, origins, occupations, genders, and ages, along with other information, of all the inhabitants of each ED. The wealth of information contained in the EDs helped us to develop a clearer profile of Norvelt in 1940. However, for reasons that remain unclear, the White family, the only black family in Norvelt, is listed as racially white.

According to Rebecca Kraus, a historian who works at the U.S. Census Bureau, "many people are finding that African Americans were missed in the 1940 Census." She adds, "you've discovered one reason why—enumerator [the person recording the data] error!"[37] The White family was the only black family to live in Norvelt. Once members of the family moved away or died, Norvelt became and remains a white community.

We invite you to read and learn about the unique and heretofore largely unknown community of Norvelt. We believe that the story of Norvelt broadens our understanding of a variety of issues, ranging from Eleanor Roosevelt's positions and advocacy, the New Deal, and the Roosevelt administration's involvement in the subsistence homesteads program to how one group of people in southwestern Pennsylvania came together to build and sustain a community and hope in a time of crisis and despair. The story of Norvelt has implications for today. It offers proof that government intervention can effectively address poverty, empower a desperate group of people, and (re)integrate marginalized and overlooked people into the body politic.

Chapter One

The World of Coal Mining, Coking, and Patch Communities in Southwestern Pennsylvania, 1880–1920

Driving through or flying over Westmoreland County in southwestern Pennsylvania today, one is struck by the bucolic aspect of the rolling hills and shaded valleys. It's a far cry from the soot-drenched air that hung over the region from the late 1800s through the 1920s. At that time coal mines and coke ovens dotted the landscape. Miners extracted coal from the rich seams, and laborers converted this coal to coke in ovens that belched waste into the atmosphere. Most of the region's coal workers and families scraped by on the low, nonunion wages prevalent in the industry during these years. They lived in patch (mining) communities, described by one author as "feudal islands," that surrounded the mines and coke ovens.[1] The mining companies established the patch communities close to the mines to ensure a ready supply of labor. Since the mine owners' goal was profit, they invested little time or money on making the communities comfortable, healthy, or pleasant places in which the mining families would live. The miners' labor generated fabulous wealth for the few who owned the mines or coke ovens. It also produced the fuel that made the iron and steel industries in Pittsburgh successful and profitable.

This chapter offers an overview of life in the coal-patch communities of southwestern Pennsylvania, the places from which many of the early inhabitants of Norvelt came. To fully understand their story, we explore where and how they lived and worked in the decades leading up to the founding of the New Deal community. What forces shaped their lives? How did their physical environment, at work and at home, limit or uplift them? How did they seek to chart their own destinies, to achieve agency in a world of constraints? To answer these questions, this chapter explores miners and their families' material realities, personal and group identities—the roles that race, ethnicity, and class played in shaping their lives—and work and community experiences.

Race, ethnicity, and class shaped the lives of the miners and their families and defined the economic possibilities and opportunities available to western Pennsylvanians in the early twentieth century. Ideas about race that existed in the United States during the early 1900s affected these immigrant and first-generation miners. Racial attitudes and practices influenced the first settlers in Norvelt, and they continue to affect Norvelters today, even though constructions of race have changed over the course of the last 110 years. In the early 1900s, most of the inhabitants of the mining and coke communities were first- or second-generation Catholic immigrants from southern and eastern Europe. As racialized others in an Anglo-Saxon, Protestant–dominated society, they were hired to work in deplorable and difficult conditions and paid extremely low wages.

The strong currents of racial and ethnic division that permeated western Pennsylvania created a fragmented society. Racial and ethnic fissures pushed people who otherwise had much in common apart from each other. Even while some patch communities transcended these divisions, most struggled with the fissures that economic deprivation and social differences generated. They succeeded best when they fought to organize unions. At the same time, the fact that much of U.S. society marginalized them strengthened the bonds between them. Their work environments, economic interests, and daily lives encouraged them to rely on each other and their families. They fought together against the mine and coke oven owners to form unions and to improve conditions in the mines, the coke ovens, and their homes and community. They turned to one another for support, solidarity, fun, and companionship.[2] Their collective histories, experiences, and outlooks contributed to Norvelt's endurance as a community.

Norvelt lies atop the Connellsville coal bed, which is part of the larger Pittsburgh coal seam. Difficult work conditions in mining and coking and the impoverished circumstances of the patch communities shaped the people who worked and lived there, just as their labor and struggles transformed both the society around them and themselves.

The Pittsburgh Coal Seam and the Connellsville District

In the first half of the nineteenth century, the northern United States accelerated its transformation from a primarily agriculture-based economy to an industrial one. Increased industrialization, with its attendant need for improved systems of communication and transportation, both required and sparked the development of greater and cheaper sources of fuel. Up until the 1880s, Americans relied on timber more than any other energy source. However, between 1850 and 1880, the use of coal to produce energy in the United States increased from 9.3 percent to 41 percent, while timber declined from 90.7 percent to 57 percent. As the 1800s

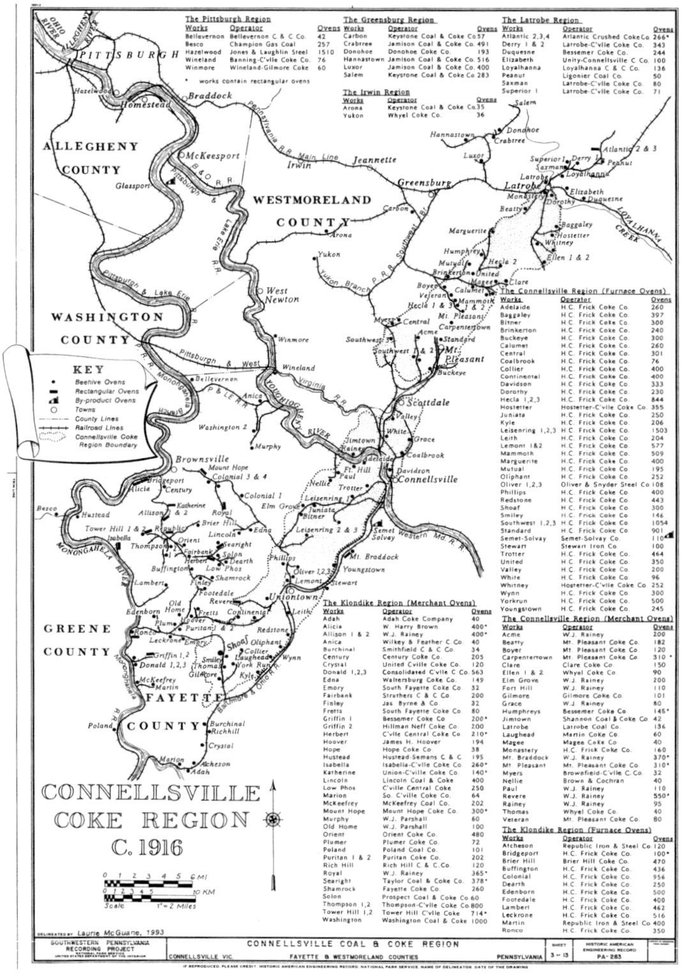

MAP 2

The Connellsville coal seam in southwestern Pennsylvania. Library of Congress, Prints and Photographs Division, Washington, D.C., HAER PA, 26-CONL.V, 1 (sheet 3 of 13).

ended, coal—and its byproduct coke—emerged as the preferred source of energy due to its availability, relatively low cost, reliability, and abundance; the United States had the largest deposits of coal in the world.[3]

In the late 1800s and early 1900s, the Pittsburgh seam, located in southwestern Pennsylvania, held some of the richest deposits of bituminous (soft) coal in the world. The Connellsville coal bed, which is part of the Pittsburgh seam, extends roughly thirty miles south of Connellsville, in Fayette County, to West Virginia and thirty miles north into Westmoreland County (where Norvelt would be built). (See map 2.) In 1913, the Connellsville basin was the leading supplier of fuel to the nation's blast furnaces; it contributed 47 percent of the coke produced in the United States overall.[4]

The bituminous coal found in southwestern Pennsylvania was particularly valuable to industrialists because it could be converted into coke comparatively cheaply. One observer characterized it as being "physically and chemically nearly

TABLE 1 **U.S. production of steel, bituminous coal, and coke, 1876–1920**

Year	Total raw steel produced	Bituminous coal nationally	Bituminous coal in Pa.	Coke production
1876	597,000			
1880	1,397,000	50,757,000	16,564,000	3,338,000
1890	4,779,000	111,302,000	40,625,054	11,508,000
1895	6,785,000	135,118,000	51,818,112	13,334,000
1900	11,227,000	212,316,000	79,318,362	20,533,000
1905	21,880,000	315,063,000	119,361,514	32,231,000
1910	28,330,000	417,111,000	148,770,858	41,709,000
1915	35,180,000	442,624,000	157,420,068	41,581,000
1920	46,183,000	568,667,000	166,929,000	51,345,000

SOURCES: U.S. Bureau of the Census, *Historical Statistics of the United States*, 693–94; DiCiccio, *Coal and Coke in Pennsylvania*, 62–63, 80.

perfect for producing beehive coke." Coal becomes coke when the gas, water, and impurities it contains are removed. This distillation process took place in beehive coke ovens, which were built close to the coal mines. Coke workers loaded the coal in the ovens and burned it at temperatures of 2200 to 2800 degrees Fahrenheit for twenty-four to forty-eight hours. Each coke worker tended or "pulled" three ovens a day, laboring in extremely hot and challenging conditions.[5] Once the process was completed, workers loaded the coke into railroad cars located nearby, which carried it to Pittsburgh and other industrial cities.

As the national demand for iron and steel increased, so, too, did the need for coke. Table 1 illustrates the parallel growth in the production of steel, coal, and coke. Steel is made by first reducing iron ore to pig iron, which is then converted to steel in the blast furnace, a procedure that requires intense and sustained heat. Iron and steel manufacturers prized the Connellsville coke because it provided sufficient heat to satisfy the enormous demands of the blast furnaces and was hard enough to sustain the enormous weight of the ore. The Connellsville coke was so abundant that it provided "essentially all of the coke consumed in western Pennsylvania and eastern Ohio, and more than 85 per cent of the coke for other iron and steel districts of the United States."[6]

H. C. Frick Coal and Coke Company

The mining of coal and the production of coke generated enormous wealth for those who had the capital to invest in it. Henry Clay Frick, Andrew Carnegie,

FIG. 1
H. C. Frick Company logo. Michael Cary, "75th Anniversary Booklet."

and Andrew Mellon all obtained some or much of their wealth from their holdings in the coal and coke industry of southwestern Pennsylvania. Realizing the economic possibilities that such investments signified, entrepreneurs opened a dizzying number of mines and built a multitude of coke ovens throughout the region. In 1916, the year of peak production, 40,000 coke ovens in the Connellsville district consumed 33,792,256 tons of coal and produced 22,489,056 tons of coke.[7]

One of the most successful of these entrepreneurs was Henry Clay Frick, the "King of Coke."[8] As the single largest owner of coke ovens in the area, he exerted a significant amount of control over the lives of the coke workers. He ruthlessly opposed workers' attempts to unionize and mining and coke families' efforts to improve their conditions. Frick both embodied and marshaled the forces arrayed against the mining and coke communities of southwestern Pennsylvania.

Frick was born in 1849 in West Overton, a small town in Westmoreland County about nine miles from Norvelt. In 1870, he started the H. C. Frick Company, and by the late 1890s he owned or controlled "two thirds of the district's sixty thousand acres of coal and 18,000 ovens." He employed "more than 12,000 men and owned 3,500 dwellings" in the company towns he established for his workers. In 1882, he joined with Andrew Carnegie to form the H. C. Frick Coke Company. The partnership provided Frick with an infusion of capital and Carnegie with an assured and cheaper supply of coke for his steel works; it also created the largest coke company in the world. In 1892, it was estimated that Frick's holdings were worth somewhere between $5 million and $8 million. When he died in 1919, he was worth over $75 million.[9]

Today, many remember Frick for his philanthropy and the Frick Collection, the outstanding art collection that he donated to New York City. Although his public image may be positive, he did not acquire his extravagant wealth by being generous to or considerate of his workers. Guided by his thirst for profits, he paid his workers as little as possible, housed them in dwellings that lacked hot water and electricity, and forced them to buy from the company stores located in the patch communities; all the profits flowed into his coffers. To ensure tight control over the workforce, he evicted striking workers and tirelessly fought unionization. He adamantly opposed making concessions or acceding to the demands of workers. As one admiring biographer enthused, Frick "never truckled, never yielded, and . . . seemed impervious to either threats or dangers of assaults." For example, in February 1891, mine workers in the Connellsville area struck when the Frick Coke Company refused to agree to their demands for an eight-hour day and "an advance of 125 percent in wages." When miners marched on the local Morewood mine, National Guard troops fired on the group, killing seven of them. Instead of showing remorse for their deaths, Frick wrote to the manager of the Morewood mine, "the strikers got what they deserved."[10]

Frick's disregard for the murdered workers in this incident reflected his quotidian lack of concern for his employees. It also reveals the enormous challenges the workers were up against on a daily basis. Frick's objective to amass as great a fortune as possible thwarted their goal of improving their basic standard of living.

Frick paid his workers an average of twenty-five to twenty-six dollars a month in the 1880s. From this sum, Frick deducted rent, which typically ran one dollar (occasionally two dollars) per room. Since most houses in the patch communities had four to six rooms, monthly rent usually was about four to six dollars. In addition, miners and their families had to cover their expenses at the company store, including any food that they consumed; clothing, tools, and explosives and fuel the miners needed to do their work; as well as any fees that accrued when the blacksmith sharpened tools. Thus, much of what Frick paid his workers in wages came back to him as rent and payments at the company store. In 1898, the H. C. Frick Coke Company received $200,000 from rent on its patch houses.[11]

Visitors to the Frick Collection in New York City may revel in the wondrous artworks exhibited there and feel grateful to the man who donated so much of his wealth to make it possible for them to see and enjoy such treasures. However, miners, coke workers, and their descendants have a much different impression of the man who paid them so little and opposed their efforts to improve their working and living conditions.

Margaret LaPenta Bartolomeo grew up in a patch community. Her father worked for a short time in the mines, and then he and her mother ran a grocery store in the community. If miners needed a place to stay after Frick evicted them, her father let them stay on their property behind the store. When asked what she thought of Frick, she forthrightly declared,

> I would never want to go see anything that belonged to Frick because he made that [fortune] from slave laborers at the mine. They went to work before the sun and [came home] after the sun came down for how much? Sure, they . . . built these company houses, gave them cold running water. People had a little yard . . . they made a garden. They made every bit of that ground count. No . . . I don't feel like he [Frick] ought to be glorified. I'm eighty years old and my heart hasn't softened in that direction yet.[12]

Catholic Immigrants, Racialized Workers, and the Coal and Coke Industry

By the early twentieth century, most of the miners and their families were first- and second-generation Catholic immigrants from southern and eastern Europe. The idea that southern and eastern Europeans were of different, perforce inferior races than northern Europeans permeated a wide swath of U.S. society in the late 1800s and early 1900s. The mine operators used this racialization to justify lower salaries for the immigrants and to deny them the privileges accorded to "racially superior" workers. These attitudes and the practices they engendered constituted yet more challenges that the coke and mining families had to confront as they struggled to raise their standard of living and be viewed and treated as equal human beings. This section first discusses racial classification in the United States in the early 1900s as it related to the miners. In order to convey how deeply these notions of race penetrated U.S. society, it then examines a range of voices, from U.S. government officials, to college professors, to H. C. Frick, to the Ku Klux Klan.

The increased production of coal and coke generated a greater demand for laborers. In 1890, there were 192,204 coal and coke workers in the United States; in 1920, there were 639,547. The number of coal and coke workers in southwestern Pennsylvania reflected national trends, only at a much higher rate. In 1870, there were roughly 16,000 coal and coke workers; by 1909, that number had increased to 186,000.[13] The vast majority of these immigrant workers were from eastern Europe and Italy.

The demand for workers attracted immigrants fleeing poverty in their countries. Eastern and central European migrants' willingness to leave their homes between 1860 and 1910 reflected important changes taking place in Europe as well as their desire to achieve a better life. For one thing, the significant increase in population (over 75 percent) and the "explosions in births" led to the growth of the "agrarian proletariat," or peasants who had no land. Large numbers of these landless peasants chose to migrate elsewhere when they realized that they could not reasonably hope to obtain land in their own countries. Eighty-five to 95 percent of those who left chose to come to the United States.[14]

U.S. agents representing coal interests traveled to eastern Europe to entice peasants to travel to the United States, knowing that coal companies could pay immigrant workers far less than they paid those already working the mines. Coal companies also recruited newly arrived immigrants in Eastern Seaboard cities who had come to America in search of work. Though they earned low wages, immigrants made significantly more than they received in their own country. In the United States, they garnered $1.50 to $2.00 a day, while back home they had been paid only fifteen or thirty cents a day. Many of the immigrants hoped that they would earn enough money so that they could return to their country of origin and purchase land, a reality that failed to materialize for many.[15]

Italy became a nation in 1860, but unification did not ameliorate the lot of the peasant population that predominated in the country. Southern Italians were particularly disadvantaged by the formation of the nation, which facilitated northern Italian domination of the south. Although the vast majority of the more than 4 million Italians who emigrated to the United States between 1880 and 1920 settled in urban centers, a significant number of them also sought employment in the mine and coke ovens of southwestern Pennsylvania. They first came to the coalfields in 1874, when the mine owners brought them in to break a strike.[16]

The arrival of these immigrants represented far more than a mere expansion of the workforce; it signified a profound transformation in the composition of the laborers. During most of the 1800s, miners and their families had been white, Protestant, and either born in the United States or immigrants from northern Europe, primarily the British Isles. By 1890, the ethnic background, origins, and religious affiliations of the mine workers had changed, as immigrant workers from southern and eastern Europe replaced the experienced workers who had previously worked in the coalfields. (One U.S. Congress report refers to this transformation as "racial displacement.") In 1890, these newly arrived immigrants constituted one quarter of the mine and coke workers in southwestern Pennsylvania. By 1909, they made up 76 percent of the laborers. In one typical western Pennsylvania mining community, they constituted 82 percent of the residents.[17]

The eastern and southern European immigrants fled impoverished circumstances in their countries of origin and arrived penniless in a country in which they did not speak the language. They were Catholics in what was still considered a Protestant nation, and members of what many in the United States considered inferior races.[18] Most of the immigrants had little formal education in their native country and spoke little to no English. These factors put these Catholic immigrants at a disadvantage in the U.S. labor force.

Unlike the English, Scottish, Welsh, and German miners who preceded them, the new immigrants had been farmers or farm laborers with no prior experience working in mines. Despite their lack of training, the owners of the mines and coke ovens welcomed these workers because they were "very industrious and regular in their work." Furthermore, the new immigrants' vulnerability and lack of experience offered the owners a greater measure of control. As the Dillingham Report noted, the mine companies found the immigrants "tractable and less inclined to give trouble than the older immigrant races."[19]

Because the new immigrants were "more tractable," the owners determined that they could pay them less than they did the "native-born" workers, an arrangement that generated increased profits for the owners and created conflicts between the different groups of laborers. The immigrants arrived in the United States with no (or very little) money, which made them generally willing to accept the jobs offered them. Their inability to speak English undermined their ability to more effectively protest their conditions, at least initially. As the Dillingham Report notes, these workers "could not easily communicate their discontent, or act as a body upon any grievances."[20]

The immigrants' lack of experience in the mines, their financial needs, their "race," and their status as newcomers unable to speak English all contributed to the construction of a tiered work situation and pay scale. The more recent arrivals were, of course, on the low end of both. The pay scale that emerged in the mines and coke ovens reflected the worker's "race" and time of arrival. The "Native-born of native father, white" earned an average of $2.36 a day. The "Native-born of foreign father" (from England, France, Germany, Ireland, Scotland, Sweden, or Wales) earned $2.21 a day. However, the foreign-born from eastern and southern Europe earned less, as the following daily wages illustrate: northern Italians, $1.90; southern Italians, $1.88; Magyars, $2.07; Poles, $2.03; Russians, $2.04; and Slovaks, $2.10. The percentage of workers of different ethnic groups who earned over two dollars a day in Pennsylvania tells the same story. Seventy percent of white, native born of native fathers miners did, while only 48 percent of Croatians, 55 percent of southern Italians (but 71 percent of northern Italians), 64 percent of Magyars, 54 percent of Poles, and 55 percent of Slovaks did. The issue was clearly race rather than newness to the United States, since 84 percent of the foreign-born English earned over two dollars a day, while 86 percent of the Scots, 82 percent of the Welsh, and 72 percent of the French did as well.[21]

The construction of race is necessarily fluid; it continually evolves according to changing power dynamics, social attitudes, and demographic trends. It reflects and reifies the hierarchy of peoples by designating some as superior and others as inferior. David Roediger discusses the construction of race in the United States primarily along the white/black divide. He notes that following the Civil War "racial precedents and racial language" were employed against "darker ethnic groups" to equate blackness with the "new immigrant groups." The new immigrants who poured into the mining communities of southwestern Pennsylvania hardly fit the description of "darker ethnic groups," with the possible exception of some southern Italians. Nevertheless, the notion of racial hierarchies that had characterized the United States since the 1600s both predisposed and enabled the "Native-born, whites" and the foreign-born from northern Europe to define these new immigrants as members of different races, and American courts attempted to codify various groups as either white or nonwhite up through the early twentieth century.[22]

W. Jett Lauck, who worked with the U.S. Immigration Commission, compiled a detailed study of the miners and coke workers in western Pennsylvania. His report betrays the implicit and explicit belief that the southern and eastern European immigrant workers lacked education, were largely responsible for the accidents that occurred in the mines, and were so downtrodden that they were unlikely to protest their conditions. Lauck writes that immigrants from these "races" are illiterate and unable to speak English; as a result, they are "unable to read printed notices or comprehend oral instructions." Therefore, he concludes, "mining accidents result from the ignorance and carelessness of employes." Lauck also writes that the "standards of living of southern and eastern Europeans . . . [are] so low that neither the conditions of employment nor the rates of pay have as a rule constituted grounds for dissatisfaction."[23]

In 1908, Annie Marion MacLean, a sociologist, wrote about the immigrant men, women, and children living in the bituminous coalfields of southwestern Pennsylvania. MacLean's writing reveals her concern that the immigrants lived in unfortunate conditions, were marginalized from "American culture," and were dominated by the Catholic Church. She referred to the immigrants as "men, women, and children—most of them of Slavic races, who have brought over to this country the manners and customs of a lower civilization than ours and who are living under conditions which tend to perpetuate their civilization instead of raising them to the level of ours." To explain why, in part, the "Slavic immigrants" were simultaneously isolated and ostracized, she added that "the Americans and the immigrants of Anglo-Saxon and Celtic origin . . . will have nothing to do with [the Slavs]; many of [the former] have the strongest dislike, even contempt, for the Slavs."[24]

Her perception that the "Slavs" were different from and inferior to "Americans and immigrants of Anglo Saxon or Celtic origin" was not unique. William Leiserson, a professor of political economy at the University of Wisconsin, discussed the benefits of unions for mine workers in southwestern Pennsylvania in the early 1900s. Discussing immigrant workers ("Slavs") and the production process, he noted, "The second effect of the influx of Slavs is that their lack of intelligence makes improved machinery and a perfected organization of the mining processes absolutely essential."[25]

Other sectors of U.S. society expressed their feelings toward these immigrants more directly, more viscerally, and with more palpable hatred. Anti-Catholic, anti-Jewish, and anti-immigrant sentiment, along with the enduring hatred of blacks, galvanized a number of Americans to join or sympathize with the Ku Klux Klan (KKK) in the 1920s. Nationally, some 4 to 5 million people joined the KKK; estimates place the number of members at over a quarter of a million in Pennsylvania.[26]

A reader today of newspapers from southwestern Pennsylvania in the 1920s may be startled by their portrayal of the Klan as both legitimate and commonplace. Articles detailing Klan activities can be found alongside descriptions of local social activities, such as weddings, visits, and deaths.[27]

The Klan was formed in the late 1860s to uphold the system of white supremacy that the Civil War had undermined and to attack newly freed African Americans. In the 1920s, the Klan portrayed itself as the defender of Protestant America against Catholics and immigrants, which in their minds were the same thing. In southwestern Pennsylvania, the massive influx of southern and eastern Europeans stoked hostility and fear among Klan members and supporters. These immigrants were willing to work for extremely low wages, and some laborers who had previously worked in the mines and coke ovens resented their arrival, holding them responsible for their own loss of jobs. Others defined the United States as a Protestant nation and felt threatened by the growing number of Catholics in their midst. As an article in one Connellsville paper noted, "The fundamental appeal of the Ku Klux Klan is native Americanism and Protestantism. It is essentially an anti-alien movement, an organization of sentiment against foreigners. That this sentiment has existed, the growth of the Klan is sufficient evidence."[28]

The Klan particularly targeted the coal and coke workers in southwestern Pennsylvania because they were Catholics and immigrants. Although the Klan had klaverns throughout the state, the group was strongest in the coal-, coke-, and steel-producing region of southwestern Pennsylvania. Allegheny, Westmoreland, Armstrong, Fayette, and Washington Counties, the heart of the coal, coke, steel, and iron industries, were the "imperial heartland" of the KKK in Pennsylvania. One of the region's most effective Klan recruiters was a Protestant minister from Latrobe, a town located just a few miles from where Norvelt would later rise.[29]

Peter Dupey started working in the coke ovens as a boy to help his father. He remembers visits from the Ku Klux Klan. "They were anti-Catholic and frightened people" by "rid[ing] through the patch with white sheets over them[selves]. The Klan members carried torches while they rode." One day, young Peter decided to find out who they were. So he "rigged a rope across the road. . . . The horses stumbled and the men fell into the ash road. The next day all the members were limping and wore bandages on their faces and arms." Dupey claims that this allowed him to find out who the Klan members were; luckily, they never found out who put the rope in the road.[30]

Working Conditions in the Coal Mines and Coke Fields

As the previous sections discussed, the coal operators and the owners of the coke ovens exploited the workers and families to amass profits. In addition, these immigrants and their children confronted negative racial assumptions and hostility from a broad swath of U.S. society in the early 1900s. However, the workers faced one additional and overwhelming challenge: the conditions in which they were forced to labor.

Working conditions in the mines and at the coke ovens were exhausting, dangerous, and oppressive. Miners worked ten to twelve hours a day until the 1930s, extracting coal from the rich underground seams that ran throughout southwestern Pennsylvania. Surrounded by darkness, except for what light their lanterns provided, many miners went to work before the sun rose and returned home after it set. They continually breathed coal dust and were constantly threatened by accidents, cave-ins, faulty equipment, or just plain mistakes. Many miners passed much of their day stooped over, crawling through poorly lighted tunnels, carrying their work gear with them. They spent countless hours driving their picks into the seams, drilling holes for the dynamite needed to loosen the coal, and loading coal cars to send up to the shaft's mouth. Miners often complained that operators "underweighed" the cars and thereby diminished the miners' pay.[31]

Andrew Zaksek started working in the mines when he was fifteen years old. His Slovenian father and Slovak mother had immigrated to the United States, "hell, in 1800 something." He was born in 1913 at Continental Mine #3, in Fayette County in southwestern Pennsylvania. When he was fifteen, he joined his father working in the mines. Although he wasn't afraid to go into the mines, he remembers that "it was kinda hard, sore back." He recalls, "I never saw daylight until Sunday. You wouldn't believe it. We worked six days trying to make six or seven dollars a week."[32]

Although the transformation of coal into coke took place above ground, it, too, was marked by appalling conditions. Placing the coal into the ovens was hard work. The extreme heat of the ovens was overwhelming. In addition, coke workers were continually exposed to the noxious fumes and toxic waste that the ovens spewed out as they burned the coal or when the workers opened the doors to "draw" out the finished coke.

Peter Dupey, the boy who had strung a rope across the road to trip the Klan, was born in 1912 of Slovak and Russian parents. He started working on the coke ovens to help his father when he was ten or twelve years old. To get the carbon out of the coal, he poured water over the "red-hot coals." When the coke was silvery, that meant it was ready. At that point, he would put the "coke in a wheelbarrow and wheel it up to the jumbo [railroad] car." He remembers that "the coke inside the railroad car was sharp and would hurt me when I fell in." To make sure that he had gotten all the coke possible, he used a "scraper" that weighed about sixty pounds to clean out the oven. When that task was complete, "boys ten or eleven years old daubed the mud on the ovens" and started the process all over again.[33]

Charles Karwatsky's father also worked on the coke ovens. He recalls that his father worked outside, tending the ovens, regardless of the weather. But he never complained, even if there was "snow on your back, [if it was] rainin[g], freezin[g]. You kept on workin[g], there was no stoppin[g]." His father, like other men, never needed to shave, since the intense heat burned their facial hair. Although mainly men worked in the coke yards, some women did as well. Karwatsky's grandmother worked in the coke yards, and his parents met working on the ovens. Karwatsky recalls that his grandmother "would fork coke and put it in wheelbarrows in her bare feet. [S]he would fork and my Dad would wheel, as a young fella."[34]

FIG. 2 Men working in the coke ovens in the Connellsville mine seam, ca. 1870. Pennsylvania State Archives, Harrisburg, Pennsylvania, MG-219.2. Philadelphia Commercial Museum Collection.

Ed Bilik was born in Standard, a patch community in Westmoreland County, which belonged to H. C. Frick. His father was Russian and his mother was Polish, and they both emigrated from Austria to southwestern Pennsylvania in the late 1880s. Bilik used to watch his father work on the coke ovens. After he pulled the coke from the oven, he would "fork it into the wheelbarrow and then haul it up to the top of the railroad car. He pushed the wheelbarrow up about eight or ten feet and dumped it and then brought it back down. He went up and down, slipping and sliding, rain and shine."[35]

The men, women, and boys did this work because they had to; it was one of the few jobs available to these immigrants.[36] Because the work was so difficult, miners and cokers developed a strong sense of camaraderie among themselves. Their mutual trust and dependency allowed them to function together in the demanding and dangerous mines and coke ovens. The shared, horrendous work and living conditions and the tight bonds of solidarity they produced help to explain why the mining communities' tenacious struggles to improve conditions and unionize persisted, despite the determined resistance of the mine owners and, until the 1930s, of the state and federal governments. They also explain the willingness of

FIG. 3 Miner in the Calumet patch community, ca. 1934. Library of Congress, Prints and Photographs Division, Washington, D.C., LC-USF33-006005-M1. Farm Security Administration/Office of War Information Collection. Photo: Ben Shahn.

people in Norvelt to work together to build a thriving community and transform their lives.

Life in the Patch Communities

Sharing deplorable working conditions and low pay in the mines and coke ovens built bonds among laborers. Living in the relatively isolated patch villages, which Paul Nyden refers to as "separate communities,"[37] fortified ties among the mining and coke families. They also shaped the values and attitudes of their inhabitants, ethics and ideals that would, among other things, contribute to the formation and endurance of Norvelt.

Labor leader John Brophy lived in patch communities in southwestern Pennsylvania in the 1920s and '30s. He echoes the idea that conditions in the mines and communities fostered tolerance. "In spite of the differences of language, nationality, and religion, there was a good degree of mutual acceptance among the miners. We were so few and so bound together by the mine, that we got to know each other well and more or less had to get along. Ours was one of only two Catholic families in the town; the others were Protestant or Orthodox. But nobody paid much attention to differences of religion. There was no church to go to, anyway."[38]

FIG. 4 Children in a company house in Scotts Run, West Virginia. Library of Congress, Prints and Photographs Division, Washington, D.C., LC-USF34-015457-C. Farm Security Administration/Office of War Information Collection. Photo: Elmer Johnson.

Ed Bilik's values and worldview were shaped by his childhood in the Standard patch community. He grew up in a family of nine children (one of whom died), with a father who worked in the coke ovens and a mother who spent much of her day cooking, trying to keep the house and clothes clean in spite of the soot from the ovens and the dirt from the unpaved streets, and tending to the house and kids. Just as the men relied on each other in their jobs, the women looked to one another for support as well. When Bilik's mother baked rolls for supper, she always gave some to her neighbor, Mrs. Bailey. (The Baileys were the only African American family in the patch.) When Mrs. Bailey's chicken laid eggs, she gave several to Mrs. Bilik. Bilik doesn't remember any prejudice against the Baileys or anyone else in the community. What he does recall is that "people looked out for each other" and treated one another with respect.[39]

Because the patch communities were small and poor, inhabitants turned to each other for help, comfort, and entertainment. Everybody knew their neighbors and what was going on in their lives because they were in daily contact with each other. For example, if Bilik's mother needed something, she would send him to the company store to get it. On his way to the store, he passed other people, and they in turn saw him. "I walked [to the company store], there were no automobiles, and on the way I would see fifteen or thirty people I knew." When asked if people locked their doors, Bilik recounted what the former mayor of Mount Pleasant, Bill Potoka, said: "I grew up in the old coal patch and we never locked our doors. If someone came to rob us, we followed him around to see what he could find."[40]

The mining companies established the patch communities close to the mines so they could have access to and control over an assured supply of labor to extract the coal and convert it to coke. Uniform construction and similar layout characterized the houses and villages. Most patch communities consisted of one hundred to two hundred semidetached houses. Each structure typically housed two families, who, in many cases, also took in boarders. Since the mining companies built the houses, they used the cheapest materials available to keep costs low. The homes generally had four to six rooms. Most houses lacked electricity, running water, or any other amenities until the early twentieth century, when some acquired them; the sole source of heat was the fireplace or stove in each home. People bathed in a tub placed in the kitchen, and a shared outhouse was the only bathroom they knew. They obtained water from an outside faucet or pump and carried it to the house.[41]

Although many communities had a school or a church, the streets were not paved, nor was much offered in the way of amusement. However, they all had the H. C. Frick Company–owned store, which many miners referred to as the "pluck-me store."[42] The Union Supply Company (the name of the "chain" company store) stocked many of the goods that the mining and coke families needed, but at a higher price than stores in the area towns charged. Since the stores were in the patch communities, it was easier to access them than to travel to the closest town, a trip that company security, the Coal and Iron Police, often forbade. If residents lacked the necessary cash to pay for their purchases, the store extended them easy credit and payment was deducted from the worker's next paycheck.[43] Most patch families were in debt to the store, the income from which, as noted above, enriched H. C. Frick and other shareholders.

Francis Lukas grew up in the patch community of Hostetter, located in Westmoreland County in the northern section of the Connellsville coal bed. His father worked in the mine, and the family bought their goods from the company store. Lukas recalled, "You had to buy everything from the company store. You weren't allowed to go to Latrobe [the nearest town] to buy it." When asked what happened if someone did go to Latrobe to buy things, Lukas replied, "they got arrested by the police. They watched real close, so you couldn't get out [and buy things] by train or streetcar."[44]

The stores generated profits for the mining companies and served as a mechanism of control. Because the mine owners did not allow non-company stores to set up shop in the patches, there was no competition. "The miner had to do all his shopping there and the company expected you to spend all of your earnings at the store . . . or [else] you would lose your job. If the mine superintendent found out that you weren't [shopping there], he would give you less work or else harder jobs."

TABLE 2 **The native white and African American population in Westmoreland County, 1910–1930**

	1910	1920	1930
Native White	167,311	212,715	244,018
African American	2,461	4,240	6,410
Total Population	231,304	273,568	294,995

SOURCE: Dougherty, "A Reference Guide." Dougherty lists his source as the "14th and 15th Population Census of the United States." We thank Raymond P. Washlaski for sending us a copy of this document.

The owners gained insight into the personal lives of the miners because managing the stores allowed them to keep tabs on what they bought. Finally, if a family could not pay its debt or if the miner or coke worker went on strike, the company simply refused them service.[45]

One other notable aspect of life in the patch community was mobility. Miners and their families frequently moved from one mining settlement to another, in search of better living and working conditions, more or some amenities, to be near friends and family, or in the hope of finding something better. John Brophy recalls that his family moved so frequently that they lived "a gypsy life." Karen Metheny found that only 27 percent of miners in Helvetia, Pennsylvania, lived in that patch community for more than one year between 1892 and 1899.[46]

African Americans and Race Relations in the Patch Communities

The lack of documentation has made it difficult to obtain a clear picture of what relationships were like between African American and white miners in the patch communities. Few black families lived in the patch communities, or in western Pennsylvania in general, in the late 1800s or early 1900s. There were, however, enough black coke workers in Mount Pleasant, Westmoreland County, in 1884 for them to hold their own assembly of the Knights of Labor. According to the census of 1900, there were 4,885,479 persons of ten years of age and over in Pennsylvania; of this number, only 2.5 percent were black. In 1900, out of a total workforce of 180,474 bituminous coal workers in Pennsylvania, blacks numbered 1,616, or 0.8 percent. While the number of black miners grew to 1,773 in 1910, they made up only 0.6 percent out of a total of 291,746 workers, and 0.1 percent in 1920.[47] Figures in Westmoreland County show a similar proportion of whites to blacks.

The few scattered references in oral histories to blacks in patch communities indicate that their numbers were low, but the paucity of information does not allow us to draw any firm conclusions about why this was the case or what it said about race relations there. Rich Trumka and Ed Bilik both grew up in a patch community; they both deny there was racism and stress the unity of the miners and their families in opposition to the mine owners. While their recollections are important, it is also possible that their memories reflect, at least in part, their current political beliefs, a certain amount of nostalgia for the unity they remember from their childhoods in the patch communities, their own unique experiences, or a combination of all of the above. However, as we will see below, their memories do not necessarily convey the reality experienced by all black inhabitants of the mining communities.

Labor Struggles, Organizing, and Strikes

The owners of the mines and coke ovens possessed powerful tools to thwart laborers' efforts to unionize and improve their working and living conditions. They evicted fired or striking workers and their families, denied them credit in the company store, and employed the Iron and Coal Police to attack them. The Iron and Coal Police, which first appeared in the anthracite coal region of northeastern Pennsylvania of 1866, worked as the coal operators' own private force to repress the miners and mining communities. They patrolled the patch communities and, when miners went out on strike, assaulted and evicted families from their houses and drove them out of the communities. It is no surprise that mining families generally disliked and feared them. The repressive measures used by the owners of the mines and coke ovens and the abusive work conditions and impoverished living situation of the miners, coke workers, and their families encouraged the bonds of unity that the recognition of shared oppression can produce and facilitated organizers' efforts to unionize them.[48]

The union that most successfully organized the miners was the United Mine Workers of America (UMWA), which was formed in 1890 through the joining together of the National Federation of Miners and Mine Laborers and the Knights of Labor. Although the depression of the 1890s was not an easy time to organize due to layoffs and economic uncertainty, the UMWA issued strike calls, worked to organize miners, and enlisted 9,700 members by 1897, mainly in Ohio and western Pennsylvania. By 1913, the UMWA had mushroomed to 377,700 members, and in 1921 it reached 425,700.[49]

Rich Trumka, president of the AFL-CIO as this book went to press, was formerly president of the United Mine Workers of America (1982–85.) He is also a former miner from southwestern Pennsylvania, as were his father, grandfather, six uncles, and cousins. He attributes the eventual success of the UMWA to several factors. First, the conditions in the mines were "horrible. [The mine owners] put more stock in the mules than they did in the men." Life in the patch communities was also difficult, and the contrast between the lives of the mining families and those of the managers was a constant and highly visible reminder of the stark differences that existed between the classes. In Nemacolin, Pennsylvania, where Trumka grew up, miners' houses were on one side of the road, and those of the managers were on the other side, called "bosses row." At the top of the hill "were six gigantic white mansions for the managers."[50]

This contrast served to fortify ties and a shared identity among the laborers and contributed to making the UMWA one of the stronger unions in the United States. Labor historian David Montgomery places the UMWA "among the most influential organizations in the labor movement." He attributes the union's "resilience" to "the bonds among the men at the coal face, the cohesiveness of the women in the mining towns, and the impact of a vast and complex union structure with which those personal loyalties interacted."[51]

The UMWA realized that in order to organize successfully it needed to build on the common sense of oppression that existed in the mines and patch communities, overcome any tensions that racial, ethnic, or religious differences produced or could produce, and reach out to all miners and their families as a body. To that end, the *UMW Journal* was published in twelve different languages, and its 1892 constitution was written in Slovenian and Italian as well as English. Organizers either knew or learned various languages or paired up with others who did to unionize the mining region. For example, one of Trumka's grandfathers spoke French, Spanish, and Italian, while his other grandfather spoke Croatian, Polish, and Czech. They would "team up and speak to the miners in their native tongues." Trumka thinks the UMWA was successful because "we treated people equally and we gave them hope. We brought them together. We didn't discriminate because of their origin, the color of their skin, or the God they worshipped. We thought workers were workers and we wouldn't allow ourselves to be divided."[52]

However, it appears that some white miners, particularly, but not only, those of British origin, did discriminate against black miners. Mine owners frequently employed African Americans as strikebreakers, which heightened white workers' antagonism toward them. Many of these black workers were recruited in the South and enticed to West Virginia or southwestern Pennsylvania with promises of good jobs and housing, unaware that they would be used to break a strike. The UMWA attempted to undermine the use of African Americans to break strikes by encouraging them to join the union. In its 1892 constitution, the UMWA stated, "No member in good standing who holds a dues or transfer card shall be debarred or hindered from obtaining work on account of race, creed, or nationality." The UMWA was the first U.S. union to explicitly adopt this position,[53] which would facilitate its successful organization of African American miners in Pennsylvania in the first decades of the twentieth century. According to a 1912 study on African Americans in Pennsylvania, "all of the Negro miners in the State are union men, and members of the United Mine Workers of America. The United Mine Workers is one of the few unions in which the Negroes agree that they receive fair treatment. In some of these miners' unions, there are Negro officers, and Negroes are always in attendance at the annual meetings."[54]

Realistically, though, the written principles and the public statements of an organization and its leaders do not necessarily reflect the actual attitudes and practices of its members or its leaders. Linda Nyden points out this discrepancy in her discussion of white miners' relationship to black miners during the 1920s. She notes that the UMWA did not protest the discriminatory hiring and promotion practices that mine owners practiced against the black miners. Furthermore, she points out that for most of the twentieth century, the top leadership of the UMWA was white. "Between 1900 and 1973, there was not a single Black international officer. . . . The first [black] to hold one in the Pittsburgh district was in 1973." Black miners were not the only group of miners excluded from leadership; most of the officers in the Pittsburgh district were of Scottish or Irish background, which "did not reflect the large percentage of foreign-born miners there," as the national origins of miners listed in a previous section demonstrates.[55]

Challenging the idea that racial harmony prevailed in the mines, some African American mining families remember all too clearly the racist treatment white miners meted out to them. In 1985, miners who had been employed at the Crows Nest Mine in Bovard, Westmoreland County, gathered with their families to commemorate their work and community. As part of the program, Lillian Clark Willis talked about what work was like for black miners. She acknowledged, "Mining was hard, dangerous and dirty, with long hours and little pay for all who worked the pits." But, she added,

> the Black miners were also victims of ignorance and prejudice that prevailed at the time. In those early years Black men were prohibited from working the better jobs such as pit boss, foreman and tipple work. In fact, it has been verified over and over again that even while digging coal in the pits, a Black man working in a dry area would have to give up that spot and work in a wet spot, if a white man did not want to work in the water. There was no choice to be made. He either moved to the water spot or he was told by the pit boss to collect his tools and he no longer had a job.[56]

Women and the Mining Communities

Many of the women and girls who settled in Norvelt had lived previously in the mining and coke communities. They drew on their gendered experiences as wives and daughters in the patches to build new and better lives for themselves, their families, and the new settlement that would become Norvelt.

Gendered ideas and practices ordered most people's lives in the coke and mining communities. Although women did not work in the mines, and only a few labored in the coke ovens, they were essential to the functioning of the mines and the survival of the patch communities and mining families. Women's work sustained the family and made it possible for the male members of the family to work in the mines or coke ovens. As David Montgomery points out, the miners' ability to extract coal was directly related to, and made possible by, the "home economy."[57] Women's largely unpaid labor included growing food in the gardens and preparing meals for the household; washing the family's clothes, which in the soot-drenched environment of the patch communities was a horrendous task; maintaining the house; and taking care of boarders to supplement their husbands' income.

Mary Mae Lulich lived in a patch community, and her husband was a miner and union organizer. Some months he only worked a few days a week, and at other times he only worked "one day a week. Then they [the mine operators] give you ten cents per person to live on for a week." In order to make ends meet, she, like many of the patch women, "had chickens and . . . a big garden. I used to can a thousand quarts of stuff." The (male) miners depended on their families for physical and emotional sustenance on a day-to-day level. Without that, it would have been very difficult if not impossible for them conduct strikes or unionize.[58] Strikes in the southwestern Pennsylvania coal region were family and community affairs; they were not struggles engaged in solely by male miners. Women's support was critical to sustaining the family, especially at a time when the loss of the miners' income made doing so an extraordinary challenge.

Women actively supported the strikes because they understood that unionization would improve their lives and those of their families. Since Mary Mae Lulich's husband was a local labor leader, he was frequently away from home working for the union. In his absence, Lulich ran the household, took care of their children, and braved the attacks to which they were subjected by antiunion forces. According to her, "we were bombed four times. Our furniture was all ruined, and the home was all ruined." Although she was often scared and occasionally asked her husband to stop, many other times she was "ready to go fight with him."[59]

Women engaged in direct actions to advance the miners' demands. On at least one occasion, they threw stones at replacement workers, whom they called scabs, for which they were arrested. They also joined together with their families to block the roads so scabs could not get through to the mines.[60] When the men went out on strike, the companies evicted them and their family from their homes. Instead of acquiescing to being thrown out of their houses, some women fought back.

The 1910–11 strike in Westmoreland County illustrates the roles that women, families, and the community played in unionization struggles. It is particularly relevant to this study because this is the area where many of the miners who would be among the original homesteaders in Norvelt worked. From March 1910 to July 1911, bituminous coal miners in Westmoreland County went out on strike. On March 4, 1910, when roughly four hundred miners in Westmoreland County joined the UMWA, the Keystone Coal and Coke Company, their employer, promptly fired forty-eight of them. On March 9, the newly constituted local met and demanded "that the discharged men should be reinstated, that the company should pay the Pittsburgh union scale," and that working hours be lowered from ten to eight a day. Over the course of the next month, the strike spread, and by May, local UMWA unions were organized throughout the county.[61]

In an attempt to undermine the strike, the mine operators evicted the mining families who lived in company houses. During the first few months, from late spring through summer, the union relief fund provided tents for the now-homeless families. Privacy and other basic comforts such as a stove or a washbasin vanished. As winter approached, the union was able to build "shanties or shacks" for the striking families, which were better than tents. However, since they were "of very cheap frame construction," the families "endured many hardships," particularly during the winter months. During the course of the strike, women gave birth to nearly one hundred babies; care for both them and their mothers was "inadequate." A Mrs. John Pierce Fox of Pittsburgh spent eight weeks in the region, observing the strike and the conditions in which the strikers lived. As she later testified before Congress, in the time she was there "there were eighteen women expecting children, not one of whom had a nightdress with which to clad the prospective babies."[62]

Women and children played important roles in the strike activities. They joined with striking miners and marched in downtown Greensburg, the county seat, to publicize their demands. Boys and girls led a parade of at least two thousand marchers at the end of March 1910. According to one report, "the boys carried dinner pails and wore caps with small mine lights. The girls carried banners bearing various inscriptions, among them: 'Give us our daily bread,' 'All we ask is justice,' 'Equal rights to all men.'" In July 1910, deputies appointed and paid by the Keystone Coal and Coke Company refused to let a "procession" of miners and their wives march through Greensburg, despite the intercession of the chief of police of South Greensburg, who said they had the right to do so. A "riot" ensued; the police fired pistols and the strikers threw stones. At the end, one deputy was injured, one striker was shot, and "many persons were arrested and charged with riot, aggravated riot, and inciting riot." Undeterred, "the strikers and many of their wives and children formed a procession and marched . . . through [the] principal streets" of Greensburg.[63]

The strike gained national prominence. Mother Jones, the labor leader and organizer for the UMWA, traveled to Westmoreland County to support the strike. As part of her work, she joined with a group of women who were "hooting at the scabs" in front of the Export mine. Following their arrest, the women, with their children, were sent by streetcar to Greensburg, some ten miles away. They sang the whole way, and continued singing while they were confined to their jail cells. After five days and, according to Mother Jones, sleepless nights for many of the inhabitants of Greensburg, the women were released. Despite their sacrifices and their struggles, the miners and their families lost the strike since "the operators made no concession."[64]

Conclusion

This chapter explores the historical context, material conditions, and political struggles that shaped the lives of many of the inhabitants of the patch communities, the place from where many of the first settlers of Norvelt drew their roots. It shows the challenges they faced as exploited laborers in the mines and coke ovens and as destitute inhabitants of the patch communities. Although these miners and coke workers extracted much of the coal and produced much of the coke that made the iron and steel industries possible, they received very little of the substantial wealth they generated in the process. Instead, they lived in isolated and impoverished patch communities that dotted southwestern Pennsylvania.

The chapter also discusses the obstacles they faced as Catholic immigrants from southern and eastern Europe in a predominantly Protestant nation. In the early 1900s, many in the United States believed that Anglo-Saxons were the superior race and Protestantism was the superior religion. They viewed the Catholic immigrants as racially beneath them and as products of an inferior civilization. These attitudes, in turn, dovetailed nicely with the interest of the coal and coke operators to pay their workers as little as possible.

Yet the abysmal work conditions that prevailed in the mines and coke ovens, along with the deprivations suffered by the families living in the patch communities, combined to create strong bonds of unity and solidarity among the mining and coke workers and families. They joined together to challenge the abusive conditions to which the mine operators and owners of the coke ovens had consigned them. In so doing, they not only helped to forge the United Mine Workers of America, they effectively established themselves as people who were aware of their rights and willing to fight for them.

One issue that is not clear is how the immigrant families and their children identified themselves in relation to African Americans in the mines and patch communities. What is certain, however, is that by the early 1930s, many of these immigrants had adopted notions of race that defined them as part of the dominant and superior white race in opposition to African Americans. One convincing example of this, as we shall see in a later chapter, is that the first settlers of Norvelt voted to reject the petition of a black family to become part of the community.

The numerous strengths and attendant weaknesses of these people's experiences as laborers and as members of a community who worked and struggled together bore directly on their ability to build and maintain Norvelt. But they could not create Norvelt or the lives they wanted on their own. They needed the additional support and resources of the federal government to turn their lives around and generate the kind of community and employment that would sustain them and their descendants. And it took the devastation of the Depression and the widespread unrest that it engendered to foster a climate and elect officials that would make massive federal government intervention possible.

CHAPTER TWO

The Crisis

The Great Depression in the Nation and Westmoreland County

Historians and economists disagree on many aspects of the Great Depression, from its causes to its remedies, but they share a consensus that it was the worst economic collapse since at least the Civil War and probably in the nation's history. It devastated individuals, families, communities, and the nation. Moreover, it was a worldwide economic calamity that touched hundreds of millions in Latin America, Europe, and Asia as well. This chapter explores the general contours of the Great Depression in the United States before focusing more narrowly on the economic situation in Westmoreland County, Pennsylvania. We address the Depression's causes and its effects overall, and then pay special attention to the struggles it caused in the material conditions that subsistence homesteads sought to improve: housing, food, and unemployment. The Depression created extraordinary circumstances that demanded innovative and far-reaching responses. Norvelt's establishment can only be understood in that context.

The Depression intensified, but did not create, the miserable conditions in which many mining families in Westmoreland County and southwestern Pennsylvania lived. Their standard of living, which was never very high, began to decline in the 1920s, as the demand for coal declined. It plummeted to a new low once the ravages of the Depression hit the coalfields and the mining communities. The federal government sponsored the development of Westmoreland Homesteads, subsequently known as Norvelt, in response to the desperate situation in which the mining families in Westmoreland County lived.

Causes

No consensus exists on the Great Depression's causes. Popular interpretation identifies the stock market collapse on October 29, 1929, as a convenient and dramatic origin moment. It was, after all, the busiest day of trading in a six-week period that saw stocks lose a full third of their value. But evidence of economic collapse could be seen in many areas of the economy months and even years earlier. Wall Street itself saw such dramatic fluctuations in the weeks leading up to Black Tuesday that it would be difficult to settle on that one day even as the critical moment of market volatility.[1] The Depression resulted from a myriad of causes, though a few stand out as particularly significant.

The most persuasive explanation for the Great Depression's arrival begins, ironically, with the very prosperity that America experienced in the 1920s. High demand for American goods and services drove economic expansion that fueled a rising prosperity.

Some of that demand came from overseas, especially during and just after World War I. European nations could neither produce the goods nor grow the food necessary for their societies to survive during and recover after the war, and American companies and farmers filled the gap. By the war's end, though, European nations could no longer afford to buy goods from America. Flush with the cash that Europeans had sent over earlier, U.S. banks lent money back to Europe and kept the cycle going. European nations continued to borrow at such rates that the accumulating debt started to worry those very American bankers who lent the money. Bankers reduced the loans, and European nations could no longer buy the goods that American farmers and industrial workers labored to produce. This proved especially devastating for the farm economy, because the European market had absorbed much of the wheat and other products that farmers operating the new, highly efficient tractors and combines had cultivated so well. Net farm income fell in the latter part of the decade, and then even further as the 1930s began. It declined by two-thirds between 1929 and 1932, from $6.1 billion to $2 billion.[2] Farm foreclosures, which had risen 300 percent from 1921 to 1925, rose another 60 percent in the latter part of the decade.[3]

Demand grew domestically in the 1920s, as American industry and agriculture benefited a great deal from technological innovations in the early decades of the twentieth century. These developments made U.S. workers in both factories and fields far more efficient than they had been in the nineteenth century, and improved productivity almost every year from 1900 to 1929. Most of the increased productivity for industrial workers derived from the electrification and reconfiguration (reorganization) of factories.[4] Traditionally, workers' wages increased at roughly the same pace as their efficiency. The more productive a worker became, the higher his or her wages rose as well. Thus, workers' rising wages gave them more purchasing power, which allowed them to buy more goods and increased the demand for the products that they produced. The greater demand fueled the interest in increasing efficiency, higher wages, and still higher demand. This dynamic expanded the economy. So long as the increased wealth that the expanding economy produced spread out among enough consumers to keep demand for goods and services high, the economy did well.[5]

But the prospect of great riches proved too much for those men in a position to decide how to distribute the increased wealth. Corporate executives reserved more and more of the benefits that the increase in worker efficiency generated. The gap between the income and wealth that the richest sliver of the population reserved for itself and that available to the rest of the nation grew wider and wider.[6] Robert McElvaine reports that the richest 0.01 percent of American families made as much income as the bottom 42 percent in 1929. Put another way, the top 10 percent of American households earned 44 percent of all income on average for the 1920s, excluding capital gains (which would have distorted the distribution further).[7] Though the wealthy garnered more and more of the benefits from the expanding economy, they did not buy enough of the consumer goods that the more efficient workers produced. There was a limit to the number of cars any one family sought to own, after all, and further economic expansion required that demand never be satiated.

Workers' wages did not keep pace with their expanding productivity, and they too could not buy enough of the products that they so effectively produced to keep the factories running at full speed. More than two-thirds of American households earned less money than the $2,500 per year threshold deemed necessary to maintain the "American standard of living." One might argue about how many of these actually lived in poverty, but they were all too poor to buy enough consumer goods to keep the economy running.[8] Not enough working-class families could afford to buy even one Model A car to spread demand widely enough to keep the highly efficient assembly line moving. They simply did not earn enough to buy the goods outright.

In the short run, retailers solved this problem by offering consumers a way to buy goods without enough cash to cover their prices. Department stores, automobile dealers, and appliance stores offered installment buying and credit to consumers. For a fraction of an item's total price, a consumer might buy a product today and pay the rest off in increments over time. This boosted demand artificially and placed many families in precarious circumstances once their incomes declined. Americans bought more than 60 percent of their new cars between 1925 and 1929 on credit, and in 1927 General Motors' credit agency, the General Motors Acceptance Corporation (GMAC), financed the sale of one million GM cars. Americans bought not only cars, but also radios, vacuum cleaners, phonographs, washing machines, cabinets, and clothes, as they ran up their indebtedness from $1.38 billion to $3 billion.[9] Retailers embraced consumer credit and encouraged potential buyers not to wait until they could afford to pay cash.

Many Americans did not earn enough even to qualify for the generous credit standards that retailers established, however, and fully half the nation could not get access to this new door to consumer culture.[10] A consumer-based economy demanded mass consumption, and U.S. workers' wages did not grow enough to sustain it. The great increases in efficiency that led initially to greater income for workers and thus greater demand for consumer products resulted in a glut of consumer goods by the early 1930s. By reserving profits for themselves rather than sharing them with their employees, the industrialists and retail magnates sowed the seeds of their own demise. Demand for products fell, and inventories rose. The factories began to slow production or shut down altogether rather than add to the unsold inventories on car lots and store shelves. They decreased workers' hours and laid off employees. This further reduced these families' ability to buy products, lowered demand, and put even more families at risk. The economy slowed even more. The Depression arrived.

Effects

Historians agree much more on the Great Depression's effects on Americans than its causes. The economic collapse seemed to affect every aspect of American life, including where people lived, what they did with their time, what and how much they ate, their physical, psychological, and emotional health, their decisions to form and dissolve families, their strategies to survive life's struggles, and even whether or not life was worth living. Many people are familiar with the basic contours of economic distress that the Great Depression visited upon the nation—or at least with the standard statistics by which we have measured that distress. The lived experience of these measures has become more distant from our own experiences, even in the recent period of severe recession. It is harder and harder to appreciate the depth and scale of suffering that America experienced in the early 1930s. Robert McElvaine summarized the key decline in economic statistics succinctly. "From the top of prosperity in 1929 to the bottom of depression in 1933, GNP dropped by a total of 29 percent, consumption expenditures by 18 percent, construction by 78 percent, and investment by an incredible 98 percent. Unemployment rose from 3.2 to 24.9 percent."[11]

The statistic most familiar to readers is likely the unemployment rate, which rose to include fully a quarter of the workforce in 1933.[12] But even this figure understates the problem, as many included among the 75 percent who had jobs worked reduced hours for diminished pay, and faced unemployment for at least part of the year. Overall, American workers in 1932 earned only 58 percent of what they had earned in 1929, and they spent so little money that retail sales in America's largest cities declined by half by the following year. By 1933 the average American worker's income had fallen yet again, to only 54 percent of its 1929 level.[13] Economist and Franklin Roosevelt advisor Adolf Berle estimated the unemployment rate in the winter of 1932–33 to have reached fully 40 percent of the workforce.[14] Forty-six percent of workers in the manufacturing sector were out of work, and 45 percent in mining industries. Steel mills operated at 12 percent capacity.[15] The unemployment rate has never approached even half this height in the years since the Great Depression.

Housing

Unemployed and underemployed Americans had great difficulty staying in their homes in the early years of the Great Depression. Americans who sought to buy their own homes in the years before the New Deal had to either pay cash or borrow money under what appear to today's eyes to be draconian conditions. Absent any federal underwriting of home loans, the typical borrower had to put nearly half of the cost of the home up front, and then repay the rest of the mortgage within five years. Given the impossibility of accomplishing this, most "home-owning" families counted on their ability to refinance the loan when the big payoff came due. They went back to the bank and took out a new loan for another five years. But the economic collapse made this difficult for many, as banks would not loan money to the unemployed and families could not get the money needed to refinance their mortgages.[16] Elmer Dillinger found himself in just this situation. He was a miner who worked for the Frick Coke Company in Mount Pleasant, near to where Westmoreland Homesteads would be built. When his mine shut down, he had a mortgage on six acres of land and a house, but no source of cash income. He fell behind in his property tax, then on his mortgage payments. By November 1933, he owed $1,500 and was desperate to either get the money or sell the land. He wrote to Clarence Pickett of the subsistence homestead program and explained that "I am living a Christian life and don't mean to wrong anyone." Did Pickett want to buy his land? Did Pickett have a job for Dillinger? "I am not begging or trying to get something for nothing. I am willing to work for what I get. . . . Please give me a chance." But Pickett had nothing to offer save his regrets.[17]

To further complicate matters, so many banks closed their doors permanently in the 1930s that nine million families lost all of their savings, a total of $7 billion, money that could have been used to pay off all or part of the outstanding mortgage debt. The banks that held those mortgages then began pressing their borrowers for loans that families could not repay. Banks foreclosed on one hundred and fifty thousand families in 1930, two hundred thousand in 1931, and two hundred and fifty thousand in 1932. In March 1933, banks foreclosed on one thousand families each day.[18] Most of those who lost their houses sought to rent apartments or moved in with friends or relatives. But many had no place to go, and they became homeless. The federal government first tried to count the homeless in 1933 and estimated that 1,225,000 Americans had no place to live.[19]

Many industrial workers lived in housing owned by their employers, who often evicted them when the workers no longer worked in the mills, factories, or mines. Owners typically did not want the added risk of housing unemployed and disgruntled former workers, over whom the company held little leverage. The Depression idled many a business, and put many workers out of jobs. Coal mine companies in West Virginia, Kentucky, and Pennsylvania often evicted their miners once the mines shut down, and the families had no place to go. They settled in tents near the old mines and faced the deprivations of winter with no shelter from the cold. In western Pennsylvania, some mining families set up house literally in the idle coke ovens themselves.[20]

Faced with such severe circumstances, parents often succumbed to the stresses. Fathers abandoned families rather than face the unrelenting evidence of their

FIG. 5
Homeless families finding shelter in idled coke ovens in southwestern Pennsylvania during the Great Depression. Coal and Coke Heritage Center at Penn State Fayette, The Eberly Campus. Patchwork Voices Community Collection.

inability to provide stable homes for their wives and children. More than 1.5 million wives lived separately from their husbands by 1940. More troubling were the two hundred thousand vagrant children who traveled with adults in search of food and shelter. The number would have been even higher still had parents not dropped many of their sons and daughters off at custodial institutions, where the resident child population soared by 50 percent in 1929 and 1930.[21]

Hunger

The absence of decent housing threatened Americans severely, but not as intensely as hunger. Millions of Americans had no reliable source of food, and they suffered a range of consequences, from anxiety to physical illness, and even death. One historian identified the Great Depression as "the only time in recorded US history of large-scale famine-like conditions nationwide."[22]

But the federal government made no attempt in the early years to measure either the size of this famine or the ways that it shaped people's lives. Reports came in piecemeal from towns, cities, and states. New York City physicians estimated that 20 percent of the city's school children were malnourished. Louisiana determined that 13 percent of its white children, and fully a quarter of its African American children, suffered the same condition. One study of Ohio found that 31 percent of children statewide were underweight. Another study of Chicago's schoolchildren found 72 percent failed to meet National Research Council standards.[23]

Seasoned newspaper reporter and friend of Eleanor Roosevelt Lorena Hickok traveled throughout the nation in the early days of the Roosevelt presidency to offer a firsthand appraisal of the state of the nation to Harry Hopkins, the former social worker who headed the Federal Emergency Relief Administration, and Eleanor Roosevelt. Hickok visited the bituminous coal–mining regions of southwestern Pennsylvania, West Virginia, and Kentucky, and reported astounding conditions. In West Virginia, she encountered miners' families living for days on "green corn and string beans—and precious little of that. And some had nothing at all, actually hadn't eaten for a couple of days."[24] West Virginia opened its National Guard camps, which the Guard used only two weeks each summer, to four thousand "undernourished children, from families on the relief rolls." Hickok visited one of the camps, where one thousand boys had been in residence for a week. Camp administrators told her that the boys had gained, on average, five pounds each. Hickok stayed for supper and saw some of the boys go back for three servings. But the toll that unemployment took on West Virginians was devastating. "From long deprivation the health of the people is beginning to break down. Some of them have been starving for eight years. I was told there are children in West Virginia who never tasted milk! I visited one group of 45 blacklisted miners and their families, who had been living in tents two years."[25] A couple of weeks in summer camp was helpful, but children needed to eat every day of the year. The result was a significant rise in disease and general ill health. Hickok concluded that "the most desperate need in West Virginia is for hospitals."[26]

A woman in Chicago wrote to a relief station in 1936 about her family's struggles to survive. She shared that "I am without food for myself and child. I only got $6.26 to last me from the tenth to the twenty-fifth. That order is out and I haven't anything to eat. We go to bed hungry. Please give us something to eat. I cannot stand to see my child hungry."[27] From California, a woman wrote to Franklin Roosevelt about her struggles to feed her family. Her husband went to Los Angeles to try to find work, and she was desperate for assistance. "I am a mother of seven children," she shared, "and utterly heart broken, in that they are all hungry, have only 65 cents in money . . . provisions all gone—at this writing—no meat, milk—sugar—in fact, about enough flour for bread [for] two meals—and that's all." She told of her seventeen-year-old son, a high school student and French horn player.

FIG. 6 Girl carrying coal gleaned from a shale pile to her house in Scotts Run, West Virginia, 1938. The experiences of children like her stimulated the establishment of subsistence homesteads to improve the lives of coal-mining families. Library of Congress, Prints and Photographs Division, Washington, D.C., LC-USF34-050215-E. Farm Security Administration/Office of War Information Collection. Photo: Marion Post Wolcott.

> O, President, my heart is breaking, as I see him go from home with half enough to eat, and go all day with out a bite of lunch, to be sure he could *beg* his lunch but he's too proud to beg as long as he can help it, and I have spent the day yesterday praying God to help me bear this, and as I tried to prepare their very scarce breakfast. . . . O, what a burden and how helpless I am, how proud I am of my children, and how dark a future under this condition.[28]

President Herbert Hoover could not bring himself to admit publicly that Americans confronted such catastrophic circumstances. Though he had come to international fame through his efforts to feed European refugees from World War

I, his fear that federal efforts to provide relief or direct employment to a devastated citizenry would destroy the independent character upon which he believed the nation had been built steered him away from a sufficient response to the crisis. He was willing to provide relief to banks through the Reconstruction Finance Corporation, and he authorized hundreds of millions of dollars of federal spending on infrastructure projects, but he steadfastly resisted a direct federal role in assisting struggling Americans. According to Hoover, charitable organizations like the Red Cross and local governments were to fill that role. His efforts consisted of establishing two advisory committees on unemployment to offer insights to local relief programs.[29]

The crisis quickly overwhelmed local resources, though. Chicago's wealthy raised $11 million to provide resources for the unemployed for a full year, but saw the sum depleted in four months.[30] In Philadelphia, one hundred of the city's richest residents donated $4 million to poor relief in late November 1930. The state gave an additional $3 million, and a newly formed Bureau of Unemployment distributed the money to local charities. They exhausted the funds within a year, and $10 million more from a new pledge drive three months after that. The city spent an additional $2.5 million from the state in two more months, and then essentially gave up.[31]

The hunger persisted and deepened through the early years of the 1930s, and the municipalities' inability to feed their residents, when coupled with the federal government's unwillingness to step in, opened the door to some dramatic episodes. Local hunger marchers pressured state and local governments in Maryland, Columbus, Ohio, and Lansing, Michigan, in the spring of 1931. The nation saw at least forty such marches by summer's end. Herbert Benjamin and the Communist Party of the United States organized a hunger delegation to visit the U.S. Congress on the opening day of the December 1931 session. President Hoover and Congress feared a broad Communist conspiracy and arrested demonstrators. But Congress did pass legislation to relieve the hungry. Hoover vetoed it.[32]

Fearful that all hunger demonstrators would be associated in most Americans' eyes with communism, Father James Cox decided to lead his own march "for the divine and human right to work" from Pittsburgh to Washington, D.C.[33] The "march" started off from St. Patrick's Church in the city's warehouse district, home to the city's largest Hooverville camp for the homeless. As the caravan wound its way through Pittsburgh, spectators lined the streets to see them off. "Men shouted, women and children waved handkerchiefs and flags."[34] They traveled by car, truck, and train, though not enough vehicles could be found to accommodate the throngs who wanted to participate. Nearly twenty thousand people saw off the six thousand men who started the journey on January 5, 1932. (Father Cox worried about the propriety of men and women marching together, so he excluded females from participation—a common separation for many Catholic extraliturgical activities.)

All along the way the caravan picked up additional men. The newly elected mayor of Johnstown, Pennsylvania, hosted the group with a rally at Point Stadium.

There, Father Cox railed against President Hoover for bailing out the banks through his Reconstruction Finance Corporation while steadfastly refusing relief for ordinary people. Cox pointed out that "the government sent Al Capone to jail for cheating it out of $100,000, yet John D. Rockefeller is giving $4,000,000 to his son to escape the inheritance tax." The march passed into Huntingdon, a predominantly Protestant town between Johnstown and Harrisburg. There, in stark contrast to the hostility that characterized Protestant-Catholic relations during Al Smith's presidential run just a few years before, a local Protestant congregation offered the men breakfast. Governor Pinchot greeted the men warmly in Harrisburg once he saw the contingent's size.[35]

President Hoover was less enthusiastic about the group's arrival in Washington. He had swept into the White House in 1928 aided in part by a vicious anti-Catholic campaign against his Democratic rival, Al Smith. He did not relish the prospect of greeting upwards of twenty-five thousand Catholic protesters, upset with his determined resistance to aiding the hungry in the midst of the worst economic disaster in the nation's history. But he relented under pressure to see a delegation that included Father Cox and twelve other men. Cox excoriated Hoover for ignoring the suffering all about him, and Hoover responded that the Depression had run its course, that prosperity would soon arrive. Father Cox and his marchers returned to Pittsburgh and hosted a rally in the University of Pittsburgh football stadium that drew a crowd of sixty-five thousand people. There, Father Cox declared that "[o]urs is a battle against Wall Street and Smithfield Street," and announced his intention of running for president on the Jobless Party ticket.[36]

Hunger marchers sought to influence public policy in cities, states, and the nation. But others took a more direct route to remedy the crisis. England, Arkansas, saw the first major food confrontation, which pitted hungry Americans against relief agencies, food merchants, and, eventually, the state itself. Arkansas suffered from a major drought that pushed local farmers, who already struggled from years of falling prices for their crops, to the verge of starvation. The local Red Cross distributed some food, but not nearly enough to keep families from suffering. Farmers from the surrounding countryside trucked into town in early January 1931 to demand more food. By the time they got there, between three hundred and five hundred people had gathered outside the Red Cross office, demanding food. When attempts to talk the farmers out of their efforts failed, the Red Cross made arrangements with local merchants to provide $1,500 worth of food to the families. The crowd did not assail anyone, but they were unwilling to walk away empty-handed. A few weeks later in Oklahoma City, a mob of hungry residents broke into a grocery store and took food off the shelves. The fire department turned fire hoses on the men and women, and police arrested twenty-six. Food riots broke out in Minneapolis, San Francisco, St. Louis, and other cities.[37] A thousand hungry New York City men stormed two bread trucks in 1930, and frantic drivers threw bread and pastries into the street to assuage the crowd.[38]

Ironically, the food crisis seemed to hit the farm areas harder than more urbanized regions—at least by some measures. Farmers had a head start on the rest of the nation's fall into the Great Depression, and they suffered hunger earlier than other areas. Nutritionists had difficulty assessing malnutrition during the Depression, in part because they had no standard measures, but also because so many Americans, between 10 and 15 percent by reliable estimates, already ate poorly at the Depression's outset. Curiously, public health officials did not document a significant increase in malnutrition throughout the decade. But they did note that it seemed to concentrate in rural areas. When the federal government started a school lunch program, for example, fully 80 percent of recipients lived in rural areas of the South. Later, when Roosevelt sought to build up the military in anticipation of entry into World War II, he was startled to learn of malnutrition's impact. Of the first one million recruits, the military had to reject four hundred thousand for health reasons—one hundred and thirty thousand for reasons derived from malnutrition.[39]

Though President Hoover had consistently claimed that prosperity was just around the corner, that the agitators were subversive agents, that his policy responses were appropriate and wise, the suffering continued. People in every region of the country had stories of struggle and deprivation, but few were as grim as in the bituminous coal region in the northern Appalachian states of West Virginia and western Pennsylvania. Their stories, carried to Washington by the twenty-five thousand who accompanied Father Cox, could be seen in the cities, towns, and coal patches of many counties. Conditions in Westmoreland County, home to the future Westmoreland Homesteads project, were forbidding.

The Economic Crisis in the Coal and Coke Fields

Work in the mines and coke ovens was always dirty, difficult, dangerous, and ill paid, and life for families in the patch communities was full of privations. Conditions worsened in the 1920s and deepened further with the Great Depression. Growth in demand for coal and coke, which had soared during World War I, declined following it. During the war, coal and coke were essential to the iron and steel industries, which were at the center of armaments production. They were also critical to the production of railroad locomotives, transport ships, electrical generators, and for the delivery of goods to the U.S. allies in Europe. Given the escalating need, mine operators opened many new mines and reopened formerly marginal mines. Not surprisingly, demand for coal and coke dropped substantially when the war ended, leaving the industry with 100 million extra tons of coal already mined. The surplus coal and coke convinced mine owners to either close their mines or sharply curtail production.[40] Both policies heralded the beginning of a painfully long period of economic decline in the bituminous fields, which led to greater unemployment and underemployment for the miners and growing

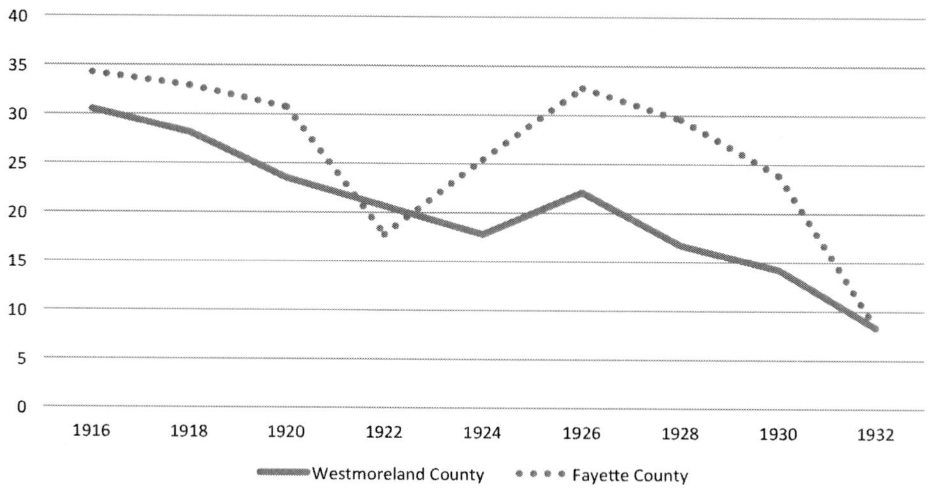

FIG. 7 Coal production, Westmoreland and Fayette Counties, selected years (net tons, millions). Schantz, *Historical Statistics of Pennsylvania's Mineral Industries*, 19–21.

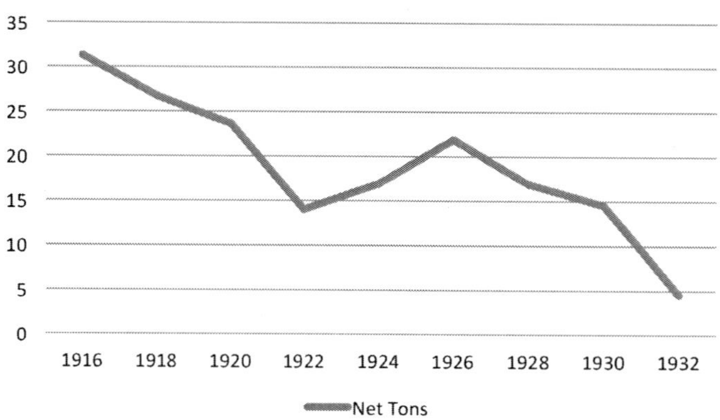

FIG. 8 Pennsylvania coke production. Schantz, *Historical Statistics of Pennsylvania's Mineral Industries*, 19–21.

poverty for mining families. The Connellsville field of southwestern Pennsylvania was especially hard hit, as figure 7 indicates. The data for coke production look similar, and the curve depicting the decline in coke production is nearly a match for the coal-production curve (see figure 8).

Two additional developments contributed to the overproduction of coal or the underemployment of miners. As mine operators sought to lower costs, they invested in mechanical mining equipment that raised per capita productivity and put miners out of work. By the early 1930s, 71 percent of all bituminous coal mined in the United States was produced by machinery, and "electrified mining machinery has reduced the number of miners from 750,000 to 250,000."[41] Further, the rise of competitive fuels in oil, natural gas, and hydroelectric power, combined with rising efficiency of coal utilization by factories and the railroads, effectively depressed the price of coal.

As the market for coal decreased during the 1920s, so, too, did the price paid for it. At one mine, for example, fine "steam coal" sold for $22.50 per ton in 1922, a time of high demand. In 1931, when the market was glutted from overproduction, that same mine sold steam coal for 15 cents per ton—less than 1 percent of the 1922 selling price.[42] Such behavior eroded the price of coal, especially where it competed with oil and gas.[43] This combination of factors—overproduction, the sharp decline in demand and price, and mechanization—resulted in unemployment, underemployment, and lower wages for coal miners during the 1920s. The poverty and hunger of the 1920s that permeated the coalfields of southwestern Pennsylvania worsened during the Depression.[44]

Toward Full Citizenship

A third factor to consider was the inability of the miners and the failure of the United Mine Workers of America (UMWA) to successfully obtain a higher wage and improved working and living conditions for the miners and their families during the 1920s. In addition to the plunging demand for coke and coal, economic competition from the nonunion coalfields of West Virginia and Kentucky in the 1920s convinced mine operators in Illinois, Indiana, Ohio, and parts of Pennsylvania that they need not and should not raise wages.

In 1920, the UMWA had established a wage scale of $7.50 a day for unionized miners,[45] but miners worked on average only 113 days each year.[46] The mine owners' refusal to extend the 1920 contract, raise the low wages, and ameliorate the grinding working conditions triggered a national strike in 1922.[47] Miners in the bituminous and anthracite coalfields across the United States, and as far away as Nova Scotia, joined the strike. Although most were not members of the union, they joined the strike hoping to secure the right to join the union and to obtain higher wages and better conditions.[48]

Nonunionized workers earned substantially lower wages than their unionized counterparts. Earnings for miners working full time in Westmoreland County averaged $1,200 a year. In unionized mines in Pittsburgh, some thirty miles away, they averaged $1,320. (In the Panhandle of West Virginia, unionized miners received $1,740.) The UMWA focused organizing efforts on Westmoreland County and the entire Connellsville coal region precisely because the nonunionized miners were receptive to the UMWA call. The UMWA sent forty "crack" organizers into the field, including Mother Jones, the famous labor leader.[49]

As could be expected, the mine owners fiercely resisted the workers' attempts to unionize and their calls for higher wages and better work conditions. *Coal Age*, a weekly magazine serving coal operators, recorded the determination of the local operators to resist the union: "There will be no capitulation to the union on the part of the Connellsville operators according to all reports from the field this week. Operators have indicated that union membership will not bar them from employment here but it also has been made clear that there will be no recognition of the union."[50]

Although the mine companies attempted to sabotage the union's efforts, organizers circumvented their plans. When barred from meeting on company-owned property, union organizers recruited so successfully in fields and along highways that about thirty thousand of the more than fifty thousand nonunion miners and coke workers of southwestern Pennsylvania joined the strike and the union.[51]

After four and one-half months, coal operators and UMWA representatives met in August 1922 in Cleveland, Ohio, to settle the strike. The union succeeded in maintaining "the economic gains acquired by the UMWA since the 1920 agreement." However, despite strong protest from southwestern Pennsylvania's representatives in Cleveland, UMWA president John L. Lewis signed an accord that did not include the nonunion strikers of southwestern Pennsylvania. The nonunionized miners continued to strike for their right to join the union for a few months, but then gave up and went back to work. In the words of labor historians Melvyn Dubofsky and Warren Van Tine, "Lewis deserted the nonunion miners of Somerset, Fayette, and Westmoreland counties in Pennsylvania, who had joined the strike, resisted to the bitter end, and refused to return to work when the August agreements excluded them." John Brophy and Powers Hapgood, two union leaders from Pennsylvania who backed the nonunionized miners, felt that Lewis had betrayed them and had thereby weakened the union, "leaving the coal industry a house divided."[52] However, miners and their families did not abandon their fight to attain higher wages and better living conditions, along with the right to unionize. They were not alone in their attempt.

In the mid-1920s, the Communist Party of the United States of America (CPUSA) determined that organizing bituminous coal miners was critical to its efforts to unionize U.S. workers. The CPUSA sought to build a revolutionary working-class movement in part by organizing a union that could effectively challenge John L. Lewis's leadership. In 1928, it formed the National Miners Union (NMU), which concentrated much of its mobilizing work, and some of the CPUSA's most experienced cadres, in southwestern Pennsylvania. The NMU held a national conference in Pittsburgh in September 1928, attended by some seven hundred delegates from Pennsylvania, Ohio, and West Virginia. Miners' willingness to join the radical union reflected their dissatisfaction with the UMWA, the growing desperation of their and their families' economic situation, and their belief that they deserved a better life.[53]

Nationally, workers and the unemployed displayed a growing readiness to fight as the deprivations unleashed by the Depression affected ever-larger numbers of Americans. According to the Department of Labor, in 1930 there were "653 disputes involving 158,114 workers." However, in the first six months of 1931 alone, there were 447 disputes affecting 132,273 workers. Of these disputes, "The most serious problems now pending, according to the department, are presented by the coal strikes now in progress in Western Pennsylvania, Eastern Ohio, and

Northern West Virginia." Of the eighty-three most serious pending labor disputes, twenty-eight were in Pennsylvania, involving 34,881 workers.[54]

It was in this context of rising protests nationally and recent pay cuts locally that the NMU initiated and led strikes in the spring and summer of 1931 in the coalfields of southwestern Pennsylvania.[55] Unemployment among miners had soared; according to one source, it had reached 75 percent.[56] By June, forty thousand miners had joined the strike.[57] William Foster, a leading figure in the CPUSA (and from 1948 to 1957 the head of the party), spent the entire five months of the strike in the area, mobilizing miners and their families in southwestern Pennsylvania.[58] This strike was a family affair. The NMU organized miners, as well as women and children. Foster boasted of this inclusionary tactic in an interview: "Another innovation [of the NMU] is the participation of 128,000 wives and children of strikers in our demonstrations and picketing."[59] In a reflection of this policy, eight thousand women and men from surrounding mining communities marched into downtown Pittsburgh in July 1931 "to show the strength of the month-old coal strike." Police, armed with tear gas and riot clubs, lined the streets, but the exhausted walkers peacefully paraded by, singing all the way. They rallied in a downtown park and listened to rallying speeches by William Foster and other labor leaders.[60]

Ironically, the militancy of the miners and the organizational power of the NMU, and behind it the CPUSA,[61] convinced the coal operators that they had to settle the strike. But not with the NMU![62] Instead, they came to an agreement with John L. Lewis and the UMWA. Coal operators' refusal to settle with the NMU, and Lewis's willingness to negotiate with the operators, isolated the NMU and contributed to the 1935 dissolution of the union. The NMU recognized its own weakness and urged its members to join the UMWA, which many of them did.[63]

The Economic Crisis and the Stranded Coal Community

The results for miners and their families were devastating. In the three decades prior to 1922, bituminous coal miners worked on average only 213 days annually, or a bit more than half of each year. During World War I they worked 243 days on average. These were the good times. In 1921, they worked only 149 days. The glut of miners and the decreased demand for their work kept the 1922–25 average workdays to between 142 and 195. The labor force exceeded the demand by roughly 40 percent for all of the 1920s. Yet the miners tended to stay in the patches, for a variety of reasons, and conditions in those communities worsened. Prices in the coal communities frequently exceeded those in the surrounding towns. Miners and their families in Westmoreland County paid 5.4 percent more for their food than did the inhabitants of nearby Greensburg. The United States Coal Commission visited coal-patch communities and found that in general the children lived below "minimum health and decency" levels. In one western Pennsylvania coal-mining town, the school principal reported that "people do not appeal to [local aid societies] until they are literally without food or resources for getting it; probably one-third of the families living in the town are living on starvation rations."[64]

Lorena Hickok's travels took her to Latrobe, Pennsylvania, within a few miles of what would become Norvelt. There she found a group of thirty or forty former miners who were too hungry, old, and broken to work in the shafts should they open again. They had no income or savings, and so had taken to living in the idled coke ovens. Hickok wrote to Eleanor Roosevelt that the men tried to cultivate small gardens near the ovens, but they were defeated.[65]

Pennsylvania entered what the *Social Service Review* editors called "the third winter of unemployment" in 1931 when Governor Gifford Pinchot ordered a comprehensive assessment of the state's economic challenges and local relief agencies' capacities to meet the demands they confronted. In its formal report, his official "Planning Committee" provided dramatic evidence of an across-the-board crisis. Nearly a quarter of all Pennsylvanians seeking work, fully 919,000 people, could find none. No industry escaped unscathed, though some seemed particularly devastated. Employment in the bituminous coal mines dropped 17.5 percent between June 1929 and June 1931. This decline in employment came on top of the already steep layoffs of the 1920s, rendering this much more than the third winter of unemployment for miners. Payrolls dropped even more precipitously, by 47 percent, over the same two years. Mine operators had often reduced hours and wages rather than let miners go completely, which preserved some measure of income. But miners could not live on the meager earnings that their reduced wages generated, and in many areas they went on strike to restore their diminished incomes. Relief agencies refused to serve strikers, though, which put their families at great peril.[66]

The result was disastrous. The Westmoreland County Unemployment Council reported in 1931 that nearly one in five workers in the county who had jobs in "normal" times could not find work.[67] (Note that these statistics reflect early efforts to gauge unemployment, and so do not match well with standard measures today. The "normal" times against which the county compared these data were already a depressed period for miners. Unemployment figures do not report the percent of those seeking work who could not find it, but rather the percent of those who in 1929 would have been employed and found themselves without jobs in 1931.) The situation was particularly bleak among the county's miners, who had been suffering for some time already. Mine operators favored reduced hours over a shrunken labor force, and so kept more miners on part time rather than fewer on full time. This reduced the employment rate in the mines by only 13.5 percent, but left the employed miners working only 64 percent of their normal hours. Demand for relief support exploded. The county spent nearly $3.5 million in 1930, much of it in short-term road-construction projects that provided temporary employment. The County Relief Board noted that unemployment "has greatly reduced the standard of living of thousands of people," but asserted that they were not alarmed. They knew of no one who had starved to death yet, though they recognized that the bleak employment prospects left many "in a highly depressed frame of mind." Moreover, while the cities had established relief agencies, the townships did not. "Unemployed miners and others in these rural districts have to depend on the generosity of the companies for which they formerly worked, on the Poor Directors, and in some cases on the Salvation Army and Red Cross."[68]

The situation quickly grew worse. If the 14,694 "extra" unemployed workers caused no alarm among county officials in 1931, the 1933 figures ought to have set bells ringing throughout the county. Fully 38,000 normally employed workers could find no job in March of 1933. The county had spent more on relief efforts in 1931 than fiscally conservative officials preferred, in part because they expected the situation to improve in 1932. They were not prepared for it to get twice as bad, and allocated only two-thirds as much to feed, clothe, and employ out-of-work workers' families as they had in the less grim year. Suffering increased dramatically. Unemployed and homeless families established legal residences in the idled coke ovens so that they might draw relief checks.[69]

Field reporters sent out to assess the situation sent back grave reports. One observed that "[m]alnutrition is prevalent. Children are in need of milk and medical care. Destitution will increase. Doubtful if local agencies can handle situation." Another noted that "[c]hildren are deprived of milk and food essential to their growth." Still another recounted that "children are not receiving sufficient food, nor are local agencies organized sufficiently to handle the situation," before predicting that "the outlook for winter is bad." In one bituminous mining district, fully two thousand people had no means of support whatsoever as the cold months approached—no income, no savings, nothing.[70]

Governor Pinchot recognized that life in the state and the country was increasingly bifurcated between the wealthy minority and the increasingly impoverished majority. Those who had resources, a steady income, a dollar to spend "may buy with it far more than at any time in recent years. Food and clothing, shelter and goods are here in unexampled plenty." At the same time, "want is abroad in the land." Wages had "fallen faster than prices, and the earnings of those who still have work bring them to a lower standard of living than before. Worst of all, millions of Americans are without the means of buying anything." Their suffering was "beyond all recent experience." The question in Pinchot's mind was not whether families could maintain their previous standard of living, but rather "whether the parents can be prevented from starving or freezing, and whether the children can be well enough fed, clothed, and sheltered to keep in health and go to school."[71]

Other public officials echoed his concerns. Senator James J. Davis told Rotary, Lions, and Kiwanis club members that the "cut-throat competition in the mining industry in Pennsylvania has reduced the living standards of miners to a point equaled in no other country outside of Russia." Unemployment worsened their quality of life even further. The state restricted relief to food only, and resisted efforts to pay cash to those in need. The result was a terrible burden on relief agencies such as the Red Cross and local communities who were left to address needs for housing and clothing. The Red Cross ran out of clothes in parts of western Pennsylvania in 1933 and handed out pieces of cloth instead. One community had workers dig up brick roads, clean off the bricks, and replant them to "improve" the roads in a "make-work" program designed to get cash into workers' hands. Families in another coal town repaired children's shoes with tire rubber. The situation only worsened by 1934, when 13 percent of the state's entire population depended on relief for all basic life necessities. Arthur Dunham noted that Pennsylvania had more people on relief than the entire population of any one of sixteen states. Its State Emergency Relief Board (SERB) spent 7 million dollars each month to support the 1.2 million Pennsylvanians who would otherwise go without food and shelter.[72]

Pinchot saw the suffering as both physical deprivation and "mental torture" for male breadwinners.

> The man who sees his family suffering for the lack of what his labor is well able to supply, and yet who can find no work, cannot be greatly blamed if he gives way to despair. And the man whose loved ones are sick, needing his help, and still he cannot help them,—his case is even worse . . . when to a man's own suffering is added the suffering of those who have a right to look to him for support, the result is often appalling. No man can understand this depression who thinks only of its bread and butter side.

Nathan Ackerman, who worked as a psychiatrist in the Pennsylvania coalfields during the Depression, agreed. He recalled that long-term unemployment had a devastating impact on the miners. "They hung around on street corners and in groups. They gave each other solace. They were loath to go home because they were indicted, as if it were their fault for being unemployed. A jobless man was a lazy good-for-nothing. . . . These men suffered from depression. They felt despised, they were ashamed of themselves. They cringed, they comforted one another. They avoided home."[73]

No policy, no program, offered dignified relief from the suffering or economic and social hope for the despondent miner and his family. By the time that most of the rest of the nation encountered the Depression, miners knew cold, hunger, and alienation well. Henry W. Francis toured the mining areas of southwestern Pennsylvania and discerned that there was little optimism among the general population for recovery programs. The problem, they told Francis, was the disposition of the miner himself. "Of course he should have work for which he is fitted—that means grubbing coal underground—but he should not be counted in on any fanciful rehabilitation scheme predicated on self-help. He simply will not fit in—he's a miner by nature and nothing but mining at good pay will satisfy him."[74] Francis concluded that he had no answers to the problem, and that no one he spoke to in Pennsylvania did either. Everyone seemed to think that coal would never come back as strongly as before, and that miners had no capacity or inclination to do anything else. But maybe they were wrong. For Francis had seen progress in West Virginia: "May not these coal diggers a few miles north have 'hidden resources,' too, in mind and spirit? Would it not be well to take stock of the Pennsylvania miner? He can't do it himself. He sees no way out—wants no way other than the work in the same old mine at living pay. . . . He'll float along if you keep him supplied with life belts without ever dreaming of getting to shore. But I suspect that once on stable ground he might find himself and for the first time be happy."[75]

But where might that stable ground be found? One answer, already under development in Westmoreland County, was the subsistence homestead community. Westmoreland Homesteads offered secure, comfortable, and attractive housing, opportunities for work, and potential for a robust community life.

Chapter Three

The Response

The New Deal and the Subsistence Homestead Program

> Whatever the outcome, President Roosevelt will live in history as a great President if only for this one fact. He not only appreciated the situation, but had the courage to grapple with the cardinal economic problem of modern life. And he did so not in the spirit of hatred manifested by the red revolutionary or the black Fascist abroad, but in the typical American spirit of great generosity and great recognition that individual life and individual homes are the precious possessions; all else is merely machinery for the attainment of a full life.
>
> —A. A. BERLE JR.,
> "The Social Economics of the New Deal"

> The setting up of a Division of Subsistence Homesteads in our Federal Government marks a national recognition of what agricultural economists in the past have called part-time farming, and city planners have called garden cities or garden suburbs. The recognition of this in federal legislation therefore injects it into our national policy at this time.
>
> —M. L. WILSON,
> "The Place of Subsistence Homesteads in Our National Economy"

The New Deal

The Great Depression began for farmers in the early 1920s and for much of the rest of America in 1929. The economic collapse was so severe, so thorough, and so overwhelming that Americans had no cache of previously successful strategies to remedy or endure it. Those who advocated waiting it out saw the economy slip further and further as time passed. What at first seemed to them to be a temporary adjustment, then a useful chastening, continued on past humbling corrective into long-term devastation. With no relief in sight, advice to let the economy fix itself went down more easily in executive dining rooms than in workers' kitchens. But by the time of the 1932 presidential election, the prospect of continued federal inaction made even the most economically comfortable Americans uneasy. Even Herbert Hoover had come to see that something had to be done, and he made plans for direct federal intervention. In the end, he proved too timid to implement most of these, and some ended up among the plethora of strategies that Franklin Roosevelt employed.

Hoover was at best a tepid laissez-faire disciple. In his youth, he declared that "[t]he time when the employer could ride roughshod over his labor is disappearing with the doctrine of 'laissez faire' on which it was founded."[1] He never warmed to the idea of an impotent federal government, but he could not countenance an activist government either. In fact, many recent conservative historians in search of a government villain to explain the Great Depression's severity and longevity have landed on Hoover's intrusive meddling in the free market.[2] Though his early attempts to reverse the Depression consisted mainly of efforts to persuade business leaders to keep prices, employment levels, and wages stable, he did turn late in his tenure to more interventionist activities. Most significantly, Hoover established the massive Reconstruction Finance Corporation (RFC) to provide government financial support to banks that struggled to stay afloat. Congress gave the RFC $500 million to loan to banks, building-and-loan-societies, and other financial institutions and authorized it to borrow an additional $1.5 billion for that purpose as well. He had put the U.S. government into the banking business in a big way.[3]

In return for steering hundreds of millions of dollars through the RFC to banks to spur them to lend money to businesses, Hoover expected that the businesses would then hire workers to revive the economy. Yet they did not, because so few consumers sought to buy the goods and services they provided. The bank bailout did not reach down to the ordinary worker, and many ordinary Americans saw Hoover as far more sympathetic to the rich than he was to the typical citizen. New York congressman and later mayor Fiorello La Guardia called the controversial RFC the "millionaire's dole."[4] But where was the federal dole for workers? What did Hoover have to offer to those who struggled to provide food and shelter for their families?

Hoover's answer to this was part philosophical, part pragmatic, and ultimately insufficient. He opposed federal welfare programs on principle, and resisted all congressional initiatives to provide direct relief to the unemployed and the poor. He worried more that free food and rent subsidies might erode individual initiative and character than that malnutrition, overcrowding, and homelessness robbed Americans of their health, well-being, and dignity. Though Hoover was by no means idle during his four years, one could not appropriately characterize his Depression response as a "program." For something so far-reaching, ambitious, and energetic, the nation needed a new president and Congress.

Franklin Delano Roosevelt fit the bill perfectly. Though born and bred in privilege, he chose not to dedicate his public life to preserving the prerogatives that this class had accumulated so zealously. Rather, he energetically championed a public policy that put the common good at its center. When he first entered the White House, he initiated a series of efforts to rejuvenate the economy and make the Depression tolerable for the many unemployed, hungry, and ill housed. The programs were often experiments in relief and economic stimulation, and they sometimes lasted only a short while. Roosevelt had few reservations about devising, implementing, assessing, then altering or even ending programs. Some of them lasted only a few years, others have endured to this day. Taken together, the programs created a "New Deal" for Americans.

New Deal as Manifestation of Cooperative Ideal

Many progressives saw the Great Depression as the product of two significant developments through the late nineteenth and early twentieth centuries. The first was the concentration of economic power, and inevitably political power, in the hands of large-scale economic entities. Newly emergent corporations, endowed by states and the federal government with incredible autonomy, prerogative, and privilege, came to dominate the economic and political landscape. They controlled so much of American life that democracy itself stood at risk. These corporations grew out of and lived by the second Depression-producing development—a predilection for garnering competitive advantages against each other, their own workers, and even the communities in which they resided. This ethic of competition, of seeking to gain advantage over others, informed every aspect of corporate activity and poisoned the body politic.

With these two developments in mind, New Deal reformers devised remedies that both displaced the ethic of competition in favor of cooperation and sought to offset corporate power by strengthening entities sufficiently to constrain those economic giants. New Dealers sought to create, in Alan Lawson's characterization, "a commonwealth of hope" in which corporations, unions, and the government would work cooperatively to achieve national and individual economic and civic well-being. They wanted to restore a national sense of commonweal that competitive capitalism and monopoly power had displaced.[5]

Reformers identified the federal government and organized labor as the most viable bodies to offset corporate dominance of American life. But the Supreme Court had systematically limited organized labor's efforts, which one historian argued had the consistent effect of "giving constitutional protection to unequal economic power in the name of personal liberty."[6] Absent federal intervention, the corporations would only continue to serve the short-term economic interests of their stockholders at the expense of the long-term health of the broader public. If only the federal government could turn corporations toward new goals and regulate their activity sufficiently to stop the recklessness with which they put society at risk, perhaps reformers could stop the downward economic spiral and build a new prosperity that shared wealth more widely and provided a sufficient measure of security and dignity to all citizens.

New Dealers did not try to destroy corporations or break them up into smaller economic entities, as others advocated, but rather accepted that they were here to stay. New Dealers sought to turn corporations to new patterns of behavior, to push them into a social compact of shared responsibility for the general welfare. The New Deal strategy was to turn these engines of competition into vehicles of cooperation. Raymond Moley, one of Roosevelt's closest advisors, recalled that the philosophical underpinning for this strategy came from Charles Van Hise's *Concentration and Control,*[7] which helped lead Franklin Roosevelt and his brain trust to the conclusion that "economic bigness was here to stay; that the problem of government was to enable the whole people to enjoy the benefits of mass production and distribution (economy and security); and that it was the duty of government to devise, with business, the means of social and individual adjustment to the facts of the industrial age—these were the heart and soul of the New Deal."[8] Moley recalled that New Dealers tried to "modify the characteristics of a chaotic competitive system that could and did produce sweatshops, child labor, rackets, ruinous price cutting, a devastated agriculture, and a score of other blights even in the peak year of 1928."[9]

The National Industrial Recovery Act (NIRA) was a prime example of this strategy. It allowed giant corporations to set prices for goods and services commonly with their competitors—to act collusively, in essence—so long as they also agreed to pay reasonable wages, establish and maintain safe working conditions for their employees, and observe their employees' rights to form unions to safeguard these standards and not undercut competitors' prices unfairly. Roosevelt had been involved in centralized war planning in his role in the Department of the Navy during World War I, and saw it as a prudent midway path between the cutthroat capitalism that brought the nation the Depression and the socialism that scared too many Americans.

Key elements of the plan came from ideas that General Electric's Gerard Swope advanced and the Chamber of Commerce endorsed. Swope had spent time at Jane Addams's Hull House in Chicago, a settlement house that sought to provide physical nourishment, cultural integration, and civic education to immigrant slum dwellers. Its progressive ideals shaped Swope's perspective, and he introduced such worker-friendly policies at General Electric as contributory unemployment insurance.[10] But he could see how his competitors achieved a competitive advantage by paying lower wages, skimping on workplace safety, and demanding longer hours. He had served with the War Industrial Board in World War I, and knew that cooperation helped to make industry more efficient. He proposed a plan to Herbert Hoover that allowed businesses within an industry to work together to set common industry standards for working conditions and wages without setting off federal antitrust actions. Hoover rejected the ideas because he thought they would allow the federal government to dictate standards to business and kill the free enterprise spirit. Roosevelt was more receptive, as was the Chamber of Commerce, which saw the exemption from antitrust enforcement as a great benefit to business. Union leaders embraced the idea because it offered the hope that businesses could offer higher wages without fear that competitors would undercut the scale to reduce costs.[11]

Congress passed the National Industrial Recovery Act on July 16, 1933, with elements that appealed to three critical constituencies. Businesses, especially large corporations, warmed to the exemptions from antitrust litigation that it offered. The president of the U.S. Chamber of Commerce called it "one of the most important measures ever presented at any time to any Congress." The National Electrical Manufacturers Association also embraced the Act.[12]

Unions embraced the intention of setting minimum wages, maximum hours, and workplace safety standards. They saw this as the best hope of curtailing the cutthroat competition that drove wages ever downward. Section 7(a) of the NIRA guaranteed workers the right to form unions, to resist company formed unions, and to have maximum hours of work per week, minimum wages, and workplace safety regulations. American Federation of Labor president William Green stated, "Millions of workers through the nation stood up for the first time in their lives to receive their charter of industrial freedom." Workplace organizing skyrocketed, including in the coal-mining regions of western Pennsylvania and West Virginia, where miners posted signs that read, "The President Wants You to Join the Union." The AFL reported in October that it had added 1.5 million new members since the NIRA went into effect.[13]

Planners applauded the central role that the federal government would play in setting industrial policies on a rational basis. Only the government could stop the deflationary spiral that crippled business development and put the nation's economy on its downward trajectory. But it would do so by stimulating cooperation between firms in the same industry. Roosevelt had explained in a fireside chat that "that organized control which we call government seems necessary to produce the same results of justice and right conduct . . . formerly achieved by the ethical conduct of individuals." The government would only step in to impose codes on industries in which the businesses could not agree among themselves.[14]

But others worried that the legislation essentially endorsed an economy built on a foundation of giant corporations that had just brought the nation to its knees. Louis Brandeis, a Supreme Court justice and longtime shaper of Democratic economic philosophy, believed the strategy would lead inevitably to the creation of more monopolies and further distress. He warned Roosevelt against the approach, and would later join court decisions that struck down the National Recovery Administration as unconstitutional.[15]

A similar strategy informed the reform of the agricultural sector. In 1920, the federal census reported for the first time in U.S. history that more people lived in urban than rural areas. But it defined "urban" as a municipality of twenty-five hundred people or more, and the 1930s saw a reversal of migration from these cities to the countryside. Fully a quarter of Americans still lived on farms in 1930.[16] America was still significantly rural, and no response to the Great Depression that focused exclusively on unemployed industrial workers could hope to succeed. Moreover, the Great Depression reached the farms at least a half decade before it hit the cities. The struggles that rural inhabitants faced were at least as bad as, and often more severe than, those of their urban compatriots. Something had to be done for the farming sector.

Roosevelt understood this clearly. He came to public service as a representative of the rural Hudson River district, in which his family's Hyde Park "gentleman's farm" fell. He launched his political career as an advocate for farmers in the New York State Assembly, and he remained attuned to rural needs throughout his life. He entered the White House convinced that any recovery program had to have two significant prongs—one that addressed industrial distress and one that restored prosperity to farmers. For in the end, if farmers could not prosper, Americans would not have the food and clothing that they needed to survive. And if farmers could not afford to buy consumer goods, then the factories too would suffer.

The problem for farmers mirrored that which industrial workers faced. Farmers had become so efficient that they outproduced demand for their products, flooded the market, drove the prices for their goods down, and reduced their incomes. However, when efficient industrial workers produced so many goods that the market became oversaturated, companies reduced their workers' hours or eliminated their jobs. They reduced the supply of goods. Nobody could fire farmers, though, or force them to produce less. In fact, when the fruits of their labor flooded the market and pushed the prices down, they responded with the opposite strategy from that of industries. Farmers produced more bushels to make up for the reduced price that each bushel brought. This pushed the price per bushel down even further, which prompted farmers to produce even more. It became an endless cycle spiraling downward.

The farm situation was made even worse by the spike in farm income that World War I generated. The war in Europe prevented farmers there from growing crops and raising livestock sufficient to the population's demand. American farmers stepped into the breach. Before the war, American farmers received 79 cents for every bushel of wheat, and they produced 751 million bushels. In 1919, they received $2.16 for each of the 952 million bushels that they produced.[17] European armies alone consumed 600 million bushels of U.S. wheat that year, and the prewar sales for hogs doubled. American farmers geared up for this by putting more land into production—especially in the lower Great Plains—and using the existing land much more efficiently. This pushed the demand for farmland up as well, so that Iowa land sold for $500 an acre. The profit margin over land value increased by up to five times the prewar level. Farmers borrowed money to buy land and machinery, and committed themselves to payments that they could only meet if the wartime levels of demand remained in place for years afterward.[18]

The war's conclusion ended this prosperity abruptly. Two months after the warring nations declared peace, England, France, and Italy canceled all orders for hogs. American farmers had already raised 400 million pounds for a market that had just disappeared.[19] The bushel of wheat that sold for $2.16 in 1919 fell to 93 cents by 1923, and to 38 cents by 1932. Farm income fell precipitously, from $17 billion in 1919 to $5 billion in 1932. In many cases, farmers had to pay more to produce their crops than they earned from their sales.[20]

The answer that most farmers came up with was to increase production even further. But farmers in 1932 had to produce five and a half bushels of wheat to get the same $2.16 that they earned for each 1919 bushel. And the cost of generating the $2.16, even accounting for increased efficiencies, exceeded that of 1919. The individual, competitive strategy drove farmers further into the economic hole in which they found themselves. Unless they joined together to withhold wheat from the market, to reduce the supply, the demand would remain too weak to justify farming. But farmers who produced nothing earned nothing, and those who reduced their output while their neighbors continued at a high pace saw no benefit from their reduced production.

The very competitive nature of commodity farming even in the flush times led farmers to implement more efficient crop-production methods. They bought the machinery, the combines and tractors, that allowed them to plant more with less effort. But farmers had to borrow money to buy these machines and the newly developed fertilizers that increased output, as well as to expand their land holdings to maximize their new machines' value. The bank required regular loan payments that compelled farmers to generate income. They could not sit out the economic down times and wait for prices to rise; they needed cash every month to meet their obligations. Their failure to do so contributed to a massive banking crisis and a further decline in demand for factory goods. Stretched farmers ordered less from the Sears catalogue.[21] Farmers operated in what Congressman John A. Martin of Colorado called "the last frontier of individualism in the sense of every fellow for himself, the devil take the hindmost. Industry and labor have fairly well learned the lesson and the need of organization. . . . [The farmer] will either take hold of his problems and work them out under this guidance or be reduced to a permanent state of tenantry and penury."[22] The message seemed clear: cooperate or suffer.

The remedy that New Deal reformers devised sought to replace the competitive ethic with a cooperative one. It sought to join farmers together to get them to produce less, to grow less wheat and corn, for example, so that the price that these goods brought at the market was higher. The strategy was to create what historian Robert McElvaine termed a "government-subsidized scarcity." The federal government paid farmers to leave acres untilled, to increase their income by decreasing their work.[23] But it only succeeded when farmers trusted that the income they earned from a combination of the crops they grew and the subsidy they received for not growing exceeded what they would have earned for planting from fence row to fence row. This was clearly the case with the low crop prices before the program started, but what about when prices began to rise? Farmers who had planted on all of their acres then would benefit from their neighbors' idleness.[24]

The House of Representatives passed the Agricultural Adjustment Act (AAA) on March 22, 1933, and the Senate did so almost two months later. Roosevelt signed the legislation on May 12, 1933. It included provisions that allowed Roosevelt to offer incentives to farmers to reduce the acres that they farmed, allowed farmers to join cooperative associations shielded from antitrust enforcement, and paid for any costs that the federal government's incentive program might incur through a special tax on food-processing companies.[25] Roosevelt's secretary of agriculture, Henry Wallace, gave a national radio address introducing the plan on May 13, during which he called the plan "A Declaration of Interdependence."[26]

Conservative critics saw red. Arthur Schlesinger Jr. recounts that Representative Fred Britten of Illinois called the bill "more Bolshevistic than any law or regulation existing in Soviet Russia." Fellow House member Joseph Martin of Massachusetts fulminated, "We are on our way to Moscow."[27] In their view, the farm bill moved too far from individualism; it diminished the farmer's individual competitive nature in favor of a large-scale cooperative ideal. When it was coupled with amendments allowing Roosevelt to manipulate currency values, even members of Roosevelt's own economic team feared the decline of capitalism. Budget director Lewis Douglas argued that in its original form it represented the "end of Western Civilization," and Bernard Baruch worried that it was "more drastic than the French Revolution."[28] Michigan's Arthur Vandenberg called it "the most revolutionary proposal that has ever been presented in the history of the government."[29]

Henry Wallace had hoped that the bill would pass through Congress by mid-March. Farmers could not wait beyond then to plant crops, and Wallace feared that they would once more plant as much as they could to make up for falling prices. The final legislation did not pass until mid-May, and farmers had planted by then. Holding true to form, they planted even more in 1933 than they had in 1932. In fact, cotton farmers sowed 4 million additional acres than they had just one year earlier, even though a year's worth of world demand for cotton sat in storage, unsold from the previous year. The depressed cotton prices were certain to fall yet again. Wallace took the dramatic step of paying the cotton farmers $100 million to plow under much of what they had already put in the ground. As difficult as this was for both farmers and the nation to digest, even more unsettling were the efforts to reduce the "production" of hogs. Wallace offered $200 million to hog farmers to kill 6.2 million young pigs and two hundred thousand farrowing sows. Newspapers across the country decried the destruction of piglets as national policy, especially when so many Americans went hungry.[30] The Agricultural Adjustment Administration would never again destroy crops or animals, but this initial effort fueled critics' declamations for years to come.

When Congress passed the Agricultural Adjustment Act, it also passed the Farm Mortgage Assistance Act. This legislation established the Farm Credit Administration with the power to refinance farm mortgages to address the foreclosure crisis that swept across rural America. It quickly arranged more than $100 million in debt refinancing that allowed poor farmers to adjust their payments to more manageable levels. In addition, it established regional banks that farmers could use to borrow money for implements and seeds. It helped to slow the massive wave of foreclosures that was pushing family farmers off their land and accelerating the movement toward greater land consolidation.[31]

Though not every aspect of the programs begun under New Deal initiatives fostered cooperation over competition, one can see the impulse informing much of what emerged from federal planners during the 1930s. This very sentiment animated the subsistence homestead program, which created Westmoreland Homesteads in western Pennsylvania. Some of the very people who helped address the response to both the industrial and the farm collapse shaped the subsistence homesteads as well. Senator John Hollis Bankhead II of Alabama included the provision in the National Industrial Recovery Act, which established the subsistence homestead program, and M. L. Wilson, Clarence Pickett, and Eleanor Roosevelt played significant roles in fashioning and implementing this innovative New Deal response to the Great Depression. Their perspectives are important to understanding the molds from which the various communities were stamped. But the communities themselves grew organically too, in response to their unique experiences and environments, as well as to the aspirations that the residents had and the efforts that they expended. It is not enough to know what the planners intended. One must also explore Norvelt's history to understand this extraordinarily human response to the struggles that the Great Depression wrought.

The Cooperative Ideal and Subsistence Homesteads

John Hollis Bankhead II would at first appear to be an unlikely sponsor of the subsistence homestead program, which he inserted into the NIRA. He worked for much of his life to build and protect a stratified society, both in his private and public efforts. He was born to a patrician family in Lamar County, Alabama, in 1872. His father represented Alabama in the U.S. Congress, as congressman and then senator, for thirty-three years. John Bankhead II earned degrees from the University of Alabama and Georgetown University and then practiced law and worked at his family's businesses for many years. As an attorney in Alabama, he represented the state's most powerful corporations—railroads and coal companies. His family later bought the Caledonia Coal Company, and he served as the president of the renamed Bankhead Coal Company for fifteen years (1911–25).[32]

Bankhead first entered public life as a Walker County delegate to the state constitutional convention in 1901, which produced a constitution committed to racial segregation. When Bankhead became state representative in 1903, he authored legislation that built on the constitution to effectively exclude African Americans and poor whites from voting. His father died in 1920, and Bankhead considered, but then rejected, the idea of running to succeed him. Bankhead did decide to run for the Senate in 1926, though, and lost to Hugo Black in the Democratic primary.

FIG. 9 John H. Bankhead II sits with his brother William, speaker of the U.S. House of Representatives. Library of Congress, Prints and Photographs Division, Washington, D.C., LC-H22-D-6389.

Bankhead tried again in 1930, this time for the other Senate seat from Alabama, and unseated the incumbent Democrat, J. Tom Heflin. Heflin had refused to support Al Smith as the Democratic nominee for president in 1928, and the party left him off the ballot as punishment. Though Bankhead won the primary and later general election handily, Heflin challenged the outcome based upon his exclusion. Bankhead eventually prevailed, and the Senate seated him.[33]

Nothing in Bankhead's early career suggested that he had become sensitive or sympathetic to the struggles that poor Alabama farmers and industrial workers faced. But he became a strong supporter of New Deal legislation that benefited poor white farmers, evident especially in his sponsorship of the subsistence homestead section of the NIRA. At the same time, he made support of New Deal programs contingent upon their exclusion of African Americans. Though section 208 of the NIRA did not specifically bar African Americans from benefiting, their general exclusion would be a constant source of frustration throughout the life of the program. Homesteads remained almost exclusively white, with few exceptions. African Americans did establish one subsistence homestead in Virginia and another in Houston, Texas, but they could not make headway anywhere else. When African Americans pressed SHD officials about this issue, the officials mostly obfuscated. The Westmoreland Homesteads story on this issue, as told in chapter 5, was no exception.

If John Bankhead moved the legislation through Congress, his influence on the program's direction once it got started shifted quickly to its initial directors and administrators in the executive branch. M. L. Wilson was the first director of the Subsistence Homesteads Division when it operated relatively freely under the Department of the Interior. Harold Ickes ostensibly oversaw the program as secretary of the interior, but he never warmed to the project, and Wilson ran it according to the ideals that he set out—with one significant exception. Eleanor Roosevelt took a special interest in the first subsistence homestead, located in Reedsville, West Virginia. She maintained a steady influence over the community that would become Arthurdale, West Virginia, throughout the entire length of its existence as a federal project, and continued her support even after it passed into the residents' private hands after World War II. She and Wilson did not differ substantially in their perspectives, and Wilson exerted significant influence over the broader program through its first year.

Milburn Lincoln (M. L.) Wilson lived and worked in agricultural settings for the first three decades of his life before moving to Washington, D.C., to work for the federal government. He was born in Atlantic, Iowa, in 1885 and grew up in the state. He earned a bachelor of science in agriculture degree from Iowa State College in 1907, moved to Montana two years later, and then left for the University of Wisconsin, where he earned a master of science degree in agricultural economics and sociology in 1920. He served in a variety of government positions for the state of Montana and then in the federal government. From 1926 to 1933 he headed the Department of Agricultural Economics at Montana State College, and he advised the USSR on large-scale wheat farming in 1929. Later colleagues often referred to him as Dr. Wilson, and noted that he was very philosophically inclined—an observation often made in tandem with one about his administrative inefficiency. He joined the Roosevelt administration as chief wheat production secretary in 1933, and became head of the Division of Subsistence Homesteads by September of that year.[34] Wilson melded his formal education and work in agricultural economics with a keen interest in social questions. Within a year of his appointment he found himself "promoted" out of the division that he led, though he shaped the program dramatically in those early months.[35]

Wilson articulated his ideal for the program in an article published in the January 1934 issue of the *Journal of Farm Economics*. He explained that the program represented a new approach to land policy that was a both a natural extension of trends in industry and farming and a cultural response against Jazz Age moral norms. Wilson saw the policy as new in that it reversed significantly long-standing federal agricultural policy, which had until then sought always to expand the number of acres in agricultural production. The oversaturation of crops that kept pushing prices and farm income down brought him to the conclusion that Americans grew too much already, and that farmers needed to reduce production. In addition, weather changes and other factors revealed that many farmers depended on what agricultural economists called "submarginal" land—land that could not yield marketable wheat, corn, tobacco, or cotton over the long term. These farmers would struggle forever unless they moved to better land. Roosevelt's land-farming policy therefore sought to take acres out of production.[36]

At the same time, the policy sought to extend long-standing farming practices. Many farmers throughout U.S. history grew crops not for markets, but for their families' own consumption. These farmers still constituted a third of all agricultural workers, according to the 1930 census, and their way of life had become more appealing as the Depression wore on. Wilson saw signs that Americans had started to abandon cities in efforts to find sufficient land to grow their own food.[37] In Wilson's view, the federal government ought to establish policies that encouraged that trend and made it more possible.

Wilson also noted a trend among industries to move away from urban centers. Wilson warmed to what economists called the "decentralization" of industry because it conceivably allowed workers to live away from cities, near factories, and on plots large enough to grow much of their own food. Workers who could grow their own food did not require the same number of hours in the factory or even wage levels as did an urban dweller who needed to buy everything. If some industries benefited from their locations near a nexus of natural resources, such as the iron industry in Pittsburgh, others were freer to locate wherever they wanted. Fabricating industries in particular seemed, in Wilson's view, to have flexibility. The push to bring electricity to rural areas made living away from cities more appealing, and might afford rural industrial workers the same level of convenience that city dwellers enjoyed.[38]

Wilson also saw rural living as more wholesome and morally uplifting than urban life. Subsistence homestead proponents agreed, he observed,

> that there are some psychological and philosophical values which attach to the soil, and that one of the most normal manners in which human beings express themselves is by carrying through the cycle of the seasons, the production of a garden. Furthermore, these fundamental values attach to the family which exhibits the skill, the initiative and the discipline necessary to the timely operations of garden production and to the consumption by the family of something which is actually produced by the family. The garden, the flowers, the fruit, the poultry, and perhaps the cow, which is possible on a subsistence homestead, is opportunity for this expression.[39]

Plus, the Jazz Age placed such powerful emphasis on materialism, on the value of things above interpersonal relationships and community, that Americans needed the comfort and security that a community rooted in rural land values could offer.[40]

The logical solution to the problems that the Depression presented, the trends that Wilson detected among both rural and urban economies, and the degenerative influence of Jazz Age values, seemed clear to him. Americans should create communities that combined recreation-level subsistence land cultivation with part-time industrial work. The work would provide the wages that families needed to buy consumer goods and household items, while the gardening would provide both the healthful foods necessary for robust living and the wholesome recreation that cultivated morally upright values and fulfillment. Wilson called these "subsistence homesteads" because they combined household food production and market wage labor within one economic model. He recognized that some might see the term "subsistence" to mean "barely eking by," but this was not how he understood it. Rather, he saw each household in such communities as sufficiently well positioned to live independent of market vagaries, cushioned from the Depression and free to join volitional communities that prized cooperation and mutual support.

Elements of the subsistence homestead program could be found in movements that antedated its specific idea. Wilson himself noted the significant role that the back-to-the-land movement played in generating ideas for the program as well as popular support for such an experiment. It helped to produce what Wilson deemed to be "deep-seated national demand" for subsistence homestead communities.[41] In addition, the garden city movement, begun in late nineteenth-century England, came across the Atlantic as a solution to urban ills found on both sides of the ocean.

Wilson saw various constituencies for the subsistence homestead communities. Farmers on submarginal land needed better land and some form of cash income. Industrial workers in overcrowded cities might never see full employment again, and large gardens would help them to live on reduced wages. Comfortable homes would relieve the cramped tenement districts in urban areas. In addition, rural industrial workers whose enterprises shut down—especially coal miners—found themselves stranded in remote locations with no economic prospects. They might flock to the cities, further crowding neighborhoods, depressing wages, and straining relief efforts. Or they could find congenial housing and food in subsistence homestead communities. The Subsistence Homestead Division established a special section devoted to this last group, the stranded industrial worker, and put Clarence Pickett in charge of their communities.

Clarence Pickett came to this position through his work with unemployed coal miners in West Virginia in 1931. President Herbert Hoover had directed the United States Children's Bureau to investigate conditions in that area, and the bureau discovered unremitting poverty. Its chief, Grace Abbott, invited the American Friends Service Committee (AFSC), the social action arm of the Quakers, to establish a pilot program to feed the children. As AFSC executive secretary, Pickett directed relief efforts in what he anticipated would be a one- or two-year initiative to provide relief in up to four specific mining communities. The federal government provided $225,000 of the first year's $400,000 budget, and the Federal Council of Churches helped to raise the additional funds. Roughly fifty-five male and female volunteers distributed food to nearly forty thousand children in more than six hundred patch towns in the bituminous coal regions of western Pennsylvania, West Virginia, and Kentucky.[42] But it was not enough. The suffering continued with staggering intensity. The American Friends Service Committee determined to do "something to permanently improve the position of the miners who will never again be able to make a living in the coal mines."[43]

Pickett's work with mining communities during the Hoover administration led to his appointment, once Roosevelt came into office, as assistant to M. L. Wilson with responsibility for four subsistence homestead communities in coal mine regions.[44] Pickett took a temporary and partial leave of absence from his position with the Quakers so that he could continue to work part-time for them even as he administered the federal subsistence homestead efforts in those communities. He explained to the American Friends Service Committee that he "would not administer the fund as the Service Committee," but he would continue on in AFSC employ and would use AFSC resources to advance the federal efforts.[45]

Unlike Wilson, who came to the program through a background in agricultural economics, Pickett brought a long history of working with Quaker social action efforts. Though he clearly sought to develop a feasible economic plan for the homestead communities and to develop the residents' gardening skills, his main concerns were to build strong cooperative communities that cultivated their members' interactive skills, their concern for each other, and their dignity. Most important to Pickett, though, was their spirituality. Villages of efficient individual farmers, living in relative isolation from each other, held little appeal to Clarence Pickett. Nor did he seek to establish merely an efficient factory town. Men and women lived for more than bread. He recalled years later that

> [w]e had a strong feeling that while we had built the façade of abundant production in this country higher and higher until its foundations had come inadequate to sustain it, we had forgotten that the hearth where the family gathers and where neighbors are welcomed is at the very heart of human life. We [in the subsistence homestead program] were trying to put the welfare of the home and the individuals who live in it in the center of our national interest. The school, health facilities, the church, adult education: all of these were very close to the central significance of the movement as we saw it.[46]

As a consequence, Pickett helped to design communities whose "educational, social and economic facilities" centered not on "securing enough wealth or education to get away from the community, but in discovering the resources, joys, and satisfactions within the community itself."[47]

Pickett came from small-town, midwestern roots, and he saw that context as especially conducive to cultivating the kind of deep religiosity that drew people away from the materialist impulse. Though he worked for the Quakers even while the Subsistence Homestead Division employed him, he never lobbied, evangelized, or sought privilege for a particular denomination. Nor did he proselytize. Yet he saw religion as central to a successful community. M. L. Wilson may have agreed. He noted in 1935 that "the Godlessness of most people who are interested in social change is a great deterrent to progress." He worried that secular reformers did "not

FIG. 10 A young boy carries water from a well to his home in Scotts Run, West Virginia. Note the condition of the housing and the distance from the well (not shown) to the home. Library of Congress, Prints and Photographs Division, Washington, D.C., LC-USF33-030146-M2. Farm Security Administration/Office of War Information Collection. Photo: Marion Post Wolcott.

have deep enough personal concerns, and allow themselves to be drawn in to petty jealousies."[48]

It was Pickett's role with a religious social action group, the American Friends Service Committee, that drew him to work among the destitute coal-mining families in Kentucky, West Virginia, and western Pennsylvania. And he tapped religious social justice and charitable networks to support those initial relief efforts with financial contributions, relief expertise, and volunteers. Early subsistence homestead activities also drew on this reservoir of resources. Pickett assigned management positions to socially conscious Quakers and tapped into the keen desire to serve offered by many young, mostly Quaker, college-age volunteers to help build the communities.

M. L. Wilson had broad responsibility for the entire subsistence homestead program, and Clarence Pickett administered four of these communities. But both came to focus most of their attention on one particular community located in Reedsville, West Virginia. The Arthurdale homestead was the first and most highly scrutinized community, and it drew special support from Eleanor (and therefore Franklin) Roosevelt. It became the poster child for subsistence homesteads, and she poured her heart, soul, and resources into it.

Eleanor Roosevelt first became aware of the acute struggles that families of unemployed coal miners in the Morgantown, West Virginia, region faced when

Lorena Hickok reported on the nearby Scotts Run area soon after Roosevelt's election as president. Harry Hopkins, Roosevelt's choice to direct the Federal Emergency Relief Administration, sent Hickok on a tour of the country to report on the human face of the Great Depression. Clarence Pickett recommended that Hickok visit the mining regions of western Pennsylvania and West Virginia to see poverty at its worst. He recounted in his memoir that he invited Hickok to Scotts Run to see the situation that the American Friends Service Committee had been working to remediate. Hickok's visit to the area stunned her. Pickett had not exaggerated the dire circumstances that the unemployed miners endured. She found thousands of men, women, and children living in tents in a region that saw temperatures drop well below freezing in the winter. They had little food, ragged clothing, and contaminated water sources. Disease ravaged the population.[49]

Hickok reported the conditions to Eleanor Roosevelt, who then joined Hickok and Pickett for her own visit to the area. The same suffering that touched Hickok and Pickett so powerfully shook Roosevelt as well. She returned to the White House and shared her dismay with readers of the *Women's Democratic News*.[50] Roosevelt had begun to articulate her position even before she visited Scotts Run. She spent some time earlier that summer in the copper-mining region near Tucson, Arizona, and saw the misery that miners and their families endured. She began there to argue that workers everywhere should earn enough from their labor to provide for life's basic dignities before operators skimmed enormous profits from the enterprise.[51] The dramatic conditions in Scotts Run confirmed her position. It was a matter of social justice rather than charity. Workers had a right to "receive in return for their labor, at least a minimum of security and happiness in life. They must have enough to eat, warmth, adequate clothing, decent shelter and an opportunity for education."[52]

By the time Eleanor Roosevelt visited Scotts Run, plans to build a subsistence homestead community on a farm that Richard Arthur owned were already in the works. They had progressed slowly, but Eleanor's engagement sped them up considerably. She visited the area in November 1933 with Louis Howe, an advisor to both Franklin and Eleanor Roosevelt who had become central in their political and personal lives. He had joined the inner circle soon after FDR came to Albany to serve in the New York state legislature, had worked tirelessly to nurse FDR back to health after polio struck him down, had guided his rise to the presidency, and lived in the White House family quarters with the Roosevelts.[53] Howe had worked with Roosevelt in the Navy Department during World War I, where he learned the intricacies and frustrations of the federal bureaucracy. He became skillful at getting things done quickly in a system that typically moved at an almost glacial pace. Both Franklin and Eleanor wanted to build the new community, to be named Arthurdale (after Richard Arthur), early enough to get residents in before winter. Howe negotiated to buy the property quickly, and then ordered fifty prefabricated cottages. These houses, designed to serve as summer cottages on Cape Cod, were built off-site and required merely to be assembled at their final destination.[54]

Howe's interest in speed may have proven counterproductive, for it marked the first in a series of setbacks that gave the subsistence homestead program's critics material on which to focus their attacks. The houses that Howe ordered were far too small for year-round family living, did not fit the foundations that future residents had already dug, had inadequate plumbing, and did not contain any insulation against West Virginia's harsh winters. They had to be refitted, which delayed rather than expedited construction and raised their costs significantly. Critics highlighted this first subsistence homestead construction as evidence of public inefficiency, rather than as a pilot project from which later communities might learn and improve upon.[55]

The houses eventually did serve their residents well, and remain inhabited today. They stand as a powerful testament to Eleanor Roosevelt's keen desire that workers live in at least modest dignity and comfort, and the community that grew around them became one of the most scrutinized and debated of all New Deal initiatives.

Eleanor Roosevelt ensured that subsistence homesteads put the residents' dignity and well-being at the center. For example, when the program first began, some proponents envisioned that at least some houses would be constructed absent modern "conveniences" that had become standard in middle-class homes but did not yet characterize those in poorer rural communities. In fact, M. L. Wilson announced in 1934 that he would save 25 percent on the cost of constructing some homes by sacrificing "improvements which I believe every house should have—electrical equipment, running water and a bathroom." He privileged budgetary concerns over the residents' health and comfort, even while he recognized and endorsed the more humane standards. Against this position, Eleanor Roosevelt insisted that all of the homes have these amenities. What kind of model would such communities provide should they require remediation the day families moved in? Harold Ickes, secretary of the Interior Department, under which the Subsistence Homestead Division fell, disagreed. Why should these homes have bathrooms when 80 percent of rural homes did not? He complained to Franklin Roosevelt, who replied that he too supported the cost-saving designs. But Eleanor Roosevelt prevailed, and all homes included bathrooms with tubs and sinks and toilets, kitchen sinks with running water, and electricity. They also included furnaces to heat the homes and provide hot water.[56]

Eleanor Roosevelt did not first conceive the subsistence homestead program, and she never held official administrative responsibility for any of its many communities, but she became the animating lifeblood and moral guardian for the entire enterprise. Moreover, though she engaged intimately with only the Arthurdale homestead, other communities across the country benefited from her strong overall support, hosted occasional visits, and held her in special regard. Some, like Eleanor, West Virginia, paid the ultimate tribute of naming themselves in her honor.

When the Westmoreland Homesteads community newsletter, the *Homestead Informer*, sponsored a contest to name their new post office, residents offered a number of options. One suggested that they name it after the first manager, David Day, but his role in resolving some tension-filled episodes in the community's early days made that an unlikely choice. Nobody recommended Bankhead Manor, or Wilsonville, or Pickett's Place. Instead, residents rallied around an amalgamation of the first and last name of the one person they felt cared most deeply about them, pushed hardest for their well-being, and personified the subsistence homestead ideal—their patron saint, Eleanor Roosevelt. They combined the last three letters of her first name with the last four letters of her last name to create their new identity. Norvelt was the product of numerous forces, not the least of which was the residents themselves. It was to be a community rooted in the cooperative spirit, a place where folks looked out for each other and invested in each other's success and happiness. To their minds, "Norvelt" conjured just the right meaning.

From the vantage point of the contemporary political landscape, the story of Westmoreland Homesteads seems improbable. It was undertaken during a time of widespread economic hardship, when money was tight and the "need" to conserve money and balance budgets received lip service from Democrats and Republicans alike. It was undertaken on behalf of the kinds of people whom elected officials often ignore, the hardcore unemployed. In this case, they were poverty-stricken bituminous coal miners stuck in abandoned mining towns. The project was undertaken by an active, expansive government that was attempting to create a completely new community by placing rough-hewn miners onto miniature farms and turning them into cultured, cooperative cultivators of the soil.

This is the story of the creation and development of that community, in all its unlikelihood, from its inception until the end of public engagement with the project, when residents dissolved the Cooperative Association and the Westmoreland Homesteads properties devolved to private ownership. That occurred in 1946. By then, the community had renamed itself Norvelt, by which name it is known today.

The Great Experiment

The Cooperative Ethos and Community Building

> Don't cling to an obsolete individualism, but realize that there must be developed a new individualism, safe guarded by the protecting wall of cooperative action.
>
> —"Advice from a Sage (University of Wisconsin President Glenn Frank)," *Homestead Informer*

> If they succeed, Westmoreland will point out a new way of living for working men's families. Similar Homesteads will be established through out the country, offering a better way of living to millions of people. If Westmoreland Homesteads fails [due to] petty jealousy or selfish desires of a few—then millions of people may be deprived of the advantages which have been offered to us. It is up to us to succeed as pioneers in a new way of living.
>
> —"Our Job at Thursday Forum," *Homestead Informer*

The western Pennsylvanians who came to live in Westmoreland Homesteads participated in a bold experiment to provide more than decent housing and land to grow gardens. Though they did not realize this at first, they joined an enterprise aimed at reforming the very competitive culture that helped to create not only the Great Depression, but also the persistent suffering that coal miners endured for decades before. Eleanor Roosevelt insisted that these communities recognize their residents' dignity by establishing minimum standards taken for granted in middle-class homes but routinely absent in coal-patch communities.

Clarence Pickett shared Eleanor's commitment. Informed by his Quaker disposition to cooperation, respect for each person's dignity, and deep commitment to cultivating community, Pickett sought to establish and nurture a new cooperative ethos in the four stranded industrial subsistence homestead projects at Westmoreland Homesteads, Arthurdale and Tygert Valley, West Virginia, and Cumberland Homesteads, Tennessee. The groundwork for this new orientation could be seen in Westmoreland Homesteads' community-education programs, cooperative economic initiatives, health-care initiatives, social organizations, and study groups.

Set against this bold experiment were the lived experiences of the residents coming into Westmoreland Homesteads, the powerfully critical voices that controlled the region's newspapers, and, increasingly over time, the administrators in Washington, D.C., whose vision for subsistence homesteads was more modest and favored efficiency above all. If Eleanor Roosevelt, Clarence Pickett, and David Day, Westmoreland Homesteads' first manager, sought to create a new ethos, most of the residents sought a foothold in the security that middle-class America could once count on: regular access to food, consumer goods, comfortable single-family houses, a bit of land. They were not hostile to the promise of a new world, and even embraced much of it, but the desire for security stood paramount in their aspirations. Many residents participated in the cooperative study clubs and social organizations, joined the community food-canning activities, and favored cooperation. But they came to Westmoreland Homesteads looking for stability above all else. They did not drive the effort to create a new ethos, though they often cooperated in efforts to bring it about.

The region's economic and cultural elite, and the newspapers they controlled—virtually all of the large-circulation papers—stood firmly against the dream of federally initiated cooperative communities. They railed against the experiment in their editorials and drenched their news coverage with powerful doses of disdain. They highlighted every perceived failing, every sign of discord within the community, every piece of evidence that the community could not thrive or even persist.

Perhaps more troubling was the division within the federal government about this innovative new plan to elevate people's lives. The U.S. Congress created the program through legislation, but numerous individual members of Congress opposed the project in principle and created barriers to its success. Though few in the executive branch outright opposed the program, many key administrators thought it was too generous to the rural poor and sought to restrain its ambitions in the name of economic efficiency.

At the heart of the differences between supporters and detractors of this great experiment lay the tension between a cooperative and an individualist ethos. This tension permeated almost every aspect of Westmoreland Homesteads' initiatives, and one can see elements of each ethos in almost all of its programs. Norvelt's story necessarily unfolds in the context of these competing value systems, with one prevailing in some moments and in some areas and waning in others. The cooperative ethos shaped Westmoreland Homesteads' earliest planning as it animated much of the community's construction and the first years of its existence. It waned in 1936, however, as evidenced in the ouster of the community's founding manager, before re-emerging less powerfully later on. In the end, Westmoreland Homesteads did not fully achieve the cooperative ideals its earliest planners envisioned, nor

FIG. 11
Eleanor Roosevelt served as the moral and political force behind much of the subsistence homestead program. She is shown seated here for a formal portrait. Library of Congress, Prints and Photographs Division, Washington, D.C., PRES-FILE—Roosevelt, Franklin Delano.

did it swing entirely to the individualist ideal. It landed somewhere between, as it found a middle way to ensuring human dignity and security more firmly in the conventional model of the American middle class. Norvelt's story can best be seen as the negotiated reality that emerged from efforts to navigate the Great Depression's treacherous realities, the emerging cooperative ethos that the New Deal fostered, and the efforts that western Pennsylvanians expended to create better, more humane and affirming lives for themselves and their families. Though the story necessarily emerges out of the Great Depression and New Deal contexts, it begins with a modest announcement in the winter of 1934.

A Homestead Project in Westmoreland County, Pennsylvania

It must have been surprising for locals in Greensburg, Pennsylvania, to learn that Homer Morris of the U.S. Department of the Interior was in town to announce a government "settlement" project. It was to be like the much-publicized community

FIG. 12
Clarence Pickett at work at his desk. American Friends Service Committee Archives, Philadelphia, Pennsylvania.

called Arthurdale in West Virginia, and was expected to provide homes and garden plots for up to 250 needy families in Westmoreland County. Morris told a newspaper reporter that a local governing board, made up of four prominent citizens, with himself as the fifth member, had been established for a new organization called Westmoreland Homesteads, Inc. An Indiana farmer named David Day, a Quaker like Morris, had been appointed as local manager for the project. Already in residence in Greensburg, Day was working to acquire "options" on nineteen hundred acres of land in Mount Pleasant Township. The news report concluded by noting that project offices had not yet been established, nor were officials ready to accept applications from "those desiring to live in the government sponsored settlement."[1]

The announcement touched off reactions that revealed the tensions between the cooperative spirit that the new project represented and the competitive, individualist ethos that capitalism championed. A *Greensburg Daily Tribune* editorial the next day framed the challenge squarely. The editors noted that while the federal government had provided land for homesteading in the past, those earlier homesteaders were "sturdy pioneers" who had "hewed the remainder of their living and

FIG. 13 Prospective homesteaders at the United, Pennsylvania, post office, near Norvelt, 1935. Library of Congress, Prints and Photographs Division, Washington, D.C., LC-USF3301-006003-M2. Farm Security Administration/Office of War Information Collection. Photo: Ben Shahn.

housing from the woods and the hills." The gift of land did not undermine their individualism so much as cultivate it. But the present group of homesteaders was to receive "modernly equipped houses" with amenities and comforts sure to lull the residents to softness and contentment.[2]

Unanswered questions certainly occupied the minds of many locals when they learned about the Westmoreland Homesteads project. Who would be eligible for this government program? Who was going to get these modern, new houses? Part of the answer came a week later, under the headline "Homestead Management Ready to Receive First Applicants." Beneath the headline was a short column summarizing Interior Secretary Harold Ickes's announcement that the project was designed for persons "stranded by the abandonment of coal mines." To underscore the need for such a project, the press release included the following information: during the previous three years, nineteen coal mines in Westmoreland County had closed, including twelve in Mount Pleasant Township.[3] The main article indicated that Day invited applications from residents of Westmoreland County, or one of the adjoining counties. He anticipated that nonmining families might also apply, and acknowledged that some *might* be accepted: "The major portion of the homesteading population in the Mt. Pleasant community will be made up of former coal miners. But others can apply and their applications will be considered on their merit. It is my opinion that those people who are stranded in villages where coal mines have been abandoned will stand the best chances of being accepted for residence in the subsistence community."[4]

In a press release from the Westmoreland Homesteads office, Day expanded on the qualifications of the ideal applicant in an official public announcement: "People now unemployed, and particularly people unemployed due to conditions in the soft coal industry are eligible to apply as prospective homesteaders. . . . There will be government assistance in the management of the unit, but democracy of spirit in all undertakings will be insisted upon. . . . The plan represents strictly a business relationship between the individual and his government and not a continuation of unemployment relief."[5]

A loan of $276,000 from the Federal Subsistence Homesteads Corporation would cover the anticipated cost of the Westmoreland Homesteads project. Other details reported included the hiring of two office staff persons, John H. Feathers, an accountant, who would earn a salary of $165 per month, and Florence Berlin, a stenographer, who would get a monthly salary of $75. Project manager Day also planned to hire three additional staff persons—one supervisor and two investigators—to oversee the applicant selection. All three were to be "trained case workers," identified with the assistance of the Pennsylvania welfare department. It was reasonable to infer that applicants would be carefully scrutinized according to some government-determined set of criteria. Interested families were asked to deliver their applications in person, but were also informed that they could mail them in if they had trouble traveling to Greensburg.[6]

Ralph and Violet May Minerd were attracted by the prospect of moving to a new home at the Westmoreland Homesteads, but Ralph was skeptical. His application wouldn't be approved, he told his family. He was an unemployed coal miner, now that the H. C. Frick Coke Company had closed the local mines, so he qualified on that score. The Minerds had moved around a lot chasing mining jobs: Buckeye, Bolivar, Garfield, Belltown, Bobtown, Jennerstown, Jenners Crossroads, and now Mount Pleasant. These were the southwestern Pennsylvania mining towns that Ralph and his family, which included seven children in 1934, had lived in over the years.[7] The Minerds had always rented, never owned, and their attachment to their lodgings was tenuous. They had been married for twenty-one years now, and it was time for something more permanent.

Ralph did not take the initiative to apply for a homestead, but Ezra Summy, his father-in-law, did. Believing that Ralph was missing an opportunity to improve his circumstances, Summy obtained an application form, coaxed Ralph and Violet May to fill it out, and then carried it to the project office in Greensburg, where he submitted it on their behalf.[8]

Ralph's intuition that it would be difficult for someone to secure one of the new homesteads proved to be correct. In the first week following Day's call for applications, more than five hundred families applied, the first of nearly two thousand applicants over the course of the project. By mid-April, new inquiries were met with rejection letters, like this one to William Beaver of Southview, Pennsylvania:

"We wish to advise you that we have . . . received ten times as many applications for homesteads as we will be able to consider. It is quite likely . . . that even though you make application for a homestead at this time, it will not be possible for you to receive favorable consideration."[9]

The story had a happier ending for the Minerds. After close scrutiny by the selection officials, the Minerd family learned that their application had been approved. Joining ninety-one other families among the first Westmoreland Homesteads residents, Ralph and Violet May selected a house and moved in during the first weeks of November 1935.[10] Ralph worked hard and showed initiative in his new "homesteader" role, and John A. Robertshaw, one of the initial local board members of Westmoreland Homesteads, Inc., took notice. Robertshaw hired Minerd to work in his thermostat factory in Youngwood, Pennsylvania, where Minerd remained until his retirement.

Selection of Homesteaders

The careful selection of homesteaders who would make the experiment a success became a top priority. Project managers sought families who could successfully "rehabilitate" and embrace the cooperative ethos—that is, willfully cooperate with one another, appreciate their new homes, carefully tend their gardens, and take advantage of adult education programs. Under such criteria, potential homesteaders were invited to apply for a place in the project. Project manager David Day's announcement stressed the importance of cooperation: "Every homesteader will be expected to be a law-abiding citizen, diligent in his work and cooperative with other homesteaders in the community."[11]

Desired homesteader characteristics could be inferred from the publication of the questionnaire applicants had to answer, which appeared in the local paper on January 17, 1934.[12] Its sixteen-question length suggested that applicants would be very closely scrutinized.

Paul M. Campbell of Pittsburgh, a 1930 graduate of Westminster College with a social science degree, supervised the selection process. Campbell and Day selected a team of eight investigators from the ranks of the area's unemployed, none of whom had a social work background. Day and Campbell sought to compensate for this lack of professional preparation by training the team for one week in late January 1934, and investigators began their work on February 4, 1934.[13]

Clarence Pickett's goal to reserve the subsistence homestead projects for unemployed miners' families alone clashed with the Division of Subsistence Homesteads (DSH) principle of local autonomy, which gave the local boards of directors a great deal of leeway. Using their discretion, the Westmoreland Homesteads board members decided instead that an 80:20 ratio of stranded workers to unemployed from other fields would result in a more balanced community.[14]

With so many area residents aspiring to become homesteaders, Campbell's screening team could not keep pace. By early March, they had interviewed fewer than half of applying families. The rigorous application process involved initial interviews by one caseworker and a second by a separate interviewer, should the family make it through the first screening stage. Next, the two caseworkers conferred to determine the final rating of the family.[15] DSH field representative Homer Morris summarized in greater detail the highly involved selection procedures:

> Homesteaders have been selected from the stranded unemployed groups upon the basis of character qualifications, experience and ability and not upon the basis of present income. The selection has been made in each case by trained social case workers according to the following procedure:
> (a) Applicant filled out rather extensive application schedules.
> (b) Social workers interviewed the applicant in his home.
> (c) Social workers interviewed referee.
> (d) Social workers after full investigations made recommendations to local Board of Directors.
> (e) All applications approved by local Board of Directors.
> (f) Applicants approved by local Board of Directors tentatively selected as homesteaders were put to work on homestead.
> (g) The homesteaders who have been recommended to Washington have been not only selected by the above procedure, but in addition they have worked on the homestead project under the direction of administrative staff from one to six months.[16]

Morris could have added that investigators consulted three references for each family, and invited homesteaders on the "short list" to small groups for evening information sessions, where they learned more about the prospective homesteading experience and the selection team observed them interacting with one another. Additional traits that disqualified a candidate involved citizenship and age. The "male head of the family" needed to be a citizen of the United States, although the wife did not. Screeners considered applicants younger than twenty-one years of age to be too inexperienced and those older than fifty to be too close to retirement to meet the long-term mortgage obligations.[17] Husbands in the first fifty selected families averaged 36.8 years of age.[18]

The age barrier distressed older unemployed miners. When Westmoreland Homesteads officials told Matthew Baker he was too old to apply for a homestead, he complained in a letter to President Roosevelt:

> Dear President, I am just writing you a few lines in regarding to a Homestead, as I have applied at West Moreland Homestead Inc. at Greensburg, Pa. and our application was not accepted on account to my age. Now I was born in Rowlesburg, W. Va. Preston County on Dec. 8 in the year of 1877. . . . I can't work in the

mines any more for I can't stand to be where there is bad air and further more the Drs. forbade me to go in the mines. I am only to[o] willing to work and pay on a home every cent of it as quick as I could. . . . [He describes his skills as a steam engineer and as a handyman willing to work hard.] We certainly would appreciate it very much. Kindly let us hear from you. I remain, Yours Truly, Mr. Matthew M. Baker, Lakelynn, Pa. Route 11.[19]

The high number of applications enabled David Day, Paul Campbell, and their team to select prospective homesteaders with great care. Overall, they deemed three traits to be "essential": "an ability to cooperate," "an interest in subsistence farming," and an ability to bring a "personal contribution to the community." David Day emphasized the cooperative aspect in an informational release for prospective applicants: "Type of Homesteaders: We are looking for families that are eager to cast their lot with others in building a new and cooperative community. People unable to give and take in good spirit need not apply."[20]

By May 1935, homestead officials had approved 774 people in 126 families, which put the average family size at about six persons. DSH officials considered children to be such important elements for successful homesteading that Westmoreland Homesteads had no childless couples, and only thirty families had fewer than three children.[21] The selection process continued into March of 1937, by which time homestead managers had accepted 231 applicants from a pool of 1484. At that point, all 250 houses were in some stage of construction (or remodeling of the existing farmhouses), and 226 families totaling 1235 people had moved into their homes. The first occupant took up residence on May 1, 1935.[22]

The Quaker Period: The Cooperative Ethos Ascendant

In the summer of 1933, nearly two full years before the first homesteader would occupy the first house, David Day was invited by the American Friends Service Committee (AFSC) to relocate to Pennsylvania to help develop the Westmoreland Homesteads project. However, Day disagreed with AFSC officials that his work would involve only "cultural, social and spiritual development" of the homesteaders rather than focusing "on the economic side." He wrote to Clarence Pickett that he saw the economic, cultural, and spiritual as being inextricably bound together. He argued that if he and the homesteaders did not "have the privilege of evolving our own organization, educational set-up, cultural life and spiritual life" out of the struggle with "economic" problems concerning such things as the layout of the buildings and decisions about livestock breeds, acreage for gardening, and which crops were appropriate, then "the whole venture had just as well not be started."[23] Despite his concerns, he and his wife Olive accepted the offer.

Once he arrived, Day worked hard to develop programs that addressed the economic, spiritual, and cultural rehabilitation of the Westmoreland Homesteads

FIG. 14 Westmoreland Homesteads, 1936. Library of Congress, Prints and Photographs Division, Washington, D.C., LC-USF34-005408-E. Farm Security Administration/Office of War Information Collection. Photo: Arthur Rothstein.

community. His efforts reflected the Quaker model of economic rehabilitation and emphasized creative forms of work, community building, education, and, above all, working together. As Day wrote, "Cooperation among the various members of the homestead is to be one of the most important phases of the program."[24]

The Quakers wanted people to become self-reliant, but they were equally concerned with promoting homesteaders' regard for the common good. To foster their identification as future members of the community, as well as to provide relief work and credit-hours, Day brought the homesteaders together on site each day, taxiing them from their coal-town houses in construction trucks. In the evenings, project management organized small group meetings at the Mount Pleasant Township School auditorium to work on practical issues, notably the organization of the Cooperative Association. Other evening meetings were of an intellectual nature. Bill and Marian Byerly, Quakers who came to help manage the project in early

FIG. 15 Norvelt carpentry shop, February 1936. Library of Congress, Prints and Photographs Division, Washington, D.C., LC-USF33-T01-000383-M5. Farm Security Administration/Office of War Information Collection. Photo: Carl Mydans.

1934 and stayed on to become homesteaders, initiated a book study and discussion group in December 1934. A lack of transportation kept many of the future homesteaders from the discussions, but those who did participate were enthusiastic about the opportunity, according to the Byerlys.[25]

Day believed that one of the key means to promote cooperation and ensure the success of Westmoreland Homesteads would be via the Westmoreland Homesteads Cooperative Association (WHCA), an organization of residents that would take the lead in generating economic enterprises for the homesteaders. As Day stated, "The Westmoreland Homesteaders Cooperative Association is the medium for this undertaking. It is planned . . . that the men and women selected shall have a trade or skill training in the shop set up by the association."[26]

Although Day's goals challenged some aspects of the capitalist, individualist ethos, they generally followed prevailing ideas about gender, as the job training offered to men and women demonstrates. Women primarily performed labor related to the domestic duties of clothing and feeding the family, while men engaged in the more masculine tasks associated with construction.

The AFSC's shop-training program exemplifies the Quakers' intertwined approach to building community and meeting the needs of the settlers. The two were so linked that David Pennell, from the AFSC office in Philadelphia, traveled to Greensburg to help set up the shop and simultaneously establish the WHCA.[27] Indeed, the shops were conceived as the key measure for gaining the participation and commitment of the new settlers to the cooperative association. Woven into the practical training program were the objectives of elevating the ideals, workmanship, and thinking of the community and advancing the cooperative movement in the community. The work emphasized the development of useful yet gendered skills: the construction of houses and furniture for men and preserving foods and making clothing for women, in a learning-by-doing environment.

The men began their vocational training during the summer of 1934.[28] They built chicken coops, cupboards, and doors in the wood shop and made roof and chimney flashing in the tinsmithing shop. In the blacksmith shop they sharpened mattocks and farm tools and made door hinges.[29] The shop trained (and employed) up to forty men per month, each working thirty hours per week, in two shifts of twenty men. They worked from 7 A.M. to noon on the first shift and from noon to 5 P.M. on the second shift, six days each week. About ten other men sometimes worked in the adjoining lumberyard, for a total of fifteen hundred man-hours of work per week.[30]

Women, in turn, earned money and credit-hours working in the gardens and preserving vegetables. Beginning in August, when vegetables ripened, ten women and two men worked full-time for about six weeks canning the produce and making sauerkraut. Women sterilized the jars and boiled the vegetables. Men finished the job, putting the lids on the jars and moving them to storage.[31] In October, twelve women began receiving paychecks to learn weaving, working fifteen hours per week.

Early designers never envisioned the New Deal subsistence homestead communities as being entirely self-sufficient. As *General Information Concerning the Purposes and Policies of the Division of Subsistence Homesteads*, published in November 1933, states, "without adequate opportunity for wage employment, failure will result."[32] The AFSC took the lead in organizing economic activities at the homestead through the economic cooperative, using articles of association drawn up by Quakers.[33] Bill Byerly, one of Day's assistants, had earned the admiration and friendship of the homesteaders for his efforts on their behalf during those first months. Byerly worked with the homesteaders to set up the WHCA, which was formally organized on March 19, 1935.[34]

The Cooperative Ideal and Community Organizations

Eager to create a cooperative ethos in Westmoreland Homesteads, early community organizers established a number of social organizations. These community groups served very specific parts of the population, such as youth, mothers, hunters, athletes, and those interested in the theater. They also aimed to embody and inculcate the broader goals of cooperation and community cohesion. Homestead officials sought to create a degree of cohesion that was unlikely to prevail in Westmoreland Homesteads or in most other communities at that time or later. In their zeal to do so, they generated a reaction among many residents against the enterprise, as we discuss in chapter 6. Nonetheless, for the most part the community groups fostered cooperation and generated a unity of spirit and identity that strengthened Westmoreland Homesteads. One can see this in the development of groups such as the Mothers' Club or the study clubs, whose entire purpose was to generate a cooperative ethos.

Study Clubs

David Day and Clarence Pickett had pretty clear ideas in 1934 about what a cooperative community might look like, but Westmoreland Homesteads residents did not yet share those perspectives when they were chosen for the community and when they moved in. The selection committee worked hard to pick residents whom Westmoreland Homesteads officials thought would be receptive to this community ideal. Once community leaders selected the right residents, the important work of inculcating and nurturing the cooperative ethos began. Day experimented with a few formats before settling on "study clubs," which formed the spine of early efforts to make real the subsistence homestead cooperative experiment.

David Day did not establish study clubs right away. He began in the summer of 1935 with Sunday evening meetings that mixed religious sentiment with cooperative study. Residents gathered to sing religious songs, listen to speakers, and discuss "idealistic concepts for community growth." But after a short while people stopped coming because the meetings had too much education and not enough religion—a complaint common to those unfamiliar with the Quaker religious sensibility and meeting style.[35] Day then shifted the meetings to evenings in the middle of the week, and he and an assistant ran them through the educational committee of the WHCA. Day also recruited a field representative from the DSH to run a "systematic adult education" program aimed at training homesteaders "in the cooperative principles, relative to the establishment of the large-scale, cooperative, agricultural enterprise." This then became a six-day school to which "native" and "foreign lineage homesteaders" came.[36]

Finally, David Day developed study clubs of ten to fifteen families who met once a month. The week prior to each study club meeting, club leaders met to determine a common focus for all of the study clubs. The night after each study club meeting, Day hosted community-wide discussions to address any questions that had come up in the study club sessions.

In his history of Westmoreland Homesteads, Paul Campbell argued that the clubs proved effective for a year and a half, until community managers came to see them as working not to cultivate the cooperative ethos so much as to provide occasions for "gossip" and generate criticisms about the community. Community managers then shut the study clubs down. But the clubs likely struggled before that point. The *Homestead Informer* reported early successes for the study clubs, such as the note in February 1936 that a "goodly number" risked the intense winter weather to attend the first meetings. At its peak, Campbell estimated that about half of homestead adult residents attended the study club meetings. But by March 1937, attendance was so bad that David Warren, David Day's successor as homestead manager, attempted to reorganize the clubs in order to draw higher attendance. He also thought that more residents would come if the housewives would bring refreshments. Paul Campbell concluded eventually that "it was impossible to find homesteader leadership capable of teaching and maintaining a continuity of constructive inspiration with the limited educational background available, and with relative unfamiliarity with the subject material."[37]

The study clubs addressed a variety of topics, from the "spirit of cooperation" to proper insecticide use on homestead gardens. The topics themselves reveal the residents' struggles to implement the ideal. Though many study session topics focused on educating residents, organizers often added exhortations to change behavior as well. One session explained how a cooperative dairy should work, for instance, so that residents could see that paying a bit more for their milk and butter would lift the entire community's prosperity. But too few residents took the model to heart, and too many saved money by buying from local farmers. The study group became a venue to inform and cajole residents to change their buying habits.[38]

If homesteaders encountered the cooperative theory most explicitly in study clubs, they imbibed its ethos in a myriad of other activities and community organizations that sought, at least in part, to privilege cooperation over competition. Even so, homesteaders would have encountered the tension between the cooperative and individualist ethos that ran so powerfully through the subsistence homestead project in each of these activities.

Women and the Mothers' Club

There can be no doubt that residence in Norvelt offered women many significant benefits, which women recognized and appreciated. Many, perhaps most, embraced the cooperative spirit and considered themselves integral members of the community. They participated in community activities and organizations and were instrumental in establishing critical institutions such as the Well Baby Clinic and the nursery school. Yet much of their lives and identities centered on their families, a focus that favored the individualist ethos and stood in some degree of tension with the cooperative spirit.

However, as was true for so much in Norvelt, the dual pulls of individualism and cooperation existed in dynamic relationship to each other. If at times they conflicted, they more frequently balanced and complemented each other, which is the key reason why the community not only survived but prospered. In many ways, the story of women in Norvelt illustrates both the appeal of the cooperative community and the draw of the individual family. One clear example of this was women's participation in the Mothers' Club. The club simultaneously fostered women's integration into the community and defined women as mothers, which reaffirmed their gendered role within the individual family.

Life for women homesteaders changed and improved after they moved to Westmoreland Homesteads, as it did for men. The new homes, washing machines, and refrigerators not only lifted women's spirits, they also lightened women's workload.[39] As a result, many women had more disposable time, which dovetailed nicely with the administration's belief that members of the community should be involved in running Westmoreland Homesteads. Women took on active roles, ranging from members to leaders in the various clubs and organizations that developed in the settlement. A number of women obtained employment in the government-financed garment factory that opened in July 1938. Women not only found jobs there, but several of them initiated and led a strike to obtain union rights later that same year, as we discuss in chapter 6.

The significant changes introduced by the move to their new homes, membership in the new community, their newfound positions of importance outside the home, and work in the garment factory, however, appear to have only slightly modified inherited gender roles. Women and men continued to have assigned responsibilities based on gender, a social arrangement that generated few questions or challenges. Women defined themselves primarily as wives and mothers, whose key duties were to ensure the smooth functioning of their households and the well-being of their families. Yet life in Westmoreland Homesteads expanded women's horizons. Faced with new opportunities, women embraced new roles, ranging from reporters for the community newspaper, the *Homestead Informer*, to elected officers of the various clubs that developed, to nationally recognized leaders of the garment factory strike.

The majority of women in Westmoreland Homesteads had not worked outside the home prior to their arrival. Forty-five of those who did had jobs in "personal service work," sales, or the clerical field. It is not clear whether any of the women who came from the patch communities had taken in boarders or engaged in other money-generating activities prior to their arrival in Norvelt. The average family size exceeded five, as the average couple had more than three children. Catherine Bosich, for example, was one of twelve siblings. Nettie Frund, a homesteader who worked in the Norvelt pants factory and helped to establish the Mothers' Club, had fourteen children.[40] Household responsibilities demanded a great deal of these mothers' time.

As we noted earlier, the managers at Westmoreland Homesteads encouraged people to get involved socially. One concrete expression of this was that by 1940 there were twenty-three clubs and associations in the community. Both the organizations and membership in them tended to divide along gender lines. Men belonged to the Volunteer Fireman's Association and women to the Mothers' Club. Women also joined the sewing club, the Health Club, the Happy Eight Card Club, and, for those of a less sunny disposition, the Grouch Card Club. Homestead

FIG. 16 Women printing *Homestead Informer.* Library of Congress, Prints and Photographs Division, Washington, D.C., LC-USF33-006366-M4. Farm Security Administration/Office of War Information Collection. Photo: Ben Shahn.

women formed knitting groups and sewing clubs, which taught young girls how to make articles of clothing and the value of being thrifty, two gender-appropriate skills that were particularly prized during the Depression. In 1937, women were the sole reporters for the *Homestead Informer*.[41]

The homestead administration backed the formation of the Mothers' Club, which began in March 1935. Alma Walker, the federally appointed nurse, helped to set it up, along with Olive and David Day. The *Homestead Informer* regularly published news of the club's meetings and activities. Residents and the administration held the club in high regard because of the important contributions members made to developing necessary services, such as the Well Baby Clinic, discussed below. As a result, when Eleanor Roosevelt visited Westmoreland Homesteads in 1937, Mrs. David Byers, the president of the Mothers' Club, was one of the select few to greet her in the nearby town of Greensburg.[42]

The women began each Mothers' Club meeting with a "collect," a prayer-like recitation that reveals the homesteaders' ideal female qualities.

> OH LORD, let us be able to assume all the responsibilities which motherhood imposes.
> May we be godly examples both to our children and to our community.
> Keep us from fault finding; and let us be considerate in word and action.
> May we not be hasty in judgment, but generous and open minded.

> Dear Lord, make us to grow calm, serene and gentle; both mentally and spiritually.
>
> Make us to see that selfishness, petty jealousies and unkindness only lead to strife and misunderstanding.
>
> Lord may we be kind, forgiving, and strive to know the Mothers—heart of all of us.
>
> Let us put away all pretense; may we grow in spirit and mind.
>
> And Oh Lord, may the words of our mouths and the meditation of our hearts be acceptable in Thy sight.[43]

The collect addresses itself to God, which reflects the founders' Christian religious beliefs. However, it makes no specific religious references so as not to favor or alienate either the Catholic or Protestant members of the community. As the collect states, women were to accept willingly motherhood and the responsibilities that it entailed. Much of the collect instructs women how to be and behave, especially toward each other. Women were to eschew "petty jealousies and unkindness" and "grow calm, serene and gentle." These proscriptive suggestions reflect ideas about gender and appropriate female behavior that homesteaders considered essential to the smooth functioning of their community: women should not be jealous of each other; they should calmly accept their situation, keep their passions in check, suppress pettiness, and work together.

The collect encouraged women to grow in spirit and mind, but did not suggest that this growth would or should lead to self-fulfillment, innovation, initiative, or independence. It counseled women to be morally upright so that they could serve as role models for their children and community and stated that women's most important contributions resulted from being virtuous women and good mothers.

Yet, even as the Mothers' Club affirmed women's gendered roles, it afforded women new opportunities to develop themselves. It provided them experience in running a democratic organization and holding positions of power. The group elected a president, vice president, secretary, and treasurer and met monthly to conduct business.[44] The meetings offered women the opportunity to participate in and manage an important organization that had no direct connection to any religious institution and in which men were not present. Members developed their ability to speak in public and write for the community; the club had a column in the *Homestead Informer*, which a succession of members wrote. Although these activities fostered talents that were not necessarily part of many women's traditional repertoire, they do not appear to have produced a break with established conceptions of gender. Perhaps many of the women understood their participation in the organization primarily as an extension of their domestic duties. They understood their work in the club not as wives and mothers who were making important contributions to the new community.

Members of the club took their duties to the community seriously. For example, in one meeting the women began to discuss the plan for health insurance

FIG. 17 Mothers' Club dinner, mid-1930s. Lois Weyandt personal collection.

for Westmoreland Homesteads. Aware of how important the plan was to their families and the community, the group felt that it needed more time to consider the proposal. "Mothers did not feel free to accept the report whole heartedly as it stood, so we decided to think about it until our next meeting."[45]

The clubs offered women the opportunity to get together with each other, share ideas, and have a good time. For one meeting, held in a 124-year-old brick house, a request to attending members read, "dress in old fashioned costumes and small prizes will be awarded. Old fashioned games will be played and topped off with a corn, wiener and marshmallow roast."[46] The meetings provided women with a space in which they could develop or improve their organizational skills and engage in the formal functioning of a group led by women.

Club members aided in the development of projects that benefited Westmoreland Homesteads as a whole as well as their own families. For example, the Mothers' Club worked with the ladies' bible class and Alma Walker, the nurse, to set up the Well Baby Clinic in January 1937. The women were central to the success of the local schools and their children's education. In one meeting, Mrs. Sara Kelley, who headed the Education Department of the Mothers' Club, suggested the club purchase one hundred lunch trays for students, while another member, Mrs. Paul Campbell, "was appointed to see about price." After the Education Department (committee) reported that lunch trays could be purchased at "$9.50 per 100," the group agreed to buy the trays. In April 1937, the Health Department administered tuberculosis tests to 152 boys and girls at the Community Center, of whom 12 tested positive and were scheduled for retesting. In May, the club set up a preschool clinic"

FIG. 18
Well Baby Clinic sketch. *Homestead Informer*, February 3, 1937.

checking the weight and general health of children getting ready to attend school. Club members sponsored the local Boy Scout troop when community men failed to provide leadership, and held an annual celebratory dinner for the boys, which included speakers and the distribution of awards.[47]

Nurse Walker evidently felt the need to educate mothers about the importance of bringing their babies to the clinic so they could receive professional attention. She acknowledged that "most babies are born well," and that "the way to tell if a baby is getting sufficient food is to watch him gain weight." Apparently, she discounted the women's perceptions about infants and felt compelled to admonish them to heed the doctor's advice. "But aren't we fortunate to have a doctor to turn to, . . . in preference of taking advice from the next door neighbor. Each baby is different and only a doctor can tell just what to do." She concluded, "Only by attending regularly and practicing the advice given at the clinic, will they [the mothers] derive the benefit that is due their baby." By the end of the month the attending doctor had registered and examined thirty-two babies. After the examination, "the clinic will be open to the entire Homesteads each Thursday from 2 to 4."[48]

Nurse Walker's paternalistic comments reflect the tension that existed between the better-educated staff that administered Norvelt and the residents. They also served to undermine women's authority. Although women established and helped to finance and staff the Well Baby Clinic, Nurse Walker argued that it was better to have a male doctor dispense advice than female neighbors. Nurse Walker, a female professional, withdrew authority from female social groups and deposited it with the male medical professional. It is not clear whether women in Norvelt heeded or rejected her advice.

Members of the Mothers' Club served as volunteers in the Well Baby Clinic and pledged to give it six dollars a month for its work. In order to raise the money, the club frequently held fundraising activities to finance its projects and benefit the community. It organized a "Bingo and Card Party" in February 1937 and a spelling bee that garnered twelve dollars in March 1937. Its efforts were successful: in April 1937 the club had a balance of $19.15, and by July the amount had reached $42.53, a significant sum for a poor community in tough times.[49]

Club members contributed to the associational life of the community; membership also enhanced their own lives and those of their families. As a result, women continued to join the club; sixty-four women attended the May 1937 meeting.[50] Women club members worked for the benefit of themselves and their family as well as the good of the entire community. The group's motto, "Through service we grow," captured this understanding of their dual role. It suggested that women developed themselves by helping the community advance. This, like the collect, reflects the idea that progress for women as individuals was intimately connected to the overall success of the community, as well as their own families.

Health Care in Westmoreland Homesteads

The communal ethos ought to have worked especially well in health care, since that was where individualism generated the greatest difficulties for families with health problems. Paying for one serious illness or injury might break a family's finances and set it back beyond the point from which it could recover readily—if at all. Even more threatening, the prohibitive cost of care might cause one to forgo treatment entirely and result in great suffering, or even death. But pooled resources allowed families to make smaller financial contributions and still benefit from treatment that cost more than they could otherwise afford. Here is where residents could both see their neighbors benefit from cooperation and profit themselves. And yet homesteaders did not embrace the plans that community managers proposed. This seemed to both baffle and frustrate Washington planners, who saw in Westmoreland Homesteads an opportunity to develop a model that might prove both beneficial for residents and instructive for other communities. The cooperative ideal proved as difficult to achieve in health care as anywhere else, and Westmoreland homesteaders' struggle to provide this resource reveals the tensions residents endured over the nature of their community.

Homesteaders worked with Dr. Robinson of the Westmoreland County Medical Society to develop two models for delivering and paying for health care in Norvelt. The preferred model, which the plan called "a medical care cooperative association," pooled subscriber resources to pay cooperating physicians a steady income for unlimited treatment. It asked each subscribing family to contribute $1 per month to pay for "hospitalization of homesteaders and their families, for consultants fees, when consultation is required, for glasses, or other corrective measures, and for a certain amount of emergency dental work." This same pool would cover a "per-diem" fee to the doctors for each day that they worked, "not to exceed a fixed sum each month." The plan also called for a $10 per case fee for obstetrical care and for the cooperative to negotiate with local hospitals to cover regular surgeries for $25 and major operations for $35. This plan required a robust enrollment to build the necessary funds to cover costs.

If not enough homesteaders joined the cooperative, Dr. Robinson recommended another option,[51] one that seemed less appealing than the first, as it assessed each family $1.50 per month to build a fund from which physicians might bill on a fee-for-service basis. In this model, physicians could charge $1 for each office call, plus an additional $0.50 if the visits required special examinations or drugs. They could charge $1.50 for house calls, $2–$2.50 for nighttime home calls, $3 for emergency calls during the day, and $3 for calls from Mount Pleasant. Normal obstetrical cases would cost the fund $20, and abnormal ones would cost $25. Homesteaders voted on their preferred cooperating physicians in the first plan, but the second had the County Medical Society appoint a Medical Advisory Board to handle care.[52]

Though the first plan clearly benefited residents financially, it depended on them to join the cooperative voluntarily. The second plan imposed a less appealing model by fiat. Homesteaders seemed to favor the first plan over the second, but did not truly embrace either one. The plans ran into two main problems. The first was economic. In order for the cooperative to work, a sizable percentage of the homestead families had to join. This meant that healthy families and families with health concerns had to join alike, with the healthy families subsidizing those in need of services. The second concern was more political. By the time that homesteaders sought to establish a health-care cooperative, a significant group of homesteaders had joined together to oppose many of the cooperative initiatives that community leaders proposed. This group formed an organization called the Protective Association, and it lobbied residents hard to stay out of the cooperative (see chapter 5).

Health-care cooperative supporters invited Dr. F. D. Mott, assistant to the medical director of the Resettlement Administration, to come to Westmoreland Homesteads to make the case for a self-sustaining cooperative in May 1937. He left believing that there was "not inconsiderable" support for the plan. But only 24 of

255 families joined the Health Care Club when residents first formed it, and heavy promotion raised the number to no more than 52 families. Mott blamed low participation "almost entirely [on] certain disruptive elements in the community" who spread the impression that "the medical care program is being forced on the community by 'management.'" In addition, they reported that the federal government subsidized medical care in the Arthurdale, West Virginia, subsistence homestead community heavily, which reduced the costs to Arthurdale's families significantly. Association members insisted that the federal government ought to do the same in Norvelt. Mott, however, hoped that Norvelt would become a model, self-funded medical cooperative that other subsistence communities would adopt.[53]

Mott recognized that fifty-two families could not sustain a health-care cooperative, especially as those families who anticipated an immediate need for medical care joined more readily than those who deemed themselves to be healthy. The pool of supporters had to include many who would not draw down the cooperative's resources in the short term in order to cover the costs of those who needed extensive care. He pushed the Health Care Club hard to draw in new members. But the club had been working hard already. They promoted their efforts through word of mouth, in formal cooperative study meetings in each residential section, and through the *Homestead Informer*. They requested and received federal funding to build fully equipped offices for a doctor and dentist in the Trade Center Building. They arranged health screenings for children in the school and in homes, and established a Well Baby Clinic in cooperation with the Mothers' Club (see above). They arranged for local physicians to commit to serving the community.[54] But the club could not pull in more than 65 homestead families at its peak membership. (By comparison, the Sportsman's Association drew 125 members into it to create a safe hunting environment in and around the Westmoreland Homesteads grounds.)[55] They determined in July that they had to raise the monthly subscription fee to $1.60 in order to cover costs, which placed an even greater burden on struggling families. As a result, the club had to delay its official start until mid-August.[56]

Mott returned to Norvelt in October 1937 and met again with residents, who shared with him the Protective Association's resistance to the plan. They also drove home the difficulty that they faced in paying the monthly subscription. But Mott did not believe that. "My own feeling is that the problem of getting families to pay $1.50 is more an educational problem, and a question of morale, than a genuine economic problem, although I am fully aware of the low income level of the mass of the families in residence."[57] Mott persuaded the Health Club board of directors to change the club by-laws to preserve the physicians' income (and therefore their participation) by adding some fees and asking residents to pay them in advance. He and the board also recommended a thirty-day waiting period from the point of first payment to when a family might draw on the club benefits. Mott and the board urged members to extend that waiting period to fully six months for pregnant women seeking maternity care—a period that likely covered all of prenatal care and potentially the birth as well.

Mott felt that Norvelt's Health Club "experiment" was "most valuable." He shared with his supervisor at the Resettlement Administration that "[i]f they make a success of this program, limited though it may be, I feel that in the long run they will be far ahead of the homesteaders in a community such as Arthurdale, where all too much subsidy has been in evidence."[58]

It is difficult to know how residents made the difficult economic decision to join the Health Club or not. But we do know that many families confronted significant health costs, especially for their children. During the same period that Dr. Mott and the Health Club directors lobbied the community hard to join the cooperative, the *Homestead Informer* reported on the combined efforts of nurse Alma Walker and Dr. Spurgeon S. DeVaux to do health screenings, administer vaccinations, and remove as many tonsils from the community's children as possible. In two years of work, Dr. DeVaux administered 738 tetanus shots and screened all schoolchildren for tuberculosis (including twenty-one X-ray follow-ups to false positive results from the skin test). Nurse Walker and Dr. DeVaux sent fourteen children to Mount Pleasant Hospital to have their tonsils removed in early June, and over the next month sent an additional twenty-one for tonsillectomies. Two state hygienists screened students before the school year ended and identified 1,367 cavities and 37 "fistulas, or gum boils." They did not treat the students, but Nurse Walker urged parents to bring their children to the dentist even when they felt that "they cannot afford this attention."[59]

Parents had no recourse but to pay cash for these treatments or to hope that physicians would forgo compensation, which is why Norvelt officials promoted the Health Club so fervently. Their lack of success prompted David Warren, community manager, to conclude in 1937 that "the figure has been kept low by the foolish action of some of those Homesteaders [read Protective Association] who have not been doing their part in the Community. Their action regarding the Health Club has been an added indication that several of our present residents must leave the project."[60]

The situation improved well enough within the year that participating physicians considered it a great success. One of the two primary physicians serving the community noted that he received more pay from the Health Club (with its fifty-two members) than he did for visits and treatments from the other two hundred families in Norvelt—even though he treated more non-club residents than those who belonged to the club. When Dr. Mott learned this, he encouraged the secretary of the Westmoreland County Medical Society to recruit physicians to sell the Health Club to residents. Mott hoped to extend the same economic successes that the Health Club had reached with primary care doctors to specialists and hospitals as well. Mott noted that homesteaders were not paying their specialist and hospital bills and forgoing needed treatments "because of inability to pay."[61]

At the same time that Mott tried to turn physicians into Health Club recruiters, he urged the Norvelt Health Club president to push complacent members off the Health Club board of directors in favor of those willing to sell memberships to other residents. He suggested spending surplus funds that the club generated through increased subscriptions on more tonsillectomies. He reasoned that the physicians would not mind, given that this would increase club membership even further and therefore the physicians' incomes and that the reserve fund had grown substantially.[62] Between forty-five and sixty-five families belonged to the Health Club throughout the 1930s, and they managed to accumulate a reserve fund of about $400, or half of a typical year's subscription total.[63]

In health care, as in other areas, homestead families faced a significant decision that reflected the tensions between the cooperative and individualist ideals. Healthy homesteaders could have joined with their neighbors in a health-care cooperative that drew down their precious resources to help sick community members—and thereby insured themselves and their families against more substantial costs when they became ill in the future. Or they could have stayed out of the cooperative and hoped to escape illness, assumed the cost of healing themselves entirely, or endured health setbacks without care. Given their precarious economic circumstances, it was no easy decision to pay the monthly premium. And the Protective Association's active opposition to the health-care cooperative muddied the waters. Association members' insistence that the DSH managers had another, subsidized (and therefore more affordable) plan for homesteaders likely encouraged some families to hold out for that more generous plan. In the end, enough homesteaders joined the cooperative for it to offer meaningful coverage. But enough stayed away for it to fall short of its goal of providing very low-cost care to most homesteaders.

Co-op Store, Barber and Beauty Shop, Dairy Lunch

The cooperative spirit infused efforts to generate economic enterprises in the community itself, as evidenced in efforts to establish and run a Co-op Store, barber and beauty shop, and Dairy Lunch. These enterprises, along with the dairy farm cooperative and the poultry and hog enterprises, aimed to accomplish dual purposes. They would exist to cultivate the cooperative spirit, and they would generate cash income that would enable homestead families to pay for housing and consumer goods that they needed to survive.

Homestead managers set the ventures up in large part to draw residents together into a strong cooperative-based community. Residents worked with Westmoreland Homesteads management and the DSH in Washington, D.C., to establish the WHCA, the economic entity that operated the store, farm, and ancillary enterprises. Residents belonged to the cooperative automatically, and the WHCA served as the vehicle through which the Division of Subsistence Homesteads invested in the community. The DSH advanced financial support to the Co-op Store, dairy farm, barber and beauty shop, Dairy Lunch, poultry operations, and crop farm through loans made to the WHCA. WHCA board president William Crawford saw potential for a profitable future. "We can build a business empire that would

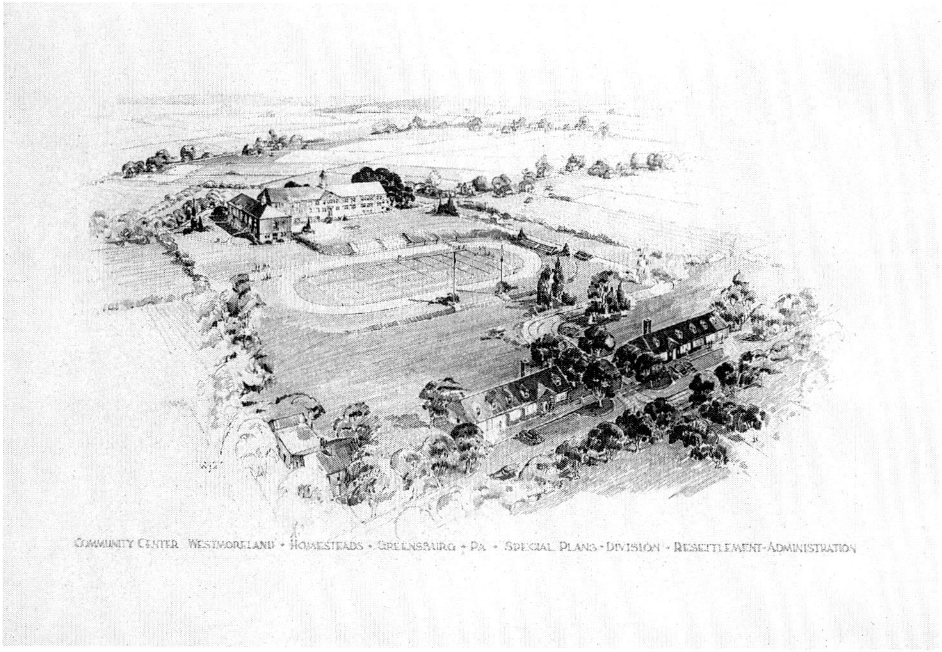

FIG. 19 Westmoreland Homesteads Community Center drawing. This drawing encompasses the Westmoreland Homesteads Trade Center, athletic field, and school as they were planned. Library of Congress, Prints and Photographs Division, Washington, D.C., LC-USF344-003852-ZB. Farm Security Administration/ Office of War Information Collection.

FIG. 20 Westmoreland Homesteads Trade Center. The Trade Center building housed various consumer co-op businesses. Earl Saville personal collection.

put the House of Morgan to shame. You have heard the call, the battle is on, now stand together through thick and thin. Victory and success can and will be ours if the ranks remain on a solid front."[64]

Later, after subsistence programs came under the auspices of the Farm Security Administration, the federal government insisted that all cooperative associations in subsistence homestead communities be converted into corporations under more direct supervision from Washington. While both the WHCA and its successor, Westmoreland Enterprises, drew their memberships from Westmoreland Homesteads residents, the WHCA operated with a greater imperative to generate the cooperative ethos. It was fully consonant with the great experiment. Westmoreland Enterprises, on the other hand, organized as a for-profit corporation, with all profits going to shareholders, Westmoreland Homesteads residents who bought the $5.00 shares of the stock.[65] Its support for the great experiment, though potentially substantial, remained almost ancillary.[66]

The Co-op Store and related ventures aimed from the beginning at more than strengthening community bonds. Community planners also knew from the outset that residents would need an income source in order for the community to survive. They had estimated that each family would need $1,000 per year to cover their costs, which meant that the entire community needed $250,000 each year. Planners believed that families who gardened would reduce their need for cash by about $150 each, or $37,500 for the whole community. Instead of $250,000, Westmoreland Homesteads would need $212,500. Planners anticipated that the cooperative enterprises would generate $100,500, reducing the need for other cash down to $112,000—all of which would have to come from work outside Westmoreland Homesteads if no factory materialized in the community. About 40 percent of residents had jobs when they came to live in Westmoreland Homesteads, and they might generate sufficient income to cover the outstanding deficit.[67]

This model placed a significant burden on the Co-op Store and other cooperative enterprises, because much of the sales from these enterprises redistributed existing cash income among those who had too little to begin with. In order to raise the cash that residents depended on to survive, they needed to sell goods and services to those outside the community—to men and women who lived in the patches and towns close enough to shop in Norvelt.

Joseph C. Haering took the lead on the Co-op Store project and predicted in his formal proposal to subsistence homestead program administrators that the store would generate significant outside business because it would be built on "a concrete highway between Mount Pleasant and Greensburg," the county seat. In order to generate the high sales numbers, Haering proposed an ambitious setup. As he explained in his formal proposal for federal start-up funds, "We felt that we wanted something different from the ordinary company store of which we have many in the particular district. Therefore, we planned our grocery department on a self-help basis, a sort of modified form of the super market idea. All goods will be on display. Attractive arrangement is secured and it will cut down on overhead

FIG. 21 The Co-op Store, 1936. Library of Congress, Prints and Photographs Division, Washington, D.C., LC-USF33-000365-M4. Farm Security Administration/Office of War Information Collection. Photo: Carl Mydans.

as we do not need as many clerks as we would in an ordinary set up."[68] He wanted sections for meat, dairy, and dry goods, all staffed by homestead residents.

But even Haering's overly ambitious predictions called for the store to generate only $1,726.46 each month in profits on $6,000 in gross sales, or $20,717.52 for an entire year. In addition, Haering anticipated that store employees would make $4,860 collectively each year in wages. This left residents roughly $75,000 short of the needed income. As late as 1939, the Co-op Store's first year to turn a profit, monthly gross sales averaged only $4,300, and the store earned a profit during that year's first six months of only $45. Income from the barber and beauty shop, the dairy farm, and poultry businesses did not close the gap.[69]

And that was in the profitable year. Before 1939 the store struggled mightily. Once the store opened in early 1937, Haering and Warren urged, cajoled, and chided residents to not only shop there, but also to support the store in other ways. As one *Homestead Informer* article noted, "To make it [the Co-op Store] successful, we must do more than a real day's work. We can all trade with it. When we see it make what we think is a mistake, we should tell our Directors or the person in charge. To complain to our neighbor or to gripe does no good, it does harm. We should all be able to think of ways to help our business. To leave it alone means failure."[70] The *Informer* concluded a bit more ominously. "*We have got to pull together, we must play ball or get off the team.*" This was no idle threat, either, given that Westmoreland Homesteads managers had just evicted five families the month before in "the best interests of the government." Not everyone played ball, though. Board members noted at the same meeting, "there is still not enough milk sold retail due to the fact that our Homesteaders insist on taking milk from Silvis and other Dairymen. If we were to get the trade we certainly should be entitled to here, our gross income would be greatly enhanced."[71] This was true enough for the Co-op Store and dairy, but not necessarily for the individual families who bought milk for their children.

Co-op store managers recognized that homesteaders were price sensitive, and tried to persuade them that shopping at the store was a prudent decision. Joseph Haering wrote, "We feel that if you check carefully, you will find that our prices are in keeping with competition, quality considered. We have a full line of everything and are now prepared to meet your needs 100%." He pointed out that the Co-op Store would deliver goods right to residents' homes.[72] Three weeks later, the Co-op Store held a grand opening with gate ticket prizes worth $5 distributed. In a stroke of good luck for the Co-op Store, nobody won a prize. Managers planned another celebration for July 3, and promised more gate prize tickets then as well.[73] Two weeks later, Haering noted that the State Bureau of Inspection awarded the barber and beauty shop a "100% rating," and urged residents to start patronizing it more. But residents did not patronize the Co-op Store sufficiently for it to make a profit. Haering commented in mid-July 1937 that "there is still entirely too much business going to outside enterprises."[74]

By October of 1937, managers began to recognize a serious deficiency in their plans. The ventures did serve as an economic stimulus for residents, whose work building the store, dairy barn, and other facilities, as well as setting up and running the enterprises, had earned 153 households an average of $621, or $95,000.00 all told.[75] But other residents took on "credit" to participate in the various enterprises. They borrowed $23,585.58 to start their poultry operations, $3,688.05 to buy from the Co-op Store, and $1,099.02 for milk and dairy deliveries. In all, residents owed $28,372.65 to the WHCA.[76] At the same time, administrators in Washington, D.C., began to apply pressure to run the homestead operations more efficiently. The U.S. Congress had fronted significant money to a subsistence homestead program about which it was at best ambivalent, and the new FSA overseers wanted to be assiduous stewards of those resources. A $28,000 debt did not look good.

To satisfy the new demand for efficiency, Westmoreland Enterprises laid off a dairy worker and saved his $40 a month wages. This marked a significant shift in the enterprises' goals. If the store, farms, and ancillary ventures once existed to provide income to residents and promote the cooperative spirit so critical to the new ethos, they now became subject to the same competitive pressures that poisoned the larger economy. Efficiency became a powerful, perhaps even primary, ideal. That newly laid-off dairy farmer could no longer support his family. And he was not alone. The Westmoreland Enterprises Board determined that labor costs were too high on the crop farm as well, and so reduced the number of farm laborers and moved the remaining employees from hourly wages to monthly salaries. In peak times, when the sewing or harvesting demanded more labor, Westmoreland Enterprises hired on a piecework basis. This new strategy reduced labor costs at corn-shucking time by 150 percent—good for the shareholders, but not for those residents who earned smaller incomes.[77] Instead of being shamed, the House of Morgan would have applauded the practice.

The cooperative managers adopted a practice that Henry Frick had pioneered in the patch communities. Board members determined that some of the farm employees bought their food and dry goods from area merchants who undercut the Co-op Store and dairy farm prices, thereby reducing the enterprises' profitability at a time when profits remained a distant aspiration. Reminiscent of coal operators' company store practices, the board adopted new rules requiring Westmoreland Enterprises employees to shop at the Co-op Store and buy their eggs and milk from the dairy farm or lose their jobs.[78] In addition, the majority of farm laborers, at least through October 1936, were paid in scrip redeemable at the Co-op Store.[79]

As noted earlier, the Co-op Store eventually did earn a modest profit. But that profit remained far too meager to bolster homesteaders' incomes. Perhaps more important, Westmoreland Homesteads officials' responses to the store's struggles eroded the very cooperative ideals that it existed to promote. Financially strapped homesteaders had to choose between low prices and community spirit when shopping for the staples upon which their families depended. However justified, exhortations to buy from the Co-op Store grew more strident over time. The Co-op Store, barber and beauty shop, and Dairy Lunch were supposed to draw homesteaders closer together, and they may have done so for many who patronized the shops. But they also raised tensions within the community.

Poultry Farm

As homesteaders moved into their houses in 1935 and began to pay their monthly rents, the project managers had still not successfully recruited any prospective industrial employers to bring to the site. Homesteaders needed some way to earn money to pay that rent. Westmoreland Homesteads and Resettlement Administration officials decided to expand the agricultural side of their operations as a way to address the employment and income problem.

On May 15, 1935, the federal government dissolved the Division of Subsistence Homesteads, and the Resettlement Administration (RA), headed by Rexford Tugwell, took over the DSH projects.[80] The RA's broader scope and larger budget made it possible to borrow funds for agricultural expansion, which switched the homestead's farming focus from a "production for use" collective farm to a larger and commercially viable "production for profit" cooperative. The planners hoped that the larger cooperative could, "with but little expense," produce "milk, meat and poultry products for sale either to the homesteaders or the local markets" and provide employment for about thirty of the settlers.[81]

FIG. 22 Westmoreland Homesteads Cooperative Association chickens on the chicken range. Library of Congress, Prints and Photographs Division, Washington, D.C., LC-USF33-015314-M2. Farm Security Administration/Office of War Information Collection. Photo: Edwin Locke.

The building and sustaining of an agricultural cooperative presented the managers and residents of Westmoreland Homesteads with significant challenges that offered no easy solution. First and foremost, the Depression and its attendant economic woes persisted. Nationally, unemployment stood at 14 percent in 1937, down from a high of between 25 to 33 percent in 1933 (right before Westmoreland Homesteads got started) but still devastatingly elevated. Unemployment didn't fall below 14 percent until 1941, as the United States geared up its war economy in preparation for participation in World War II.[82] Wages remained low. High unemployment and low wages limited the consumer market for goods the Westmoreland Homesteads cooperatives produced.

A further complication was that although a few of the homesteaders had been selected for their farming skills, and some others because their farmlands had been among the lands purchased for the Westmoreland Homesteads project, most of the settlers had minimal agricultural experience beyond gardening.[83] Their lack of experience required them to receive training in modern agricultural techniques and the use of farm equipment.[84]

The 1340-acre size of the Westmoreland Homesteads properties in 1935 allowed for 680 acres to be allotted to the cooperative farm, "of which about 520 are tillable—the balance being wooded and waste land."[85] To finance the operation, the U.S. government loaned the Westmoreland Homesteads Cooperative Enterprise $370,000, at 3 to 4 percent interest. The enterprise distributed the money among

FIG. 23 Brooder barn at the poultry farm. Earl Saville personal collection.

the following agricultural enterprises: general farms, $38,400; dairy, $31,200; hog farm, $12,400; beef herd, $7,025; poultry, $179,000.[86] Clearly, the economic planners put a lot of eggs in the poultry business basket.

The poultry business was a two-track operation, an arrangement that, like many other activities in Westmoreland Homesteads, relied on both cooperative and family-based initiatives. It consisted of a centralized poultry house and the distribution of chickens to individual families. The WHCA initially supplied each homesteader family with chickens, coops, and feed that it purchased in bulk. It then charged the homesteaders for the chickens and feed, along with monthly rental of the chicken coops. Homesteaders kept females as layers and ate the roosters that they hatched and raised. They sold the eggs back to the cooperative, with a premium for hatchable eggs. Homesteaders bought the "peeps" (baby chickens) on credit and paid for them through deductions to their account when they sold eggs and chickens back to the cooperative. The association had purchased expensive Rhode Island Red breeding stock and bought good females back from the homesteaders. Because the hens came from high-quality breeding stock, the association also sold brooders to outside buyers who wanted to improve or expand their flocks.[87]

The goal of the poultry business, as with all the cooperative activities, was twofold: to generate income and a livelihood and to build the cooperative. It sought to accomplish both by creating jobs for the homesteaders; producing goods that the residents could consume, thereby meeting their basic needs at a cost competitive with what they would have to pay elsewhere; and selling the chickens and eggs to bring in money to sustain the cooperative and the community. For example, as resident Ed Cibulas recalled, the Civilian Conservation Corps was "a big market for eggs and chickens from the cooperatives."

FIG. 24
Norvelt poultry farm brochure. Earl Saville personal collection.

> Each day a truck came in from the CCC camps. They'd come in and take maybe twenty dozen eggs every day, plus they'd take the older chickens. They took them in crates and took them up to the CCC camps where they were working, like Laurel State Park, Kooser Park, [and] Shawnee. They were taking the eggs and the chickens up to them because the CCC guys were only getting twenty-one dollars a month. They had all their food . . . and you know what, most of them sent all their money home to help their mother and dad.[88]

The poultry business got off to a successful start in March 1936, according to cooperative manager Haering, despite having "inexperienced help and all the cards stacked against us." The construction crew built the incubator room in four days, which was very fast considering the workers had never done this before. Then "the worst flood this section of the country has ever experienced" hit; nevertheless, the suppliers managed to deliver the "food, litter, coal, [and] equipment." A few days later the management distributed thirty-three hundred peeps to homesteaders and, "despite the decided change in temperature at midnight all but three [of the peeps] came through in splendid fashion." Haering concluded, "Only utter devotion to the job on the part of all who had anything to do with it as well as 100 per cent cooperation on the part of the homesteaders who received the peeps to date have made our record start possible."[89] By early May 1936, the "poultry raising activities" were "in full swing." March and April had witnessed "uniformly good hatches," and "25,000 young chicks [were] on hand."[90]

The management understood that in order for the promising beginning to develop into an ongoing success, it needed to educate homesteaders on how to take care of the chickens. To that end, it announced that the next study group, scheduled for April 28, 1936, would focus on "the care of baby chicks." It added encouragingly, "Most homesteaders will have immediate interest in this subject." In a subsequent message, the *Homestead Informer* warned residents, "Under no circumstances should the eggs be washed [with water] after they have become soiled or dirty. Use a piece of steel wool to clean them." Water suffocated the chicks still in the eggs.[91]

One ongoing problem that agricultural workers confronted was a lack of sufficient funds. For example, residents who worked in construction on the homestead in 1936 were paid fifty cents an hour, while agricultural workers only earned twenty-five cents an hour. In order for the farm laborers to earn the same amount as the construction workers, they would have had to work twice as many hours, a situation that caused "dissatisfaction." The farm advisor who reported on the conflict noted, "the only solution . . . was to raise the pay to 35¢ per hour and eliminate all hand labor possible, by the use of machinery."[92] Although this proposal cut agricultural production costs, it did not ameliorate the overall economic problems facing Westmoreland Homesteads. In fact, it led to fewer people earning incomes, thus exacerbating the problem.

Conflicts over wages bedeviled the cooperative. Government officials, homestead personnel, and residents all agreed that homesteaders needed to earn a sufficient income to support their families. However, as Ward Beckwith pointed out, the amount required to do so, even taking into consideration the community's access to the goods it produced, was "three and a half to four times the prevailing rate of agricultural wages in the vicinity." Washington bureaucrats and community managers' solution was to increase production. Yet increased production could solve the problem only if demand rose, which the poor state of the economy made impossible.

Increased production, which is often defined as heightened efficiency, typically results in fewer workers producing more goods for increased profits. It became the bureaucratic panacea for the cooperative's economic woes. In 1936, the WHCA purchased farm machinery, which "enable[d it] to prepare, plant and harvest the crops in an efficient and economical manner." In 1937, manager David Warren concluded that the "last twelve months have been unusually ruinous to poultry, due to the high price of feed and the low price of poultry products." He noted that "[t]here are 80 large poultry houses" at Westmoreland Homesteads, which was inefficient, since it demanded too many workers to tend the separate facilities. His solution? Thirty-eight of these houses "should be concentrated immediately." He also opined that part of the problem was that the homesteaders had been extended more credit "than they should have been permitted."[93]

Another incident occurred that reveals weaknesses in the cooperative ethos and viability. Residents sold chickens and eggs to "slickers" in exchange for magazine subscriptions. William Crawford, the president of the board of directors of the WHCA, sharply rebuked them for doing so. He pointed out "the salesmen took the chickens and eggs, went out and sold some, and made a nice profit." As a result, the residents "lost their laying hens, which would have produced more eggs, and lost many times the price of the magazines." He added, "not only did they lose the price of eggs, but they are also out the price of the chickens." Crawford further admonished, "Then again they sold something which belongs to the co-op."[94]

Despite these issues, the poultry business appeared to improve in June 1937. Egg production, which had "recently [been] in somewhat of a slump," rose: "34,045 chicks were incubated since February 1st," which represented an increase of "nearly 20,000 chicks" over the last year." Orders for chickens poured in "faster than they can be filled." And the cooperative produced roughly eighteen hundred dozen per week.[95]

Even when the poultry business improved, the additional income wasn't sufficient for homesteaders to make up the losses from their involvement with the for-profit cooperative venture. Westmoreland Homesteads extended credit to the 132 families who participated in the poultry program. The average homestead family owed the association about $184 for feed, incubation heaters, bedding, and other expenses, which constituted nearly a fifth of a working family's annual income in 1936. A fair number of homestead families even owed more than $500 or $600, staggeringly high debt levels.[96] The average family indebtedness to the association continued to creep up that fall, reaching $195 by the end of the year. It must have been difficult for the homesteaders to reconcile their increased debt with cooperative manager Haering's optimistic 1936 prediction that a homesteader who participated in the poultry cooperative could expect a net return of about $543 in a year's time.[97]

Just as in the Co-op Store, the poultry enterprise depended heavily on the active cooperation of homestead families and the vagaries of the overall economy. In contrast to the way the store operated, however, a larger number of homesteaders participated directly in the "production" of goods that entered the market, and therefore had a more tangible stake in the poultry farm's success. This broader participation could very easily have fortified the cooperative ethos, even if it took place mostly on individual homestead plots rather than in centralized locations. Yet even this did not ensure the level of profitability necessary to keep Westmoreland Homesteads afloat. Factors outside the community's control, such as severe weather and the vagaries of the broader market, still dictated the community's ability to generate income from their efforts. Their varying success and Washington's increasing anxiety about outstanding loans pushed managers to strive for greater and greater efficiencies in poultry operations. Families who did not obtain sufficient income from farming activities sometimes adopted individualist strategies to meet pressing obligations. Just as in the Co-op Store, therefore, the poultry business brought increasing tensions between the cooperative and the individual ethos.

Challenges to the Great Experiment

Probably the single most significant challenge to Westmoreland Homesteads' great experiment of supplanting the competitive, individualist culture with a cooperative ethos was, ironically, the very thing that highlighted competitiveness's deficiency. For if economic strain made plain the failures of this social organization, it also made successful cooperation more difficult. The Westmoreland Homesteads manager himself pointed out, as the houses neared completion and the construction jobs came to an end, that the absence of alternative income sources would strain homestead families tremendously. David Day noted that this transition from "construction to other economic life" would generate more difficulty than "anything experienced here yet." He continued, "We can pull through if in the midst of stress and strain we keep our balance and exercise patience and tolerance with each other. If a group of us get blurry-eyed and mad and fail to think twice before we act, our cooperative and with it the whole community will go to 'pot.'"[98] Day's concerns proved accurate, as the still weak economy, financial strains, the fears of not being able to maintain house payments, and anxiety about making ends meet undermined cooperative enterprises such as the health-care initiative and the Co-op Store and gave birth to a sometimes organized group of homesteaders who challenged Westmoreland Homesteads.

CHAPTER FIVE

Challenges to the Cooperative Ethos

The Depression's prolonged economic distress opened people's minds to alternatives to the "rugged" (and often heartless) system of dog-eat-dog striving. The subsistence homesteads program became one of those alternatives. As such, it encountered stiff opposition from defenders of the status quo in industry, in the press, and in government. Though anti–New Dealers held only a minority of seats in Congress as Franklin Roosevelt took office in 1933, an improving economy allowed some New Deal supporters to begin to waver. As early as 1934, Congress enacted the first impediment to the subsistence homesteads program. It came in response to Division of Subsistence Homestead (DSH) efforts to build a postal equipment factory at Arthurdale, West Virginia. Members of Congress railed against the proposal, saying it could lead to the nationalization of all industry and even to the "end of free government." The resulting amendment prohibited the use of government funds, directly or indirectly, to introduce industry on any of the subsistence homesteads projects.[1] This led to much trouble at Westmoreland Homesteads.

In addition to such external opponents, internal opposition emerged at many homestead projects as well. Many homesteaders became somewhat disillusioned after the initial honeymoon period. As Conkin explained,

> Too often the homesteaders were overly idealistic in their expectations about their new homes, and disappointed at the reality, became bitter toward the government. Almost always the early homesteaders were enthusiastic, feeling that they were modern pioneers. . . . But once on the project, things usually went wrong. Policies were changed at Washington, and the homesteaders felt cheated. The large expenses in construction often aroused fears of such high purchase prices that the homesteader could never afford them.[2]

Sometimes the cause of dissatisfaction was not that something went wrong, but, paradoxically, that things went as planned. Edward Banfield studied a number of New Deal communities in the west and found that homesteaders were confused by their relatively elevated status. On the one hand, they stood as equal citizens of a new community and equal shareholders in the cooperatives, frequently holding governing roles as board members and committee chairs. At the same time, they were subject to strict rules and stipulations given by their "bosses" on the cooperative jobs and by government overseers of the projects:

> By its peculiar character, the project threw out of kilter the well-ordered system of conventional, taken-for-granted attitudes and behavior which . . . the settlers had always depended upon elsewhere. As a farm manager, or as an owner, tenant . . . or laborer a man had always known where he stood and so had his wife and his neighbors and the world at large. If he were a laborer, he knew without thinking how to place himself and his fellow-workers and his boss in the scheme of things—a scheme of things in which certain signs and symbols had agreed-upon, identifiable meanings. [On the projects], some of the old signs were gone and others had ill-defined meanings. Habit and custom, the easiest of disciplines to bear, were no longer reliable guides.[3]

The result of confusion about role and status, Banfield concludes, was uncertainty, insecurity, and anger, despite the fact that in their private employment they had often been subjected to a more onerous paternalism.

At Westmoreland Homesteads, such fears and disillusionment can be seen in the complaints about management practices coming in the early summer of 1935, as the first houses were finished and the men on the work crews anticipated the eventual end of construction work. Homesteader worries about their monthly rental fees and what would happen if they couldn't find the cash were palpable and perhaps justified, given management's inability at that time to find enough permanent jobs for them. However, feelings of anger were encouraged and amplified by the anti–New Deal press, which publicized squabbles at the homestead and clucked their disapproval of the "Soviet" and "collectivist" tendencies of cooperatives.[4]

Another significant factor was national labor strife, as workers around the country pushed back against employers who were using desperate economic conditions as justification for cutting wages or imposing "horrendous job conditions."[5] The new worker assertiveness across the country virtually invited anxious homesteaders to imagine themselves as hapless, oppressed toilers confronting "unfair" bosses. Further, labor strikes and strident rhetoric provided a conflictual model of management-employee relations, an attitude reflected by the dissenters at Westmoreland Homesteads, who used terms like "dictators" and "Raw Deal" to describe their treatment by homestead managers.[6]

The first open and publicized conflict broke in late May 1935, characterized in typical fashion by a local newspaper as a case of the "rugged individualism" of angry homesteaders rebelling against the burdensome "socialism" inherent in Westmoreland Homesteads rules and policies.[7] At the heart of the dispute was the credit-hour system. Homesteaders selected for the project could find employment in building the houses and other structures of the community, earning fifty cents an hour, paid partly in cash and partly in "credit-hours" to be applied toward the rent or the eventual purchase of their houses once they were complete. The ratio was 25 percent cash, 75 percent credit. In other words, workers were paid one dollar in cash and received three dollars in credit for each eight hours of work, to be used toward the rental or purchase price of their homes.

The credit-hour system seemed like a good arrangement for providing the unemployed homesteaders with a modest income, and putting them on the federal payroll brought them under federal insurance for unemployment compensation at the same time. The credit-hour system further enabled those without savings accounts to bank some of their worked hours in the form of credits that they could use in the future to pay their rent or their house payments. The system was therefore somewhat innovative and experimental, a response to the particular problem of the stranded group of homesteaders. The system was not without some inherent flaws, however, as David Day and others soon found out.

Under Resettlement Administration (RA) rules, a homesteader could accumulate only twelve hundred hours in the credit-hour system, and by June 1935 some homesteaders had been working on the project for a full year and had reached the limit. They worried that they were working without compensation and demanded cash payment for their labor at that time. Because of the RA quota on hours, Day had the option of dismissing them from the work crews at that point. Instead, he offered to pay them half of their hours per week in cash if they would contribute the other half of their labor for the development and benefit of the community. (This proposal was the "collectivism" to which the *Tribune* objected.) Because the eventual price that the homesteader would pay for each house was to be calculated on the basis of the costs of construction, cash payments drove up the construction cost per house. However, payments in credit-hours did not show up as costs. Day's plan was to use credit-hours to make the houses more affordable for all. The homesteaders, taking a short-term view, felt they were being "cheated."

Another irritant for homesteaders was the perception that disparities in work hours were arbitrary. Second-generation Norvelter Len Solo recalls that his father resented the process of selecting work crews at the daily "shape ups" at the construction office:

> Workers would go to the construction office where materials were stored, and the foreman would choose the workers for the day. People weren't employed on a day-to-day basis, they were employed intermittently, and my father was quite angry about that at times because it appeared to him, and to some other workers, that there was some favoritism in the choosing of the worker. And also because of the inconsistency. He, like many others, had come through the Depression and had nothing, and there was that expectation—I'm not sure how it was established—that you would be getting work.[8]

A related cause of discontent is tinged with an element of class conflict. In order to speed up house construction, the homestead management hired outside skilled workers and paid them at a higher rate than the predominantly unskilled laborers from the homestead. The wage differential generated resentment among homesteaders. Related to this perceived injustice was the policy that prohibited already employed homesteaders from joining construction crews and thus denied them the opportunity to gain credit-hours. To compensate, they were permitted to arrange for substitute workers, called "chalk eyes" in the vernacular, to work in their place. For every eight hours of substitute work the laborer received two hours paid in cash, while the homesteader received six hours of credit that he could use for future rent or purchase payments. The fact that homesteaders could find substitutes willing to labor at one-quarter of the usual wage rate indicated the severity of the unemployment problem in western Pennsylvania in the mid-1930s. However, to many homesteaders, the practice of employing "chalk eyes" seemed to both exploit the substitute workers and provide an unfair advantage to the few homesteaders already "lucky" enough to hold paying jobs.[9]

Thus, grievances accumulated. Acting upon their grievances, three disgruntled homesteaders—James O. Silvis, president of the Cooperative Association, Edward P. Raum, vice president, and Harvey Smeltzer, the fire chief—circulated two petitions protesting managerial practices. They then hand-carried the petitions to Washington and presented them to Resettlement Administration officials.[10] The first petition protested the credit-hour system and demanded cash payment for all work done beyond the twelve-hundred-hour credit-hour limit. Sixty of the 228 homestead families had signed it. The second petition called for Day to be fired as project manager. Silvis and the others claimed it represented the feelings of 95 percent of the homesteaders. However, it is hard to gauge the accuracy of this statement, since the petition had no signatures.[11]

The DSH did not ignore complaints about the credit-hour system. In 1935, administrators wrote a memo noting, "Protests from the homesteaders are being received every day, and it is absolutely necessary that a solution be found immediately." It concluded, "The credit hour system was harmful for many reasons . . . and certainly should be definitely abandoned." It criticized the "[i]mposition of unjust and irregular penalties on homesteaders for free withdrawal," which caused confusion in the "minds of homesteaders as to their real income" and tempted homesteaders who had off-site employment to hire "chalk-eyes."[12] The memo also recommended that all credit-hours, in cases where homesteaders left the project, be liquidated in cash at fifty cents on the dollar.

Although DSH officials addressed concerns raised in the first petition, they dismissed the second, unsigned petition with the comments that "Mr. Day positively will not be removed. He is one of the best men we have" and that Day had "carte blanche" to deal with the situation, including increasing the homesteaders' cash incomes. "We are confident that he will work out whatever readjustment of the work credit is shown to be necessary to provide homesteaders with enough cash to meet living costs."[13] Day subsequently announced new wage rates that eliminated the credit-hour system and paid workers a flat rate for the week, thus exceeding petitioners' demands.[14]

DSH officials announced that they would back Day if he decided that he needed to evict the three disgruntled petitioners "in the cause of harmony," and that is exactly what he did.[15] The *Daily Tribune*, not a paper to let an opportunity to criticize the project slip by, suggested that Westmoreland Homesteads managers operated much like Soviet autocrats sending dissenters to Siberia.[16]

Day found himself in a difficult position as a result of the June petition incident. The cooperative ethos embodied the democratic spirit and sought to inspire feelings of community and solidarity. Individuals who objected to the cooperative purpose of the project were literally "out of place," impediments to the achievement of the cooperative goals that others still supported. Was it right to eject them? From the outset, the need to remove disruptive participants was understood as essential to the success of the project, and was the main reason for using lease contracts rather than outright mortgage contracts. As M. L. Wilson had explained early in 1934, homesteaders unwilling to work cooperatively would be removed from the homestead and replaced by other willing families.[17] However, while it may have been expedient for David Day to evict the organizers of opposition to Westmoreland Homesteads management and policy, doing so seemed like a demonstration of intolerance and appeared to undermine the spirit of democracy that he hoped to impart.

Critical Press Accounts

By 1935, when the subsistence homestead program was barely two years old, reporters around the country jumped on an anti-homestead bandwagon. A spate of hostile articles appeared in papers across the country. Rodney Dutcher, who wrote a column syndicated in 750 papers, called the SH program "New Deal Mess No. 1."[18] Columnist David Lawrence, founder of the magazine *U.S. News and World Report*, wrote that same month that the subsistence homesteads program was a "palpable failure," a "passing dream of the 'planned economy' experts."[19] A column in the *Chicago Tribune* mocked the subsistence homesteads program as a utopian fantasy of Mrs. Roosevelt and a waste of taxpayer money akin to providing "electric curling irons for hillbillies."[20]

On October 14, 1935, representatives from various western Pennsylvania newspapers met in Greensburg for the district meeting of the Pennsylvania Newspaper Publishers Association. After lunching at the Mountain View Hotel, about twenty of them toured the Westmoreland Homesteads project.[21] Two days later the *Pittsburgh Post-Gazette*, a staunch anti–New Deal paper at the time, published a harsh criticism of the project. The article proclaimed that although "the families who now occupy the 72 finished dwellings" think of their community as a "utopia-in-the-making"—"it isn't." Further, the project had "failed in every way to fulfill the promises of their optimistic sponsors." Reporter W. C. Farson revisited the credit-hour dispute and complaints about Day's management, sympathetically interviewed Silvis, Raum, and Smeltzer, and noted that construction was behind schedule. His most trenchant criticism, the one closest to the mark, was given in the headline: "Homestead Plan Fails to Attract Any New Industries to Westmoreland." Farson accurately identified Day's greatest failing, the problem that would continue to fester until a "cure" was found.[22]

Critical coverage of events at Westmoreland Homesteads did nothing for the homesteaders' sense of pride, nor did it bolster their enthusiasm for the difficult work of building a cooperative community. On top of that, the physical and temporal distance between on-site managers and their Washington superiors introduced new problems, strained the relationship between managers like Day and the homesteaders, and added validity to press criticism. For example, the payrolls at Westmoreland were frequently delayed, sometimes more than a month. The payroll for the period from September 1 to September 15, 1935, was delayed thirty-six days. It did not arrive at Westmoreland Homesteads until October 21. Payroll delays had begun after the projects had been transferred from the DSH to the Resettlement Administration in June. Local managers were not at fault, but they were the ones who received the blame. Throughout the summer of 1935 Day repeatedly telegraphed his superiors at the RA seeking help:

> July 16—Just this note to assure you that conditions are growing hourly more tense. We can't maintain our people much longer. The cooperative store, with limited capital, has just about reached its limit of credit. Our cash account is nearly exhausted and feed for hens and baby chicks must be purchased today. Men are reported coming to work with partially filled dinner pails.
>
> Aug. 20—Our field payroll for the last half July left here August 6—Stop—Administrative payroll August first—why don't we get some action—Crews are restless and office staff disgusted.
>
> Oct. 14—Protest meeting of cooperatives is being held tonight. Wire information on payroll.

As an RA official noted, the payroll delays were dispiriting. "Possibly the most disastrous result of this situation has been that the homesteaders, erstwhile enthusiastic supporters of the project, look with doubt, now that their faith has been undermined by these delays, upon any new promise coming from Washington. It cannot be stressed too strongly that if the spirit essential to furtherance of our plans is to be maintained, a remedy must be applied and applied immediately." David Day felt the difficulties of the situation so acutely that he applied to the County Relief for temporary advances to keep the homesteaders from going to Washington.[23]

This was not the end of problems at Westmoreland Homesteads. In 1936, Day reported to Washington that some of the younger families "tend to become cliquish and have carried on their activities to an excess at the disgust of the people."[24] The Washington office wrote that prospective homesteaders needed to have group discussions with project leaders on the advantages and disadvantages of homestead living, and should meet with families already in residence to discuss "community factors."[25] In what may have been a related effort to reach the minds of homesteaders, Day began teaching an adult education course entitled the History of Philosophy in the evenings at Westmoreland Homesteads that same October.[26]

Homesteader opposition recurred in 1937, but by then David Day was gone. Despite earlier assurances of confidence in Day's stewardship of the Westmoreland community, leaders in Washington, concerned with their perception of administrative inefficiencies, asked him to resign. He refused, so he was dismissed.[27] His removal reflected larger bureaucratic changes going on in the program. The Farm Security Administration of the Department of Agriculture absorbed the subsistence homesteads program on September 1, 1937.[28]

A number of commentators opined that Day's ouster reflected jockeying for power within the RA as it prepared for the transition. Clarence Pickett was critical of the "typical bureaucrats" who pushed Day out.[29] Pickett met with M. L. Wilson on November 28 to assess whether the cooperative, democratic vision could be revived, but Wilson pessimistically concluded that Rexford Tugwell, who had headed the Resettlement Administration, had set a tone of top-down management, which had undermined the original vision for the homestead.[30] Pickett also thought about resigning, but Wilson urged him to continue working on behalf of the stranded homesteaders when the Resettlement Administration moved into the Department of Agriculture.

As Wilson had surmised, the new manager for Westmoreland Homesteads, David Warren, leaned more toward economy and efficiency than toward community and solidarity. Paul Campbell, in charge of family selection at the time, wrote that Warren's by-the-book approach undermined the sense of community:

> [L]ocal administrative philosophy changed in scope, which change initiated a period of what appeared to be positive order. Dealings with community problems were placed on a more rigid, matter-of-fact basis and several of the families comprising this small group were advised to change their behavior patterns, or to expect to leave the experiment. Other families, who were not meeting their financial obligations to the cooperative association or to the government . . . were treated likewise. Evolving out of the frustrations of the guilt feeling and the fear of the loss of homestead status there developed a conflict that tended momentarily to threaten community integration.[31]

Warren set his tone even before he assumed leadership of the homestead. Responding to homesteader complaints that they were being "intimidated by government co-operative control," Warren warned that "those who will not co-operate sincerely in bringing about co-operative success will not be able to remain permanently in the community." However, he added reassuringly, "reasonable" and "sincere" homesteaders "who respect and care for their property and that of the cooperative need have no fear" of eviction and "can confidently look forward to a pleasant life in Westmoreland."[32]

Several of his subsequent authoritarian actions belied this promise, such as his handling of Co-op Store issues. A common, if somewhat minor, frustration among the project managers in Washington and Westmoreland Homesteads was the difficulty they encountered in persuading the homesteaders to patronize the Co-op Store. A shortage of automobiles combined with relatively long walking distances is part of the explanation. Second-generation homesteader Earl Saville recalls that Frick's Union Supply company store in Calumet was closer to his house than the Co-op Store, so he usually headed there when his mother sent him out for milk or bread.[33] Nevertheless, Warren sought to correct the problem by requiring homesteaders to turn in "sales slips" for all purchases made at the Co-op Store; he then posted a list of purchases made by each member of the cooperative. "Mr. Warren came forth with a bombshell," wrote an unidentified reporter in the next issue of the *Homestead Informer*. "Get this—from now on the amount of the purchases each Homestead family makes will be a matter of common knowledge. And the record of those who do not patronize it will be equally well known. This is Mr. Warren's first statement of future policy. It may indicate . . . the way in which other similar conditions will be faced."[34] In that same issue, Manager Warren posted another "bombshell," naming ten homesteaders who were employed by the Cooperative Association but who had not paid their dues to join the association. They had, Warren wrote, until December 15 to join if they expected to remain on the cooperative payroll.[35]

In 1937, the unyielding tone of Warren's spoken and published admonitions, given in a time of continuing unemployment, did nothing to ease homesteader anxieties. By June of that year, some of the more dissatisfied homesteaders set up a defensive organization called the "Homesteaders' Club," which Warren quickly criticized: "It appears that the real purpose of this Homesteaders' Club . . . is not for the purpose for which you and I want such an organization. It seems that the Club is proposed with the hope of organizing the homesteaders into one group, with the intent that the Club, made up of all homesteaders, would then be in a position to make demands on the Government." Warren contended the organizers were using strong-arm tactics to persuade or intimidate others into joining, and warned that "bad and destructive thought" from the club might "set back" the gains the community had already made.[36]

By late August, Warren decided that the presence of the new club constituted a threat to "the best interests of the community" and ordered five families who were members (or leaders?) to leave the homesteads project, an action reported by one newspaper with the headline "Soviet Experiment in Westmoreland County Boils Over."[37] To protest the evictions, 100 homesteaders (out of 238 families in residence at that time) left the homestead property and traveled to Laick Hall in

Greensburg.[38] Ray Newhouse, one of those told by Warren to leave the homestead, told reporters invited to the meeting that Warren was using "blacksnake whip methods of discipline" and that "[t]he community has degenerated from a haven from unemployment to a hotbed of subversive terrorism." Warren had labeled the Homesteaders' Club "communistic" to justify his actions, Newhouse added, but the manager denied making any such comment. Communism "has nothing to do with it," he said. "We've had no Communism in the community, they're just using it as a word."[39] "The forming of the organization Mr. Newhouse talks about has nothing to do with the evictions. We are not bucking any organizations. The only way the homesteaders can get anywhere is to organize for group action."[40] Asked for further clarification, Warren's reply was blunt: "This homesteads community is an experiment. The government has definite ideas on what this community can mean to the homesteaders. If some people are not fitting in, the government is justified in ordering them to leave. The contracts which the government has with the homesteaders can be terminated by either party. I would say the five families who have been ordered to leave are trouble makers."[41]

Newhouse, invoking the president, was equally hard-line: "President Roosevelt wouldn't tolerate this kind of action if he knew about it. I have enough affidavits to wreck the whole affair."[42]

David Warren's clumsy management style may have precipitated the late summer crisis of 1937, but Newhouse and his fellow dissenters recognized the underlying problems of unemployment and low pay, as one paper reported: "The chief complaint against the management . . . is that the homestead has failed to accomplish its primary purpose. That was the establishment of industry within the community to provide work for permanently unemployed men. Aggravating this fault, it was declared, are low wages for what work is obtainable, and steady losses from farming efforts by former miners as a result of poor administration."[43]

Another homesteader, unnamed but not one of the protesters, remarked similarly: "The only trouble is there's not enough work to go 'round. Half the family heads got to work outside—in Greensburg and the towns round about. All we have here is some jobs working for the cooperative and the WPA."[44]

Two of the ousted families had been told to leave the project as early as March 1, 1937.[45] As a consequence of their refusal to comply with the order to vacate their houses, U.S. deputy marshals from Pittsburgh moved their furniture to a warehouse in Pittsburgh. The legal order for eviction cited nonpayment of rent, despite Warren's earlier assertion that it was their refusal to cooperate, not rent-related issues, that convinced him they must leave the homestead.[46] Additionally, Nelson had been accused of improper dealings regarding his participation in the cooperative poultry enterprise.[47] When other families given eviction notices claimed that they were owed money for previously earned credit-hours, their evictions were postponed.[48] Despite the Homesteaders' Club's appeals to representatives in Congress and sympathetic coverage by the local press, federal marshals removed them from the homestead in late October.[49]

In early September, the dissident Homesteaders' Club had been renamed the Protective Association. According to the papers of incorporation it filed in the county court, it existed to ensure "the protection of social intercourse and maintenance and support of benevolent, charitable and educational undertakings among its members." R. A. Newhouse was named as president.[50] By the end of the year, seventy families had joined the organization.[51] Vice president William Crawford was a well-known leader among the homesteaders, having served as superintendent of the Sunday school and as president of the Cooperative Association, now renamed Westmoreland Cooperative Enterprises, Inc. Further, Crawford was one of the few persons named to greet and accompany Eleanor Roosevelt when she visited Westmoreland Homesteads in May. Crawford told reporters he didn't trust David Warren: "Warren doesn't really want us to do things for ourselves. He's afraid that if we learn to stand on our own two feet we won't need him anymore and he'll be out of a job. When we organized a protective association, he tried to dominate it. When he saw we wouldn't let him, he started this eviction business." Crawford added that Warren's power to evict was more power than one man should have.[52]

To his credit, Warren recognized the merit of the latter claim and responded by creating a grievance committee to hear issues related to possible evictions. "I called both sides into my office and had them agree to set up a grievance committee to mediate these problems. Two Homesteaders, two from the management and one impartial person. The Homesteaders are electing their representatives now."[53]

Pennsylvania in Review, a periodical sympathetic to New Deal programs, agreed with David Warren's somewhat dismissive characterization of the controversy as mere "growing pains." Noting that regional newspapers had shown themselves eager to "rend the air with prophesies of doom," the author suggested a better interpretation: "Truth is that the Homestead's conflicts are nothing more than the growing pains that characterize the evolution of the Homestead from a government project to an independent town." He also described his understanding of the long-term benefits of the Westmoreland Homesteads project: "Now that the depression clouds have lifted, the Westmoreland Homesteaders find themselves substantially better off than most of their former co-sufferers. They live in clean, healthy surroundings. They live in houses for which they pay an amazingly low rental. Life is not all milk and honey for the Homesteaders. There are many knotty problems of homestead life that still demand solution. The project has its faults, but that only means it is alive and growing."[54]

Westmoreland Homesteads official Paul Campbell later wrote that project management had anticipated the possibility of conflict between homesteaders divided by nationality (foreign-born vs. U.S.-born) and/or by religion (Protestant v. Catholic), but had not anticipated the emergent "generation gap" as posing a threat to "homogeneous community thought." Strife along religious and national lines failed to appear. Instead, Campbell echoed Day's comments about *younger* families being cliquish, noting that some of these families' defiance of community norms and consequent fears of eviction had led them to organize the Protective Association.[55]

Protective Association tactics included both the carrot and the stick. To recruit new members, the Protective Association promised homesteaders protection against the possibility of eviction. It also tried to gain control of managerial positions in order to reward Protective Association members with patronage jobs. According to Campbell, the Protective Association also tried to intimidate homesteaders into joining, threatening to fire homesteaders from their co-op jobs and to evict their opponents from the homesteads once it had "gained control of the project administration."[56]

The power of the Protective Association peaked in January 1938, when it gained control of the Westmoreland Community Enterprises (WCE) board by electing five of its members. In addition, the Protective Association also won many of the 1938 offices of the Activities Council. The backlash against the Protective Association's blunt power play turned electoral successes into Pyrrhic victories. Homesteaders more aligned with management purposes resisted the advances of the Protective Association by forming two new organizations. Those employed by the WCE cooperative formed the Cooperative Association Employee Union, banding together to protect their jobs. And more generally, anti-PA homesteaders created the "Civic Club" to promote "a civic spirit" and the "good reputation of the community."[57]

During the year that the Protective Association controlled the Cooperative Association, attendance at monthly meetings dwindled to the point where only the officers attended.[58] The agenda for the November 1938 meeting of the Cooperative Association (Westmoreland Community Enterprises), held in the auditorium of the newly finished elementary school, included a discussion of the recent strike at the garment factory. Only fifty-seven members showed up, so the meeting was delayed for lack of a quorum. Some of the members in attendance were able to raise a quorum by knocking on doors until they persuaded an additional seventeen persons to attend.[59]

The Protective Association blamed the poor attendance at Cooperative Association meetings on Westmoreland Homesteads officials. "The reason why the members are not turning out is that they are tired of hearing the 'soft soap' of Cooperative Manager Joseph Haering," an unidentified critic told the local newspaper. The specifics of his complaints against Haering involved poor management of the agricultural activities, resulting in economic losses, and, more pointedly, Haering's prediction that homesteaders could expect to earn several hundred dollars profit each year raising chickens, which had not yet occurred.[60]

Warren resigned as manager in February 1938, and Ward Beckwith replaced him.[61] The more conciliatory style Beckwith brought to his managerial duties helped to ease tensions. Beckwith understood that a measure of "heterogeneous thought," including a degree of dissent and disagreement, was a normal and healthy process of community development, and under his tenure the influence of the Protective Association waned.[62]

In 1939 and 1940, the Civic Club overpowered the Protective Association and placed its members in the majority on the boards of the Cooperative Association

FIG. 25 Meeting of the cooperative board, February 1936. Joseph Haering is seated second from the left; William Crawford is standing, third from left. Library of Congress, Prints and Photographs Division, Washington, D.C., LC-USF33-000365-M1. Farm Security Administration/Office of War Information Collection. Photo: Carl Mydans.

and the Activities Council. In addition, because the Civic Club had successfully defended the Cooperative Association's jobs during the period of the Protective Association's control of the co-op board, the Cooperative Association Employee Union disappeared in 1939.[63]

Local newspapers were eager to print homesteaders' charges of corruption or ineptitude on the part of Westmoreland Homesteads managers. After major Republican victories in the November 1938 elections, including in the Pennsylvania governor's race and in state and national legislative contests, the *Tribune* published a letter (about thirty-five column inches long) calling four Westmoreland Homesteads officials (Beckwith, Campbell, Haering, and agricultural specialist Walter Funkhouser) "Raw Deal dictators" and commenting that they (presumably Democrats) should "have learned a lesson from the November elections, but it seems they haven't." The writer's main focus of complaint was a ban on hunting on homesteads property, which conceivably annoyed quite a few homesteaders as well. In defense of the policy, Beckwith explained that in past hunting seasons "a valuable 450 pound sow was shot! Last year four corn shocks were deliberately burned and several farm employees working in the fields were endangered through the discharge of firearms close to them, and one man to this day carries a lead pellet in his hand!"[64]

In what had by now become familiar Protective Association style, the writer of the letter about hunting also alluded to monetary losses in the agricultural program, implying that the "dictators" were to blame. Stronger charges along those lines appeared the following day in another letter, in which an unidentified homesteader calling himself "the wise old owl" called for "an investigation of the reckless way in which the federal government is wasting [taxpayer] money at the Homesteads in trying to regulate the lives of the homesteaders." Among other things, he charged that the oat crop that year was "practically worthless," that the financial statements that Mr. Haering presented to the WCE board were unreliable, that the wheat and corn crops were spoiling because of improper handling and weevil infestation, and that the management had failed to support the garment workers in their quest for union representation.[65]

By 1940, as attendance at the regular Protective Association meetings dropped to fewer than a dozen homesteaders, the PA began to understand its unpopularity.[66] However, lack of support did nothing to lessen the group's oppositional stance. On September 4, 1940, the *Tribune* published an anonymous letter similar to other Protective Association critiques. The tone mirrored the anti–New Deal cast of earlier *Tribune* editorials in suggesting that Norvelt officials were "un-American" and possibly disloyal. The letter quoted Mr. C. B. Baldwin, an FSA administrator, saying that communities like Norvelt were "fertile soil for those agitators and sympathizers of foreign philosophies who're trying to plant seeds of discontent and doubt about our American system."[67] Another letter published on November 20, 1940, charged that manager Ward Beckwith was a leader in the Socialist Labor Party and had not voted in the November election and that Joseph Haering had violated the Hatch Act by using his personal automobile to transport Norvelt voters to the polls.[68]

Ward Beckwith responded to the September 4 letter by noting that the writer had misquoted FSA administrator Baldwin and distorted his intended meaning. Rather than painting homestead projects as seedbeds of radicalism, Baldwin had written something quite different: "We are dealing with the most underprivileged, poverty-stricken part of the farm population. This group might provide fertile soil for those agitators and sympathizers with foreign philosophies who're trying to plant seeds of discontent and doubt about our American system. . . . The most effective way to combat these activities is to give our underprivileged farm folks some security and some stake in the country. FSA is doing just these things."[69]

Several months earlier, on May 14, Protective Association president Frank Klosky had contacted Major John O. Walker of the Resettlement Division, declaring the Westmoreland project "a failure" and informing him that "a majority" of homesteaders were hoping for an "investigation" of management practices at Westmoreland. He further argued that many of the homesteaders at Westmoreland were "underprivileged" and "poverty stricken." Walker replied to Klosky that the FSA had already concluded an investigation and had found that homesteaders enjoyed "better housing and living conditions, regular employment and community services which are not enjoyed by the majority of people in the same status of life in this vicinity," and that relief wages on the homestead exceeded the $52.80 WPA monthly wage scale by $17 or more, depending on the size of the family.[70]

After 1940, mention of the Protective Association disappears from the documentary record. Occasionally hints of similar tensions did emerge. For example, when the government sought to liquidate its interest in the homesteads through the formation of a representational group of homesteaders, some Norvelters demanded that election to the board be determined through a secret ballot, not by federal designation. But a half century later, few knew about the Protective Association. Informal polling by one of the authors of about a dozen second- and third-generation homesteaders at a Norvelt Historical Society meeting drew only blank stares and puzzlement.[71]

Racial Tension and Harmonious Coexistence

The Protective Association constituted the last organized internal resistance at Westmoreland Homesteads, and it emerged out of the economic anxieties in which the residents lived. Looming over the stresses and subsequent tensions that economic hardship imposed on the experiment in cooperative living were the inherited ethnic, religious, and racial prejudices that planners expected to find among residents. The ethnic and religious divisions did not manifest themselves in ways that planners feared they might, but race did play a distinctive and divisive role in Westmoreland Homesteads.

Helen and Chauncey White, who, like all other applicants, wanted to live in a good house, applied for admission to Westmoreland Homesteads several times.[72] Although they met the standards required for selection, they were not initially admitted for the simple reason that they were African American. Their story reflects the tensions that existed in Norvelt between the cooperative and individualist ethos, refracted through the lens of race.

The Whites' experience at Westmoreland Homesteads mirrored that of other black families in other subsistence homestead communities. The official DSH policy with respect to race was liberal for its day. According to acting general manager E. B. Johnson, the division practiced a policy of nondiscrimination:

> [T]his Division has followed a policy of not discriminating as to race, creed, color or political belief. . . . [No] project should . . . limit the homesteaders to any particular race or group. In areas where a project is being planned and where there is a reasonable Negro population, a Negro employee of the Planning Section Staff, in addition to a white employee of the staff, is to make a survey as to the participation of Negroes as homesteaders in the project, and their respective reports are to have consideration in the planning of the project.[73]

Despite such a promising statement, DSH projects commonly reflected Jim Crow attitudes. For example, Arthurdale, a subsistence homestead in West Virginia, only accepted white settlers, although a number of black families applied.[74]

As DSH correspondence with those advocating racial integration reveals, "The Reedsville [Arthurdale], West Virginia, project, as you know, was the first to be planned. Commitments were made in regard to homesteaders at a very early date and no Negroes were among those chosen. In case the project is expanded so as to require the selection of additional homesteaders, the choice will be made without regard to the applicant's color or race."[75]

Early DSH projects were particularly susceptible to racial bias, given that project directors and the DSH sought to defer to local self-government as much as possible, even when local whites exercised their predilection to discriminate against African Americans. Westmoreland Homesteads shared that experience, with an important caveat. In his press release inviting applications for the Westmoreland Homesteads, project manager David Day stressed "democracy of spirit" with regard to project administration. He discussed the admission of black homesteaders with the members of the Homesteaders' Cooperative Association. He told them he was "desirous of having Negro homesteaders in this new community" but allowed the settlers to decide the matter themselves. A majority voted against admitting blacks to the project. Day then informed the black families that the "sentiment was opposed to them becoming homesteaders."[76]

But even had the white homesteaders voted to integrate their community, few African American families would likely have made it past the local selection committee. Though they were under no formal instructions to admit only white families, committee members scrutinized black families much more intensely than they did whites. The committee found that roughly 14 percent of white applicants met the criteria for admission to Westmoreland Homesteads, but only 5 percent of blacks. "Only this family [the Whites], of the 20 negro applicants, compared favorably with the other selected families under the same selection standards," said Paul Campbell, senior selection supervisor.[77]

Even the Whites did not make it initially, but they refused to let the rejections deter them. Helen White wrote directly to President Roosevelt, describing their situation and asking for his help. According to Norma Williams, one of the White children, President Roosevelt "wrote back that there would be no discrimination in Norvelt. Things moved along pretty quickly after we got that letter."[78]

DSH officials in Washington agreed with Roosevelt, and David Day communicated their disapproval of the community's exclusion of blacks to the homesteaders.[79] Day told the homesteaders that the DSH officials had decided to eject homesteaders who displayed racially prejudicial attitudes. "The letter [from DSH] states that homesteaders are all on trial during the construction period and if a homesteader has prejudices that are not in line with the plan of the project the only action open to him is withdrawal from the project. Consequently, equal opportunity will be given to all races."[80] The Whites' determination, combined with presidential insistence, Day's support, and DSH threats, convinced the board that the best policy was to reverse their vote and accept the Whites, who moved into Westmoreland Homesteads and lived there for decades.

FIG. 26 The White family home in Norvelt. Earl Saville personal collection.

The Whites participated in community life in many ways. Chauncey White was elected chairman of the co-op chicken houses committee and a member of the Education Committee. Ellis White, one of the children, came in third in the competition to see who produced the most eggs. Helen and Chauncey attended a meeting of the Section D (the area of Norvelt that they lived in) study group and joined with their neighbors in a "covered dish supper" after the meeting. Sarah Brown, née White, remembered that her mother was famous for her delicious pies, and one of the highlights of her life in Norvelt was the day her pie won the best pie award in a community contest.[81]

Sarah Brown has very fond memories of growing up in Norvelt: "I have nothing but good things to say about Norvelt. We were the only black family in Norvelt. When I went to Hurst High School, I was the only black person in that high school. And my brother was the next one. All of us went through Hurst High School and we were just treated royally. So I have nothing but complimentary things to say about Norvelt."[82]

She added that the Whites "were respected as a family." Because she lived in Norvelt, "most of my friends were in Norvelt, they were all white." Norma Williams, her sister, shares her primarily positive memories. When the Whites moved in, they faced "obstacles and the disapproval of many. Some of the neighbors were fearful, but it was OK after everyone got to know us. I'd have to say we led a pretty quiet and happy life there."[83]

FIG. 27 Westmoreland Homesteads children's party with three of the White boys, 1941. Earl Saville personal collection.

On another level, neither they nor their white neighbors ever fully crossed the color line that ran through most American communities. Earl Saville, who was a youngster when the Whites moved in, lived across the street from the Whites. He recalls, "Chauncey White and Hal White [one of the White sons], they were the nicest people you were ever going to meet." Yet, for reasons Saville could not explain, "they [the Whites] kept to themselves." Saville remembered another incident that reveals the persistence of the racial divide. "Of course, us kids would get together and they [the Whites] would stand on that side of the road and we'd stand on this side and I'd throw a stone over there. 'You black people!' You know how kids do. We talked, and we got along; just some of the things we'd do."[84]

Race mattered most starkly when it came to more intimate relations. For all their friendships and happy childhood, the Whites always knew they were black and looked to "our own" when it came to dating and, perhaps, shared cultural tastes and practices.

> Well, when we grew up I can remember my mother and father talking to us, and trying to tell us [about relations with the white kids], and we were just all buddies [with the other children in Norvelt]. But then you come to that age [teenage]. So we had a car and my brother knew how to drive. So we would go to Mt. Pleasant [a town about five miles from Norvelt], where there were other black people. I remember we would go to the skating rink, on Monday or whatever day it was. Then we would go to Uniontown [a town about twenty-nine miles

away] to dances. I can remember going there, it was a big deal, Duke Ellington was playing. My brother could drive a car, so that's how we got around it as we grew up. To come and be with our own.[85]

Carol Davis, the daughter of white homesteaders, confirms Sarah Brown's memory. When asked if any of the white kids would have dated anyone from the White family, she replied, "Oh no, God no." In fact, they "would not have thought about it; [it was] out of bounds."[86]

Conclusion

Westmoreland Homesteads faced a series of external and internal challenges. Many of the local newspapers, which were ardent foes of the New Deal, never missed an opportunity to criticize the cooperative community. They characterized it as a Soviet-style collective farm and reported any apparent failings or internal dissent. And indeed, some of the homesteaders expressed varying degrees of dissatisfaction with the project. Some of them even organized the Protective Association in order to defend themselves from what they perceived to be the arbitrary and unjust policies of the federally appointed administration.

The internal tensions were both inevitable and, ironically, evidence of how successful the community was. One of the key sources of conflict was the early management's attempt to build a democratic ethos based on their definitions of what that democracy would look like and how it would function. Surely it is no coincidence that the well-educated administrators held certain notions of how the community should run that arose from their vision of the world, but did not necessarily reflect the views of the homesteaders themselves. Ironically, though, the dissenters appear to have absorbed some of the lessons the management wished to impart to the homesteaders. They aired their complaints, convinced others that they were valid criticisms, and organized the Protective Association to lobby for their demands. Ultimately, however, the majority of homesteaders rejected their critique and opted to align themselves with management and the community project.

The inclusion of a black family in Westmoreland Homesteads posed another type of challenge to the community. In Arthurdale, the white homesteaders had refused to let black families be part of their settlement. Although it appeared that history would repeat itself in Westmoreland Homesteads, Mrs. White wrote to the President Roosevelt, who interceded on the family's behalf. Notions of race did not dissolve in Norvelt, nor did they anywhere in the United States during these decades, but the Whites did move in and become members of the community. In this case, as in the others discussed in this chapter, challenges emerged, but the power of community and the spirit of working together to build something better prevailed. Westmoreland Homesteads not only survived, it thrived.

CHAPTER SIX

Becoming Norvelt

The Triumph of the Middle Way

The bold experiment in communal values at Westmoreland Homesteads did not prevail entirely. David Day did not even survive as community director beyond the early, formative years. But neither did it fail, really. Though many Westmoreland Homesteads residents did not join the community health cooperative, flock to cooperative discussion meetings, or patronize the Co-op Store sufficiently, they did not reject the cooperative ethos in favor of unbridled individualism. Far from it. They favored what might reasonably be called a middle way, a path that tempered their enthusiastic embrace of communalism with the hard struggle to husband scarce resources in the oppressive context of severe economic deprivation. Though it made good sense to support the homestead cooperative dairy by buying milk and butter at slightly higher prices than local farmers charged, the penny saved on a gallon of milk might make it possible for a family to pay for the medical care that a sick child needed. Similarly, though that child would have received less expensive and more accessible care had every family joined the health-care cooperative, most families redirected those health-care premium dollars toward food, clothing, or equity in their homes. Families did not reject cooperative programs in favor of individualist choices, but rather made hard decisions about what to forgo in order keep their heads above water.

For the most part, those choices allowed homesteaders to stay in their homes, keep the creditors at bay, feed and nurture their families, and reach out to each other. They created something good amidst the strong tide of suffering that washed over southwestern Pennsylvania. It was not paradise, for sure, but it was a lot closer to heaven than the surrounding coal patches from which many homesteaders had come. And if local newspapers were reluctant to acknowledge this, Eleanor Roosevelt herself made it clear when she visited Westmoreland Homesteads in the spring of 1937.

FIG. 28 Eleanor Roosevelt escorted by local officials during her May 1937 visit to Westmoreland Homesteads. Lois Weyandt personal collection.

"Give to People a Better Chance to Live Decently"

With these words Eleanor Roosevelt ended her one and only visit to Westmoreland Homesteads.[1] As we pointed out in chapter 3, Roosevelt was a central figure in the development of the federal subsistence housing program. Her sincere concern for the plight of the destitute and desperate motivated her to devote countless hours, energy, and personal funds to making sure that the impoverished not only had homes but a dignified life that would allow them to flourish. In addition to generating humane home and work lives for working families, the homesteads would also undermine the growing unrest among miners in places like Westmoreland County.

During her visit to Westmoreland Homesteads, Roosevelt clarified that private industry needed to get involved in the construction of similar communities. The federal government neither could nor should be responsible for financing the construction of homes for all those who needed them. The subsistence housing settlements were "examples for private industry to follow," and indeed, "already a number of steel companies" were doing just that. In an attempt to simultaneously appease her critics and urge them to adopt the policies she favored, she added, "If the government attempted to rehouse all the people who need to be rehoused you would certainly hear some howls."[2]

On May 21, 1937, Eleanor Roosevelt, accompanied by her frequent traveling companion, Elinor Morgenthau, the wife of secretary of the treasury Henry

Morgenthau; Marion Dickerman, her friend and principal of the Todhunter School of New York City; and ten former students of the school, stepped down from the train in Greensburg, Pennsylvania. Some 150 well-wishers and local politicians greeted them. Rejecting the offer of a police escort, Roosevelt insisted on driving her own car to Westmoreland Homesteads, some eight miles away.[3]

A delegation of local officials greeted her when she arrived in Westmoreland Homesteads and escorted her on a tour of the settlement. The welcoming committee consisted of "[David] Warren, manager; Paul Campbell, executive secretary; Mrs. David Byers, president of the Mothers' Clubs; William T. Brown, regional credit advisor; William Crawford, president of the Enterprise Corporation; Mrs. Alma Walker, nurse; Miss Florence Ammon, home economist; and J. C. Haering, cooperative manager."[4]

For the next three hours the group visited the four-, five-, and six-room homes of residents Mr. and Mrs. George Miller, Mr. and Mrs. William Riddle, Mrs. and Mrs. John Kelley, and Mr. and Mrs. John Terney, respectively. They also toured community buildings, such as the nursery school, the homestead school, and the trade center, along with various agricultural projects such as the hatchery, brooder house, dairy, and chicken range.[5] As Mrs. Kelley recounted years later, the visit was exciting and offered her and other residents the opportunity to demonstrate what they had accomplished.[6]

Mrs. Kelley's memories of that day provide a glimpse into the economic realities in which the homesteaders lived, as well as her (and presumably other homesteaders') sense of pride in their accomplishments and admiration for the first lady, and the gender roles that were an intrinsic part of Westmoreland Homesteads society. As Mrs. Kelley remembers, when she found out that hers was one of the houses that the visitors would tour, "I gave thanks to God that I had just finished the spring housecleaning." Her husband, John, "got up at 5 a.m. to make sure the yard was clean." She, in turn, "scurried around making certain the curtains hung fresh, the carpets were clean and there was no dust." When the house was clean and tidy, the family "got all dressed up as best we could. Now, remember, that was Depression time. There wasn't money for fine clothes. I just put on my best housedress that was clean and starched. We were all bathed and bright as new pennies. Then we stood at the door and waited."[7]

Since Eleanor Roosevelt had insisted that the houses in Westmoreland Homesteads, as in all the subsistence projects, be built well and have modern amenities such as indoor plumbing and electricity, she and her group made a point of closely inspecting the homes in the community "from cellar to roof."[8] Anticipating that they would do so, Mrs. Kelley had borrowed her mother's Fiesta ware. She was particularly gratified when the visitors "looked in her closets and remarked on them."[9] Roosevelt was pleased with the houses. Before she left, she remarked that the community was "very well planned, and the homes well constructed."[10]

Eleanor Roosevelt saw the homestead as the fruit of her efforts and the inhabitants as people in need of her ongoing help and advice. They, in turn, saw her as

FIG. 29 Eleanor Roosevelt's visit to the Westmoreland Homesteads nursery school, May 1937. Lois Weyandt personal collection.

their benefactress and conduit to the federal government. When she saw a baby asleep in a room with the windows closed, she remarked, "That is a wicked thing. No child should sleep in a room without air." The local nurse, Alma Walker, noted, "there had been difficulty in awakening some homesteaders to the value of fresh air." David Warren, the project manager, suggested an explanation and took the opportunity to press her for more money. The windows were closed, he pointed out, because there were no screens, and there were no screens because, despite the homesteaders' efforts, there was "no money forthcoming" from the federal government to purchase them.[11]

Eleanor Roosevelt demonstrated special interest in how the inhabitants, particularly the young, were faring. Reflecting her dual interest in health and children, she particularly sought to find out how many children had been inoculated and attended the health and baby clinics.[12] Mrs. Kelley remembers that Roosevelt "pulled [her] aside and asked her about her needs." Mrs. Kelley took the opportunity to point out that "the youth were leaving due to lack of jobs." Like David Warren, she saw Eleanor Roosevelt as the community's intercessor with the federal government and did not want to miss the chance to ask for more support.[13]

Eleanor Roosevelt left with a favorable impression of Westmoreland Homesteads. At the close of her visit, she commented, "It is very well planned, and the homes are well constructed. The homes are a great deal better than many I have seen."[14] She described her visit in her My Day newspaper column and concluded, "the people in charge had really accomplished a very remarkable piece of work."[15]

From Westmoreland Homesteads she and her party drove to Arthurdale, West Virginia, the site of the first subsistence homestead that she had helped to establish.

Eleanor Roosevelt came to Westmoreland Homesteads and endorsed the community's efforts. She did not lament its failure to embrace fully the cooperative ideals early planners had set out to achieve, condemn the racial imbalance within the community, nor decry the cooperative dairy's precarious financial status. She did not demand that more families join the health-care cooperative, or question the Protective Association's motives. She came to Westmoreland Homesteads open to seeing it as it presented itself and found it to be attractive, affirming, and successful. The residents had achieved the extraordinary goal of becoming a community committed to each other's well-being. Despite its failure to fully realize its ideals, Eleanor Roosevelt pronounced the great experiment to be a success. She endorsed Westmoreland Homesteads. In time, the residents would affirm her judgment, her sanction of their efforts, by adopting her name.

Naming Norvelt

Although the homesteaders agreed that the name "Westmoreland Homesteads" was "too lengthy" and "implies little meaning," it took them at least one year of public debate to determine a fitting name for their community. The *Homestead Informer* announced a naming contest, to which residents sent in a wide variety of names. One person liked White View because "the houses are white and we have a wonderful view." Marian Byerly, the president of the Mothers' Club, who was part of the delegation that escorted Eleanor Roosevelt on her visit to Westmoreland Homesteads, recommended that "Home" be part of the name. In response, Mrs. Dewey Honse, the wife of the pants factory janitor and watchman whose reinstatement was one of the demands of the 1938 strike (see below), put forward "Homeville," and another resident suggested "Hometown."[16]

Addah White was a homesteader who "had been appointed by the Federal Emergency Relief Administration to conduct home economic classes in sewing, cooking, and canning." She must have thought that the name should honor the people whom she considered responsible for the development of Westmoreland Homesteads, since she suggested "Eleanorville (Eleanor Roosevelt); O'Dayville (Olive Day); Norvelt (which is a combination of the last two syllables of Mrs. Roosevelt's name)." Addah White's last entry won the contest, and Westmoreland Homesteads became Norvelt, "the name of the project's most enthusiastic patron."[17]

On July 24, 1937, Westmoreland Homesteads held a special flag-raising ceremony. The area's state representative, Mr. Allen, spoke at the ceremony and urged everyone to register to vote because it is "our responsibility as citizens of the Commonwealth."[18] At the close of the event he announced the community's new name. Harry Ellis White, in an article in the *Homestead Informer* describing the occasion, concluded, "we are proud of the name Norvelt."[19]

The homesteaders were understandably grateful to Eleanor Roosevelt for the work that she had undertaken on their behalf. At the same time, by naming their community after her, they asserted their direct connection to the first lady. They had come a long way in a few short years. They were no longer marginalized outcasts, living in isolated patch communities or part of the millions of the unemployed or underemployed, desperately seeking employment, food, and shelter. Now they were citizens whom their local representative exhorted to vote. They were proud of what they had accomplished and the path they had chosen, and they appreciated the work of Eleanor Roosevelt, the Roosevelt administration, and their own efforts. The choice of name affirmed and proclaimed this vision of themselves and the community they had built.

Homesteaders did not achieve this success easily, as the continuing story of its early years reveals. The struggles to establish a successful factory, navigate the political conflicts that uncertainty sparked, plant and cultivate robust gardens, and, finally, to come to own their homes outright reveal the path to the middle way that Eleanor Roosevelt endorsed.

Factory

The early twentieth-century American factory system epitomized the competitive ethos at its most extreme. Though workers and owners ostensibly strove together to create products intended to enrich all, in reality the entire process pitted individuals in direct and consequential competition with each other. Companies sold their goods in a competitive market that generated intense pressures to drive costs down. Labor constituted one of the ripest areas in which to cut those costs, and employers regularly pitted their employees against each other to prevent them from rising collectively to demand higher wages. In times of slack demand, employers reduced their employees' wages or let them go altogether. Factory machines posed great physical risks to employees who tended them, and employers kept costs lower by chasing ever after greater efficiencies that eschewed workplace safety. And yet Westmoreland Homesteads' planners knew that the community's residents would not be able to provide for themselves and their families without some source of wage income. They needed a factory. The great task was to entice a manufacturer to come to Westmoreland Homesteads, and then to persuade that owner to run a humane shop. This proved to be the most difficult of all the subsistence homestead's hurdles to surmount.

General Information Concerning the Purposes and Policies of the Division of Subsistence Homesteads, published in November 1933, states matter-of-factly what everyone connected to the program knew very well, that "without adequate opportunity for wage employment, failure will result."[20] The need for cash income was never far from David Day's mind, judging from his frequent and recurring efforts to find suitable industrial ventures for Westmoreland Homesteads. Had he been able to solve the problem early on, many of the Westmoreland Homesteaders' disappointments and conflicts might have been forestalled. Two promising employment prospects in the spring of 1934 nearly resolved the problems well before the first homesteaders moved onto the site.

One prospect involved an enamelware factory proposed by a Mr. George Abersold, a successful Pittsburgh businessman interested in expanding his operations to Westmoreland County. Abersold told project officials that his proposed factory would employ 150 men and women and that he would invest $70,000 of his own money in the venture, sufficient to build the factory and provide operating capital. Officials in the national office approved the proposal, and the local Westmoreland Homesteads board did as well. But it appears that Mr. Abersold died suddenly, and the enamelware factory never materialized.[21]

The second early prospect involved the expansion or relocation of a small factory in Somerset County, Pennsylvania, that made craft items that sold well even in the Depression. Homesteaders would make Christmas cradles, children's furniture, latticework, trellises, and garden pergolas. C. W. Beam proposed to manufacture these craft items using hand labor, a proposal in line with the Quaker approach that appealed to Clarence Pickett a great deal. But Beam wanted the Division of Subsistence Homesteads (DSH) to build his factory, and the local Westmoreland Homesteads board rejected the proposal outright.[22]

Later proposals never made it even to the voting stage, as one flaw or another disqualified them from serious consideration.[23] Most of these failed for lack of investment capital, which the banks did not offer because of the Depression and which the comptroller general had forbidden the DSH to provide. Despite progress on other fronts, the failure to find a source of cash income worried the Westmoreland homesteaders and later provoked conflict between them and project management.

It appeared that the factory would not come easily, and perhaps would not come at all, unless the federal government put up seed money to get the enterprise going. Early struggles to entice factory owners to Westmoreland Homesteads drove home the need to approach the project very practically. Though establishing a factory that somehow embodied the cooperative ideal—that elevated the workers' experience and income above the ordinary model prevailing in America—would have cheered community planners and residents, the need for any income-generating factory trumped that sentiment. On this critical score, the subsistence homesteader planners grounded their ambitions firmly in the practical and most expedient path. Unlike the Co-op Store, dairy and poultry farms, and Dairy Lunch, which all started out with a goal of strengthening the cooperative ethos and made compromises along the way to accommodate pressures from Washington and market woes, the factory began with the explicit understanding that it would engage fully in the competitive market. The cooperative ideal might call for a less hierarchical workplace arrangement with local and widespread ownership, but the imperative was to create income sources in this one piece of the bold subsistence homestead community experiment to enable the broader vision to succeed. On a very mundane level, families needed to pay rent, buy food, and secure services as soon as possible. The quickest path was to entice an existing manufacturing company to open a factory in Westmoreland Homesteads, and community administrators set out to do that right away. Their success would help ensure the community's survival. At the same time, the triumph would necessarily erode the idealistic cooperative ideal in favor of a middle way.

The ultimate solution took the form of a garment factory that employed women primarily. Three companies expressed keen interest in operating a factory in Westmoreland Homesteads once the federal government committed to financing the factory's construction and early operating costs. The first promising lead turned sour when a Resettlement Administration official discovered that the interested company had just declared bankruptcy. The second potential investor expressed great interest, but also worried that the cooperative ideal and federal government involvement might require the company to pay its employees more generously than did other area factories and that Westmoreland Community Enterprises, Inc. might usurp the factory once it started generating profits. But the third company succeeded in opening in August 1938.[24]

Klee Oppenheimer's Washington Manufacturing Company of New York committed to operating the factory that the federal government lent Westmoreland Community Enterprises, Inc. the money to build. In a complex financial arrangement, Westmoreland Community Enterprises, Inc. secured loans to build the factory and then leased it to the Westmoreland Garment Corporation, Inc. to operate. Because Norvelt residents needed to learn how to operate the machines and could not run them at sufficient efficiency for some time, the Westmoreland Garment Corporation borrowed additional funds from the Resettlement Administration to cover initial operating costs. In the final tally, the federal government lent roughly $400,000 for factory construction and early operating costs.[25]

When the U.S. government loaned Westmoreland Community Enterprises, Inc. $260,000 to build and start operating the factory in 1938, it effectively made 123 homesteaders stockholders in the industry. Each family owned about five dollars' worth of stock in the factory.[26] Further, according to the original agreement, "the first 20 percent of the factory's net profits each year goes to the employes as a profit-sharing bonus." At the same time, the government held the stock of the homesteaders who formed the factory corporation as collateral.[27]

The Westmoreland Garment Corporation later requested and received an additional $75,000 loan from the federal government to cover operating expenses while it geared up to meet the increased demands generated by the approach of World War II.[28] The government ended its financial connection to the factory when it sold the building and machinery to the Washington Sales Corporation, a subsidiary of the Washington Manufacturing Company. The Washington Manufacturing Company in turn transferred ownership to the Amco Athletic Apparel Corporation in 1948, which had a factory in New York. The Norvelt factory then

FIG. 30 Factory workers and their male manager at the garment factory loading dock. Carol Davis personal collection.

became known as Amco of Norvelt.[29] Both ownership and the name remained until 1966, when a fire shut the factory.[30]

The factory originally produced pants; after Amco took over ownership the workers produced "athletic uniforms, emblems and kindred articles."[31] During World War II, the government awarded the Washington Manufacturing Company contracts to produce trousers for the military.[32] In 1940, the company obtained an army contract to produce thirty thousand "olive drab serge trousers" at 55.56 cents per pair.[33] This contract helped the factory generate net sales of $231,301.83 in the first nine months of the year. It also provided employment for a significant number of Norvelt residents. In 1941, 312 people worked at the factory, and 203 of them (65 percent) lived in Norvelt.[34]

The garment industry was highly competitive throughout the twentieth century and operated on small profit margins as a result. Company owners persistently sought ways to cut costs and often targeted the wages that they paid to garment workers. Companies closed facilities in higher-wage regions of the country in favor of building new factories in areas where they could pay less to workers for the same labor. Westmoreland Garment Corporation treasurer Klee Oppenheimer noted in the summer of 1939 that southern plant owners paid their workers only 25 cents an hour, while the Norvelt factory had to pay 10 cents more per hour. In addition, Oppenheimer complained to Resettlement Administration officials, the Westmoreland Garment Corporation was obligated to grant each worker an "hour and forty minutes rest period each week," or roughly twenty minutes rest during each eight-hour shift. Oppenheimer was willing to concede the rest period if he could get the employees to speed up their production. To that end, he hired an experienced superintendent with a track record of working with the factory layout and type of garment that the Westmoreland Garment Corporation manufactured.[35]

Although Oppenheimer's approach, which the Westmoreland Garment Corporation endorsed, epitomized the individualist approach, the workers, schooled in the cooperative ethos of Westmoreland Homesteads and, perhaps, drawing on their own struggles in the coalfields, banded together to form a union. From the day the factory doors opened, women constituted the majority of the workforce (which included eighty women and ten men) and served as the key union organizers and leaders. Gendered perceptions about wages prevailed at the factory, as women received 20 cents an hour while men were paid 25 cents during the three-month trial period, after which their wages rose.[36]

In October 1938, workers walked off the job and initiated a strike against the company. According to Sarah Karp, a resident of Norvelt and president of the local of the Committee for Industrial Organization, the strike was not about wages. Their demands reflected the importance they placed on banding together and standing up for one another.

1. Recognition of the Norvelt local of the Amalgamated Clothing Makers of America as the Bargaining agency for the factory.
2. Granting of a closed shop.
3 Granting of the checkoff.[37]
4. Reinstatement of Dewey Honse, night watchman who was dismissed by the factory's management Wednesday afternoon.[38]

Women dominated all levels of the strike; they organized the daily protests, strategized about tactics, and spoke to the press. They were the public face of the union and the workers. Women not only made up most of the strikers, they also led the local. Sarah Karp was the president, and "Miss Jean Eicholtz [was the] recording secretary, and Mrs. Esther Kuriz, [the] secretary and treasurer."[39]

The striking workers set up a picket line and sang songs to keep their spirits up. This was a battle they were determined to win. As Sarah Karp said, "We are not going to work until they meet our demands. All of the employees have signed up for the union, except one woman, and that makes it about 100 percent. The one woman tried to go through the picket line, but she did not get through."[40]

After being on strike for close to five weeks, the strike committee decided that they needed to mobilize federal backing for their demands. They made plans to send a committee to Washington, D.C., "to enroll the support of Mrs. Eleanor Roosevelt and officials of the Farm Security Administration in the strike."[41] It is not clear whether news of their upcoming trip reached the Washington Manufacturing Company or not, but early in November the company was ready to settle the strike. It met with officials of the Amalgamated Clothing Workers Union and agreed to three of the workers' four demands. The workers "won their fight for a union contract, a closed shop and the check-off of union dues."[42] The only outstanding issue was that of Dewey Honse, which, according to Sarah Karp, "would be taken up later."[43]

Women continued to work in the factory after the strike ended. Indeed, the number of women from Norvelt who worked outside the home as compared to women in the surrounding communities is notable. According to the 1940 census, very few women in the nearby mining towns of Mammoth, Calumet, and Kecksburg had paid employment, and the few who did primarily worked as maids. Only about five women from Norvelt worked as domestics, while close to one hundred worked in the garment factory. In addition, one worked as a clerk for the railroads, one was a bookkeeper in the retail trades, two were nurses, and one was the postmistress.[44]

Despite the changes in ownership and items produced, workers remained solidly committed to the union, for which they fought to obtain recognition. The workers affiliated with the Amalgamated Clothing Workers of America, a Congress of Industrial Organizations (CIO) union, and formed Local 354 in 1939.[45] When Amco took over the factory in 1948, the workers voted unanimously to retain a union shop.[46] The new owners, in turn, promised to keep all the employees, which numbered 130 women and men, as well as the rights and benefits the workers had won. These rights and benefits included "social security, paid vacations, six paid holidays a year, hospitalization, sick benefits, and life insurance."[47]

The construction of the factory, the single largest source of income-earning employment for residents of Norvelt, marked the changing balance between the cooperative spirit and the individualist drive. The decision of the government and management to establish a for-profit factory in Norvelt with absentee owners, an option that the majority of homesteaders agreed with, signaled the decline of the cooperative enterprises and the rise of the profit motive and individual paycheck. Yet the factory workers' determination to fight together to form a union undoubtedly reflected lessons they had learned from their cooperative living and working experience in Norvelt and, perhaps, from their fights in the coalfields. When faced with the individualist, profit-driven ethos that dominated the factory owner's approach, these workers' response was to join together to secure their rights, including the right of the fired night watchman to work.

Gardens

Westmoreland homesteaders worked out the tensions between the cooperative ethos and an individualist culture in the gardens that figured so prominently in Westmoreland Homesteads plans. After the houses themselves, the gardens stood out most prominently in the subsistence homestead template for creating a new way of living in Depression-era America. The gardens contained elements of both cooperative and individualist values, and residents resolved these tensions just as they had so many other aspects of life in Westmoreland Homesteads—they found a middle way between the two competing ideals.

The idea to use gardens as a means of providing food supplies to those in need did not originate with the subsistence homestead program. In fact, state and local governments found them to be attractive forms of food "relief" throughout the series of economic setbacks that befell America during the late nineteenth and early twentieth centuries. They promised both economic efficiency and moral uplift, two characteristics that appealed powerfully to societies buckling under the intense pressure of economic collapse. For minimal cost, relief agencies could provide seeds to the hungry and encourage them to sow, cultivate, harvest, and preserve their own food. In addition, gardening demanded hard work. For those who worried that giving food to the hungry directly would erode their will to work, gardening constituted a near-perfect alternative. As M. L. Wilson wrote, "there are some psychological and philosophical values which attach to the soil; that one of the most nearly normal manners in which human beings express themselves is by carrying through the cycle of the seasons the production of a garden; that there are fundamental values which attach to a family exhibiting the skill, the initiative and the discipline necessary to the timely operations of garden production and to the consumption by the family of something which the family produces."[48]

Those living on the margins of society had long strategized innovative ways to sustain themselves. Coal miners maintained vegetable gardens wherever the soil permitted, for they knew the strain that buying food in the company store placed on their depleted budgets. American cities, counties, and states regularly offered gardens as a form of relief for the unemployed from the 1870s up through the Great Depression. Garden historian Laura Lawson points out that these relief gardens sprang up during times of crisis and then disappeared rapidly once more economically flush times arrived.[49] The Great Depression followed the same pattern.

Americans recognized the economic depression's severity and devised public policies that supported gardening to provide sustenance to the unemployed. Lawson saw two types of gardens at the Depression's outset: the work relief garden, which employed men for wage labor on large-scale garden projects, and family subsistence gardens in plots reserved for individual families. Within a few years, Lawson points out, the wage labor garden had largely disappeared in favor of the subsistence garden. By 1935, even most subsistence garden programs had ended in favor of different kinds of federal relief.[50]

At their peak, relief gardens offered food to millions of Americans. The Federal Emergency Relief Administration noted that Americans cultivated fully 328,456 acres of gardens to produce $47 million worth of food in 1934. At least 80 percent of states sponsored some kind of gardening program. The New York State Temporary Emergency Relief Administration, for example, supported subsistence gardening in "backyards, vacant lots and large tracts of land" as early as 1932. In 1933, such gardens provided food for 41,149 needy families. By 1934, New Yorkers planted between 65,000 and 75,000 such gardens. Cities and towns sponsored the vast majority of these by dividing large tracts of land into smaller plots of one eighth of an acre. The towns organized these gardens on what they considered a "cooperative" basis, in which they paid those who tilled the gardens and the welfare commissioner distributed the vegetables to the "needy unemployed in the community." The program also included 6,000 "industrial" gardens, in which corporations financed gardens to feed their unemployed and part-time workers.[51]

Lorena Hickok, a close friend of Eleanor Roosevelt, toured southwestern Pennsylvania and West Virginia for Harry Hopkins in 1933 and found gardens used throughout the region. In West Virginia, she wondered how they could have planted some of them, given the steep hillside slopes to which they clung. One mining family sowed four acres with only a pitchfork and a spade. Hickok saw the gardens as one of the few bright spots in an otherwise grim landscape. She relayed that in Westmoreland County, Pennsylvania, "I visited some of the gardens—including a backyard garden in a mining town where the soil, so far as I could see, consisted almost entirely of coke ashes! Even the men living in the abandoned coke ovens at Latrobe had gardens—pathetic little patches of tomatoes and cabbages. By and large, the happiest and most contented people I saw were those working in the gardens." But even these unemployed gardeners shared that they would rather have paid work than toil in the garden.[52]

Given the positive role that gardens played in relief efforts before the New Deal, it is not surprising to find them in the subsistence homestead program. The original plans for each subsistence homestead included space for a substantial garden, often designed to be roughly one acre large. The DSH intended that each family would grow enough fruit and vegetables to feed the family for much of the year. Homestead staff established classes to teach women to preserve the produce that they did not consume right away, and various homesteads held group canning events during which women gathered to work on this together. The goal was for each family to grow and can enough food to offset the need for wages significantly. Men could then earn less money without putting the family at risk. Once the homesteads got up and running, the DSH anticipated that they would become models of dispersed populations in strong communities, rooted in the land, employed in small factories, committed to a cooperative rather than a competitive ideal.

The DSH intended the plots in various projects to look something like figure 31, with ample space for garden vegetables, fruit trees, grape arbors, chicken yards, and even a pasture for those homesteaders who had their own cow. This particular plan located the fruit trees in the front of the plot, beginning along the street's edge and stretching along the house's side parallel to the vegetable garden and halfway to its end as well. The small orchard ended in the middle of the chicken yard, a good distance from the house's back door. The trees served to shield the "working" parts of the homestead from the street, and offered a pleasant appearance to the plot. The pasture took the least maintenance of all other parts of the property, and the landscape designer put it farthest from the house itself. The vegetable garden would get regular use in the preparation of meals, and it sat just beyond the house's backyard, relatively close to the kitchen that it supplied every day. Those crops that the homestead family might sell or barter with others rather than consume lay

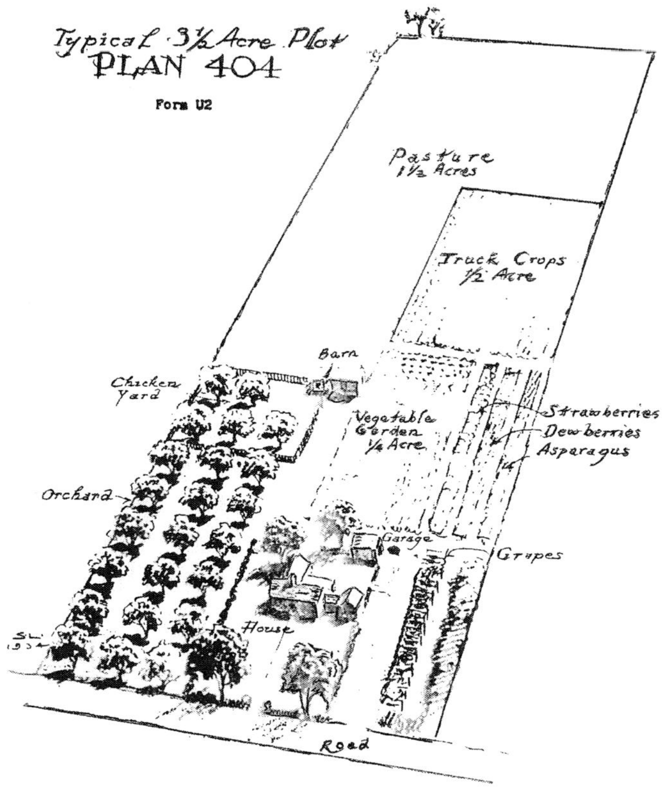

FIG. 31
Model subsistence homestead plot with garden. The Division of Subsistence Homesteads produced this design for homesteads like Westmoreland Homesteads. Note the placement of the garden relative to the house and the pasture for homesteads with cows. *Homestead Houses*, 65.

beyond the vegetable garden, more convenient to residents than the pasture, but farther away than the supply of food that the family would bring into the kitchen. The plan reflected its designers' careful consideration of the way that a homestead family might live.

The Department of Agriculture also suggested a model for laying out the plot of a subsistence homestead in northern areas of the country (see figure 32). This plan resembles the DSH design, though it places even greater emphasis on convenience. The vegetable garden lies even closer to the kitchen than in the previous design. There is no pasture, presumably because there would be no cow, and the orchard takes the space farthest from the house. In this design, the orchard would take the least regular maintenance, and so placing it farther away from the homestead family posed little difficulty. The trees around the house offered a hint of what lay at the property's back, though, with a pear and apple tree foreshadowing the orchard. The chicken coop and poultry run lay far from the house itself, making the morning run for breakfast eggs a good stretch of the legs. Both the Agriculture Department and the DSH designs included garages for residents' cars, though the design depicted suggests that the garage would also house "tools."

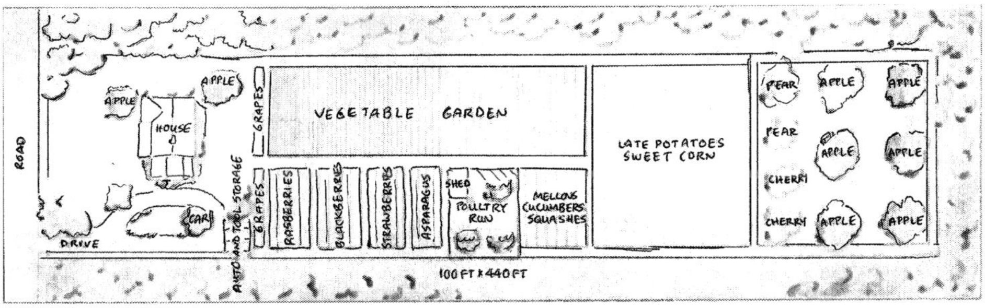

FIG. 32 Model northern subsistence homestead plot, including garden. Note that this plan specifies the location of each vegetable and puts the chicken coop (poultry barn) far from the kitchen. Wilcox, *Planning a Subsistence Homestead*, 4.

Architect Paul Bartholomew's drawings for homestead plots in Norvelt envisioned somewhat smaller gardens (see figure 33) located in close proximity to the houses. But he included a practical consideration that the previous designs neglected, a designated area for the underground dispersal of the human effluent emanating from each house's indoor plumbing. This had to be located close to the house to limit the distance waste traveled with each flush. The Norvelt houses had plumbing, but they did not connect to a common sewage system. Each homestead retained its own waste. Bartholomew deemed it best not to plant the carrots, lettuce, and beets in this field, but this decision pushed the garden farther from the kitchen and lengthened the distance from field to table.[53]

Bartholomew also left open the garden design's interior specifics to the residents, as he delineated only the space that the garden might occupy. The DSH plans and the Department of Agriculture map not only identified locations for the gardens, but also specified where certain types of vegetables ought to be planted.

Bartholomew's drawings, like those of the DSH and Department of Agriculture, put the chicken coop at the far end of the immediate backyard, beyond the garage. Later designs gave the two a shared wall and brought the chicken coop closer to the house. At least one Westmoreland Homesteads family apparently brought the chickens closer still, as the *Homestead Informer* featured a warning in 1937 against keeping chickens in the basement. Though it might be convenient, Paul Campbell warned, "this is so unhealthy and can only be spoken of in terms of filth." He added that the homestead management would not tolerate the practice and that "there is no possible excuse for it." But Norvelt residents recalled that there was a reason, as their families brought chicks in from the coops to their basements and kitchens to keep them from freezing to death on particularly cold spring nights.[54]

Norvelt residents did not have cows on their individual plots, but they did have chickens, fruit trees, garden vegetables, fruits, and grape arbors. By any measure, life on a Westmoreland homestead from April through October was hard work, with days filled with plowing, sowing, weeding, harvesting, tending the chickens,

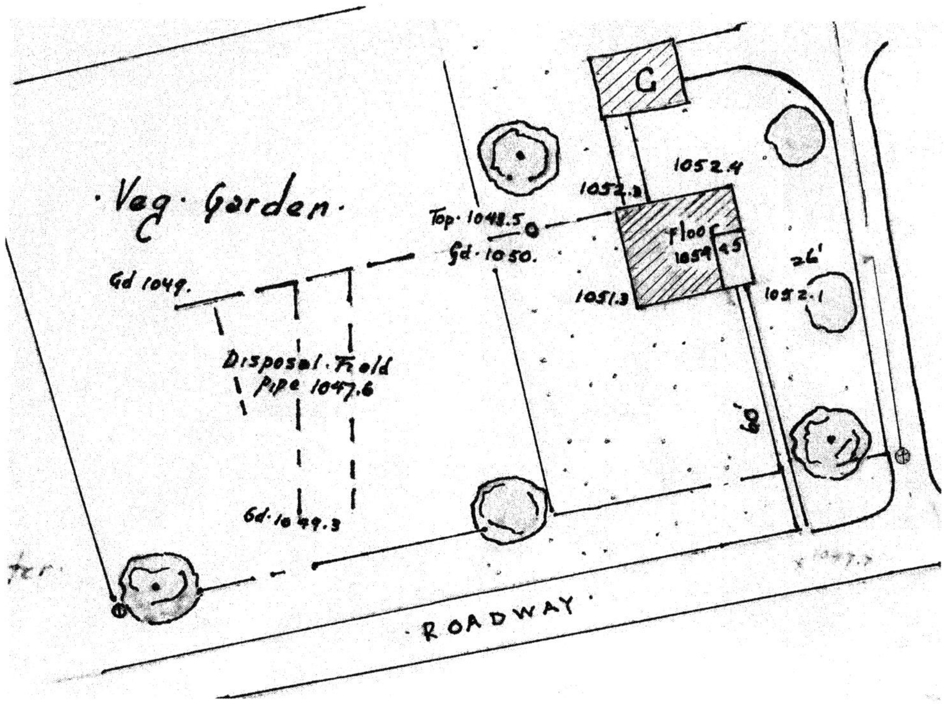

FIG. 33 Residential plot plan in Westmoreland Homesteads. Note that architect Bartholomew included the "disposal field" to the left of the house, with the vegetable garden behind the septic area. The plot drawing extends far to the rear of the vegetable garden and the house, with more than an acre of land that residents could have used for grazing cows. No residents actually had cows on their property, though. National Archives and Records Administration, College Park, Maryland, RG 96.

and preparing and canning food. Valeria Wolk, who moved to Westmoreland Homesteads as a young girl, recalls that "no one was afraid of hard work" when she was growing up. Though the fathers plowed and planted the gardens and the mothers canned the output, the children had to weed and clear the plants of bugs daily. It was laborious work, broken up occasionally by breaks for refreshing homemade root beer.[55]

Though every single adult man and woman among Norvelt's initial residents professed significant gardening experience in the review process to select residents, the level of cultivating that the DSH envisioned was closer to small-scale farming than gardening. Only a small fraction of the homesteaders had actual farming experience.[56] The residents thus did not have the kind of knowledge and experience that made for ready success in the large gardens on their lots. The Westmoreland Homesteads management sought to remedy this with services, classes, and instructional materials. W. L. Funkhouser, who served as Westmoreland Homesteads farming director in the mid-1930s, offered regular instruction through the community newsletter, the *Homestead Informer*, about gardening strategies and techniques. He offered advice on when to plant lawns (fall rather than spring), when to plant various vegetables, where to plant fruit trees, how to care for the gardening tools that the federal government provided to residents, and how to fertilize the gardens with chicken manure.[57]

It is less clear how residents responded to the gardening opportunities. T. Swann Harding noted in his study of subsistence homesteads that residents generally did not take to gardening even when they needed the food, and that "[i] n practically every case . . . as the family income passed a certain fairly well-defined point—say, for example, a hundred dollars a month for a family of four—most desire to dig in the soil vanished, and the subsistence features of the homestead subsided."[58] This may have been the case in Norvelt as well, for, as Charles Loomis observed in his assessment of subsistence homesteads, "[i]t is not easy . . . to get the average American family employed in urban industry to farm small plots of ground intensively."[59] Norvelt residents report a more nuanced story, noting that some families embraced gardening because they depended on and enjoyed the food. Others recall hating the hours spent in the garden, though they did put in the hours. Ward Beckwith, the Westmoreland Homesteads community manager, noted in a 1940 report that "only an occasional family is able to utilize for subsistence purposes the whole of the average 2 1/4 acre homestead lot. It is now evident that an average lot of one acre intensively cultivated will provide as much land as an employed family head can find time to cultivate, unless the family composition is such that the other members of the family can provide the necessary labor."[60] But even the extra hands did not necessarily guarantee gardening enthusiasm. By 1939, twenty-three families, or roughly 10 percent of the Westmoreland Homesteads families, had abandoned the gardens altogether, and another 15 percent gardened on less than a quarter of an acre. Fully half either did no gardening or gardened on less than one half of an acre. At the other end of the spectrum, however, a quarter of all families cultivated more than an acre.[61] During World War II, when families could afford store-bought produce, many more Westmoreland homesteaders curtailed their gardening considerably, while others continued to grow vegetables and keep chickens.[62]

The Resettlement Administration established new selection criteria in January 1936 for residents in homestead projects, with "special criteria applicable to Westmoreland Homesteads." These criteria expressed preference for families "with some gardening or farm experience."[63] It is difficult to tell from this whether the Resettlement Administration understood the existing gardening experience in the community to be sufficient or too little. Within a few years the emphasis on gardening background waned considerably, as the criteria shifted dramatically toward families with enough income to pay their monthly home fees and buy food without credit at the Co-op Store. The income ceiling rose from $1,200 per year to $1,600, and that figure became an average of the previous five years' income rather than simply from the previous single year. This allowed families with incomes even higher than $1,600 in the previous year to enter the community, so long as they had experienced a sufficient economic deficiency earlier. These families would have incomes well above the threshold that Harding suggested allowed families to lose interest in farming. There was little concern about attracting these more comfortable families to Westmoreland Homesteads, as the desire to get a home in the community remained high throughout the early years. Fully 1,689 families applied to live in one of the homestead's 250 houses, and 400 families applied for homes even after Norvelt closed the application list in August 1937. They hoped to replace families that moved away, which a few did—usually to pursue work opportunities in other areas.[64]

Even had Westmoreland homesteaders been enthusiastic farmers, their activity would have put them in tension with the cooperative spirit that the subsistence homestead program sought to cultivate. The original plans for the initial subsistence homestead in Reedsville, West Virginia, called for cooperative farming on common plots. Houses were to be grouped together on higher, less fertile land, with the lower, richer areas reserved for communal farms. But this smacked too much of socialism or communism for policy makers in the DSH, who insisted on individual plots for each family. Wanting a program that bolstered rather than undermined American individualism, they spread the homes over the entire area, on good soil and bad, and encouraged each family to cultivate land that would one day be their own.[65]

Westmoreland Homesteads inherited this latter model. Each family was responsible for raising its own food on individual lots. Homesteaders might assist one another with their gardens, share the produce with each other informally, and seek advice on gardening strategies, successes, and failures, but the bulk of the work fell on the parents and children in each home. They worked their own gardens for their own benefit.[66]

The rejection of the communal garden in favor of the individual family garden constituted one more compromise of the cooperative ethos that early subsistence homestead planners had sought so intently. The family garden represented a miniature version of the sturdy pioneer homestead family farm that the subsistence homesteads' conservative critics extolled. It required disciplined application of effort and strategy to plant, cultivate, harvest, and store each garden's produce. Gardens meant work, done by nuclear families, for their own benefit. And yet the cooperative ethos did not disappear entirely. Women gathered together to can what they grew and shared their expertise with each other. Families shared their produce, especially their prized products, with their neighbors freely, without compensation. Families shared gardening tools. Westmoreland homesteaders found a middle way.

Selling Norvelt: Privatization

The tension between the cooperative and competitive ethos existed throughout Norvelt. One could see it in the gardens, the factory, the co-op dairy and store. But it emerged most powerfully in the homes themselves, and in their unusual and arcane ownership status. Nothing loomed as powerfully for the community's residents as their desire to own their own homes. But this proved to be an elusive goal for at least a full decade. At the beginning, no residents could afford to buy the homes. The subsistence homestead program sought to assist those living on the economic margins, after all. But residents paid a sort of rent on the houses in which they lived, and they understood that rent to constitute credit toward ownership of their homes—even if the legal arrangements remained somewhat opaque. The residents did not merely "rent" the houses that happened to fall within the community's boundaries; they invested in the broader Westmoreland Homesteads enterprise. They participated in the cooperative community, yet they aspired to own their homes, to move that property from the community to the individual family. World War II increased incomes sufficiently for residents to achieve that goal, and the war's conclusion created the opportunity, finally, for that to happen.

The federal government sought to exit the housing business after World War II, moving quickly to sell houses that it had built over the previous decade. It had built some to provide living accommodations for factory workers employed in industries deemed vital to the war effort. These projects were often linked to specific factories or mills, similar in purpose to factory towns. It had built others for low-income Americans in urban areas, who were also expected to work in war-related factories. It had built resettlement plans to move people from urban areas to more rural settings, or off submarginal farm land to land that would produce more readily. And it had built subsistence homesteads with the intention of developing mixed industrial and farming activities in cooperative communities that honored their members' dignity and sought to lift them to humane lives. After the war, the government put nearly everything up for sale, including Norvelt, Pennsylvania.

Local editorialists did not see Norvelt's sale as part of the broader federal effort, but rather as a direct rejection of Westmoreland Homesteads' ideals and practices. Newspapers that had railed against the project steadily from its inception in the early 1930s through its first decade of life—as nearly all local newspapers did—saw in the sale a validation of the positions that they had promoted for the previous decade. In their view, the federal government had judged this particular community a failure and had come belatedly to the position that it was time to cut its losses and get out of the community-building business.

The papers all evaluated the plan as a business model and asked whether the federal government had made or lost money on the deal. For the most part their calculations showed huge losses, and they therefore deemed Norvelt to be a total failure. Though we argue that Norvelt cannot be judged entirely or even primarily as a business venture, an attempt at a final financial accounting is useful to understanding the broader story. The accounting itself is elusive, though, as the subsistence homestead program moved from one department to another, and those with fiduciary oversight became increasingly removed from the expenditures for which they held responsibility. Just making sure that the archive of records followed along with the program as it moved from department to department proved to be a substantial task.

The subsistence homestead program started out as its own Division of Subsistence Homesteads in August 1933, where it lived for four months before coming under the loose supervision of the Federal Subsistence Homestead Corporation, a quasi-private corporation formed to allow local subsidiary corporations (like Westmoreland Homesteads) to operate relatively free of federal bureaucratic delays. Administrators believed—correctly, it turned out—that the local managers could move more quickly to build the houses if they did not need to seek approval from Washington for each purchase and contract. Federal attorneys soon determined this arrangement to be unconstitutional and struck down the corporation arrangement. The program moved to the Resettlement Administration in May 1935, where it stayed for two years. It then moved to the Farm Security Administration within a different cabinet department (from Interior to Agriculture). It stayed there through most of World War II before coming under the wing of the Federal Public Housing Authority (FPHA), which sold its properties after the war ended. The figures upon which the local papers based their calculations came from the FPHA, which had no role in the community's planning, construction, or even management for the first ten of its dozen years of existence.

The figures that most newspaper accounts put forward suggested that the houses, outbuildings, communal structures (school, Community Center, poultry and dairy barns) cost $2,010,043.53 to build. The FPHA sold the houses to the newly formed Homestead Association of Westmoreland for $542,314, which then sold each of the 251 houses to its resident family. Most papers therefore subtracted the purchase price for the homes from the building cost and determined that the federal government lost roughly $1.5 million. The *Daily Courier*, the *Monessen Daily Independent*, the *Greensburg Daily Tribune*, and the *Pittsburgh Sun-Telegraph* roundly condemned the loss as proof that the utopian fantasy constituted a fool's errand from its beginning, and that taxpayers suffered the consequences.[67] *The Daily Courier* went even further in its condemnation the following year, when it used roughly the same numbers to reach the new conclusion that the homestead had lost fully $2,000,000—virtually everything spent on the homestead construction had become a liability.[68]

Not everyone drew such dire financial conclusions, however. The *Bulletin Index* pointed out that the actual purchase price for the homes was $828,203, not the $542,314 that others cited. The discrepancy in cost derived from a unique work arrangement that the federal government established with future homesteaders. In the "credit-hour" system, discussed more fully in chapter 5, residents constructed the homes and received diminished pay for their efforts. The future residents earned only a portion of their wage in cash, and the rest of their "pay" came in the form of credit, which went into a virtual bank from which residents might draw to pay a portion of their rent. These payments built equity in the home against the day, which arrived finally in 1946, when the homeowners purchased their houses. The federal government determined to honor this contract with the residents, and so reduced the prices by the amount that they had paid already. Residents had already paid $285,889 by January 1946, which, when subtracted from $828,203, resulted in the $542,314 purchase price cited most often. But using the actual purchase price reduced the "loss" on the homes to $1,181,780, and it came down further still when one added in the sale of the community buildings and grounds, which had been included in the $2,010,043 original construction cost. The *Bulletin Index* calculated that the federal government would be out $760,000, not the $1.5 million that most papers claimed and certainly not the $2 million figure the *Courier* reported. Moreover, the *Bulletin Index* noted,

> it must be remembered that the men who constructed the Homesteads were taken off relief. It is a good guess that the 1,200 people living in Norvelt would have eaten up many hundreds of thousands of assistance dollars long before their breadwinners found work. Leaving aside the social value of planting a model homestead in a slatternly mining community, of rescuing these families from the slough of the depression, and the value of the project as an experiment, it is doubtful if the net dollar-and-cents cost of Norvelt to the taxpayers was more than a trifling sum.[69]

The Farm Security Administration records indicate an even more favorable balance than the *Bulletin Index* reported. The cost of the homes themselves, including outbuildings and land purchases, came to $999,898.68.[70] This was $171,695.68 more than the FPHA received in payment for the homes. While still a significant sum, it falls far short of the $1,500,000–$2,000,000 figures cited in the press. The entire Norvelt project cost more to build than the figure just cited for the houses, and it is against this larger sum that critics account for Norvelt's deficit. But the costs for much of the work that the federal government paid for in Norvelt, to grade roads, construct a reservoir, build a school, were costs that government entities often assumed for new private developments. Counties often extended roads and sewer and water lines to developments, and school districts regularly built new elementary and high schools that benefited the children from only a portion of the district. (The federal government donated the school it built in Norvelt to the wider Mount Pleasant school district in 1940, and Norvelt's critics did not then condemn the Mount Pleasant district for this socialist incursion.) When critics measured Norvelt's cost in the broadest strokes, they inflated the deficit that it ran relative to other communities.

The larger point is that one should not measure Norvelt's success on a financial ledger alone. The question had never been whether the federal government could turn a profit on housing the poor. The answer to that was clearly no. The real question was whether the federal government could help citizens improve their lives by leveraging the construction of humane dwellings and providing the opportunity to cultivate cooperative communities. Was the society that this effort helped to create a better—more personally and socially fulfilling, enriching, creative, humane, just—community than was otherwise available to Westmoreland County's unemployed working-class citizens? The answer was clearly yes, and the evidence can be seen in some key aspects of Norvelt's sale.

The most powerful evidence came from the sales themselves. By all accounts, each and every family that lived in Norvelt in 1944 bought their homes in 1946. Not a single one of the 251 families sought to leave their homes and neighborhoods for any of the privately developed patches, towns, or cities against which Norvelt's critics compared the community and found Norvelt wanting. One critic saw the home sales as evidence that "resettlement is unpopular" and that "the ordered lives of those communal colonies appeal to comparatively few people."[71] But people clamored to get into Norvelt—fully 400 families applied for the waiting list even after the last house had been occupied. Once the houses went up for sale, every single resident chose to stay rather than leave for neighboring towns or patches. The homesteaders' primary concern was not whether to stay, but rather under what conditions they could solidify their presence in the community through the purchase of their homes. (Norvelt residents did battle over the purchase plans—more on that later.) Moreover, the purchases did not constitute speculation. They did not seek to make a real estate killing by purchasing underpriced homes (as some suggested the houses had been) and reselling them soon after. Homesteaders simply and decisively wanted to remain in Norvelt.

Homesteaders came to Norvelt expecting one day to buy the homes in which they lived. This had been the stated goal for Westmoreland Homesteads from its earliest inception. The question was never *if* residents could buy their homes, but rather *when* and under what conditions. Nothing in the residents' experience dissuaded them from their desire to make their lives in this "New Deal experiment." They offered the most eloquent statement on Norvelt's success by rooting themselves in the community.

Rumors of plans to sell the houses to the homesteaders circulated throughout the community periodically, and heated up dramatically in the early 1940s. The Norvelt Activities Council, which consisted of representatives from various community organizations, pushed the federal government hard in 1943 for a commitment to sell the homes. Government officials agreed at that time, but then delayed making firm plans for a year.[72] The 1944 plan, which did not get under way officially until 1945 and then spilled into 1946, maintained many of the elements of earlier models. It called for the formation of the Homestead Association of Westmoreland at Norvelt, which would consist of all resident household members. A board of seven of these members—the same who constituted the Norvelt Activities Council in 1943—was to administer the sale and then manage the community as a cooperative. Each household would own one of 251 shares in the cooperative, and the cooperative would then sell the homes to the resident families through the further extension of the monthly "rent" payments that residents had been making. Some of the families had done well enough financially during World War II to save enough money to buy their homes outright, and they would be able to do so under the plan. Others needed to borrow money to cover the outstanding balance on their homes, and the federal government offered to step in as mortgager for them.

More than 400 residents agreed in principle to the plan at a meeting on Sunday, June 11, 1944, but then balked at details four months later.[73] The Federal Public Housing Administration worked with the early board members, which consisted of five men and two women, to devise the specific plans for the sale.[74] These board members shared plans for the transfer of ownership with the broader community in mid-October 1944. It is not fully clear from surviving records why, but homesteaders rose up in opposition to the plan, the cooperative's by-laws, and its board membership at a meeting on Thursday, October 12. It may have been due to their discomfort with the process, which would delay direct purchase of the homes. Board President J. Watson Sisley responded by affirming both the board's intention to expedite sales of the homes and its determination to halt any agreement with the federal government until a "majority of the residents of the community evidence the desire to purchase their homes under the plan as presented." Sisley conveyed further that the federal government would not go forward with sales until either the community members reconciled with the current board or elected a new board. The homesteaders' reaction to the original plan and board troubled representatives of the FPHA, and it determined not to proceed with the sales until residents had voted formally on a new set of by-laws that also met with FPHA approval. Given the strong reaction against the plan at Thursday night's meeting, the board determined to hold the vote via secret ballot delivered to each homestead (returned in a sealed envelope) and to appoint a neutral committee to conduct the election.[75] Later reports indicate the residents favored a more rapid transfer of deeds from either the FPHA or the Homestead Association to residents than had been originally proposed—that they preferred to own their homes outright sooner rather than own merely shares in a cooperative.[76] The homesteaders voted in an almost entirely new, all-male board of directors (there was only one holdover from the previous board), and the plan went forward in 1945.[77] Newspaper accounts indicate that it did not change in substance from the previous plan.

The average cost of each house came to $2,161, and the actual price varied according to the house and lot size. The smaller, two-bedroom houses cost least, starting at about $1,778, and the largest, six-room houses cost the most, topping out at $2,578.[78] The purchasers got title to the house, the outbuildings (garage, chicken coop, grape arbor), and the plot as they had been drawn up in 1934.

The sales did include six deed restrictions that constrained the ways homesteaders could use their property even after they bought the land and houses outright. They reveal that homesteaders had come to see themselves more as a middle-class suburban community than a rural agricultural town. The deed restrictions required that all waste be disposed of via septic tanks or sewage lines, that any additions made to the houses be consistent with the original designs, that no building be constructed within twenty feet of a property line or within thirty feet of a street, and that no building on anyone's property be used for either a "malodorous occupation" or for "the manufacture, sale or distribution of malt or alcoholic beverages."[79] The restrictions clearly thwarted anyone's industrial ambitions for his or her property, but they also appeared to preclude expanded farming activities. It is difficult to imagine how one might maintain a barn with cows or pigs without offering "malodorous" offense. In fact, even chicken coops, present on every single plot in town, generated unpleasant odors. Norvelt had become, and its residents wanted it to remain, a suburban community from which most workers commuted to their jobs. One news report described the "tenants" as "engaged in various lines of endeavor in various communities near their homes."[80] The *homesteaders* had moved far down the road to becoming more typical *home owners*, albeit in a community with a very strong local identity and a powerful commitment to social engagement.

Homesteaders asserted by their insistence on buying their homes that they preferred some elements of the individualist ideal to the cooperative ethos. When the Federal Public Housing Administration proposed a plan to transfer home ownership to a newly formed Homestead Association of Westmoreland at Norvelt, homesteaders rose up to protest and eventually forestalled that plan. They rejected the cooperative ideal (communal ownership) in favor of the more individualist (direct home ownership). But they did not reject the cooperative ethos outright. They did not flee the community once they had sufficient funds to buy homes in Mount Pleasant, Latrobe, or other nearby communities. They wanted to stay in what they had helped to build in Norvelt. They embraced the middle way.

Chapter Seven

Living in Norvelt

Domestic Architecture

Visitors to Norvelt notice the houses before all else. Even today, when substantial additions have altered most homes' outward appearance, one can see the essential character of these Cape Cod–style houses lined up neatly along the curvilinear streets. This physical landscape constitutes Norvelt's most enduring legacy and most visible manifestation. The houses themselves are the first and most prominent aspect of this landscape, and any history of the community must account for not only how they came to be, but also the residents' lived experiences in those homes. The houses sheltered, protected, and joined Norvelt's residents to each other, but also offered privacy and refuge from the community.

The subsistence homestead model aimed to relieve material suffering through the provision of comfortable homes, reduce reliance on wage labor through subsistence gardens, and create affirming communities that enriched residents' lives through an enhanced ethic of cooperation and mutual concern. The Norvelt houses, layout, and landscape design incorporated a number of features that worked toward and away from these goals, existing in tension with the broader social aims.

The program's primary aim of strengthening community through the elimination of deprivation succeeded. The homes offered residents a level of dignity, comfort, and stability that few had experienced in their lifetimes, and none enjoyed in the midst of the Great Depression. Absent the burning anxieties that the inability to provide sufficient shelter and food caused parents, they became freer to join with others in common endeavors to strengthen the social bonds at the heart of the subsistence homestead ideal. Though the homes were extremely modest by middle-class standards even in the 1930s, they offered comfort, convenience, and aesthetic beauty to hundreds of western Pennsylvanians. Moreover, their common economic situations and relatively shared housing conditions formed a foundation of shared experience that reinforced community ties.

The subsistence homestead plans contained other components that did not work as well to strengthen community bonds—sometimes because they did not succeed as planned, and other times because the very plans themselves privileged individualism over community. The large-scale gardening at the center of the subsistence homestead ideal took a form that militated against community formation, and Norvelt residents soon wearied of the substantial commitment that it required. All but a few of the original houses remain standing even today, and the families that inhabited them in the nearly four generations since their construction have maintained them extraordinarily well. But most gardens gave way to lawns within a decade or so of their establishment, and few can be found today. Moreover, as discussed in chapter 6, aspects of the gardens themselves pulled people away from their neighbors to the sustained duties that planting, maintaining, and harvesting individual plots demanded. The Division of Subsistence Homesteads (DSH) gave in to outside pressures in the early years of planning and forsook communal plots in favor of individual gardens for each family. The hours spent in sustaining the gardens afforded an abundance of vegetables and fruits for each family, but also demanded that they toil in isolation from each other to produce the food that they often later shared with one another.

This chapter explores Norvelt's physical landscape in an effort to more fully explicate the community's most visible characteristic. It begins with a brief history of planned communities in American history, and then narrows to a concentrated focus on Norvelt's homes.

Antecedents to the Subsistence Homestead: Planned Communities

Americans had been building "planned communities" for centuries by the time that Paul Bartholomew sat down at his drafting table to draw up the landscape and home designs for the Westmoreland Homesteads in the early 1930s. The purposes, physical designs, and character of these communities changed over time until they finally came to be divided between one of two central forms. The first aimed at economic efficiency and profit maximization, and the second sought to establish and sustain strong community identity and democratic ideals. The story of the development of these two aims makes Norvelt more understandable.

The earliest planned communities were likely religious communes, such as those established in 1732 in Ephrata, Pennsylvania, and in 1824 in Old Economy, Pennsylvania.[1] The more prevalent models for someone planning a community in the early twentieth century were the various company towns established for economic purposes—and the reformers' efforts to humanize these towns, which had gained prominence in architectural circles by then. John S. Garner discerned a pattern of planned community development, a "morphology" of planning, for the New England region. Figure 34 lays out the developments in that morphology, though these dates suggest a specificity that dissipates under close scrutiny. One

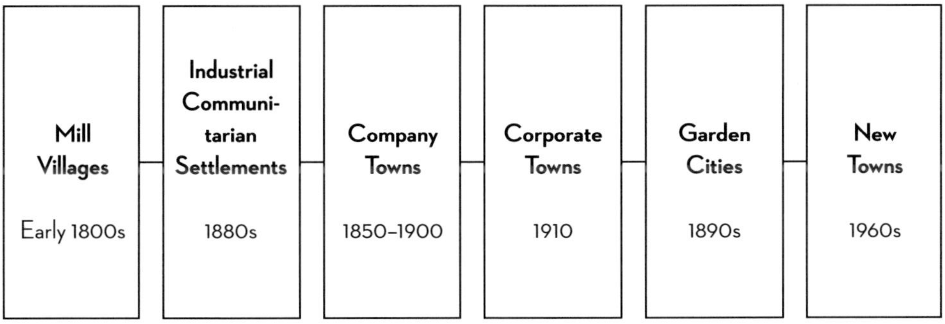

FIG. 34 Garner's "morphology" of planned communities. Drawn by Timothy Kelly based on information in Garner, *The Model Company Town*, 4. Garner's morphology follows closely one that Morris Knowles suggested in 1920. Knowles's evolutionary model consisted of the following: Mill Tenements; Mining Camps; Early Industrial Towns; Garden City Movement; Newer Industrial Towns. *Knowles, Industrial Housing*, 6–7.

might find examples of each of the types that Garner lists outside of the period that he associates most closely with them.

Most relevant to Norvelt's design were the company towns whose characteristics Norvelt was intended to improve upon. For the century preceding Norvelt's construction, most planned communities took the form of the company towns built around a mill or factory site to accommodate the laborers needed to work at these for-profit economic enterprises. Most shared a paternalistic and exploitive bent, rooted in the drive for economic efficiency and racial and ethnic prejudice. A few aimed at improving resident comfort and happiness. Margaret Crawford estimates that fully 2 million people lived in company towns in 1930, the decade in which Norvelt was built. Crawford identifies three periods in the development of company towns throughout American history. She argues that the second period began with the construction of the town that George Pullman named after himself (and his Pullman Car Company) in 1883. This "model company town" aimed at eliminating labor strife by building towns with "significantly better living conditions." But the tension over wages and company control of workers' lives both in the factory and the community led to bitter conflicts. Even Pullman himself came to the conclusion that his company town did not achieve his goals, and he discouraged other capitalists from following in his footsteps.[2]

Chastened by Pullman's failures, industrialists moved to a modified version of the company town in which the companies laid out the town streets and house plots but sold the homes to workers (or any interested buyers) rather than holding onto them. Crawford points to places like Gary, Indiana (U.S. Steel), and Vandergrift, Pennsylvania (Apollo Iron and Steel Company), where the companies tried to stay out of real estate ownership after establishing the town layouts.[3]

In part as a response to the failures evident in places like Pullman, Illinois, and in part as a logical outgrowth of the Progressive movement, the third period of company towns emerged in 1914. It relied on professional architects, town planners,

Initial Company Towns	Model Company Towns	"New" Company Towns
Began in 1820s	Began in 1880s	Began in 1914

FIG. 35 Crawford's three periods of company town construction. Drawn by Timothy Kelly based on information in Crawford, *Building the Workingman's Paradise.*

and landscape architects to design "new" company towns that hid the towns' industrial origins. Crawford sees a marked improvement in the typical company town after the move to the "new" plans, which included elements of the garden city ideal.

Though elements of the garden city ideal had existed for decades, Ebenezer Howard's 1902 *Garden Cities of To-Morrow* is generally cited as the primer for the movement.[4] Howard's blueprint called for satellite cities of no more than thirty-two thousand residents connected by high-speed rail lines to urban hubs. The garden cities were to have central parks, lots of green space, and curvilinear street patterns along which workers' houses would be built. Factories would rim the circle of streets around the central park and workers' homes, and farms, forests, and pastures were to preserve the land beyond the factories.[5] Despite its towering presence within the urban planning community, only two garden cities ever actually came into existence, both in England. But designers took elements of the garden city when building suburban towns in England and America.[6]

It is important to note that even when Americans intended to build garden cities to improve workers' living conditions, middle-class residents almost always reaped the benefits. Construction costs invariably drove house prices above workers' budgets.[7] Such was the case for Forest Hills Gardens in New York and Mariemont, Ohio, a Cincinnati suburb. It was also the case for Chatham Village near Pittsburgh, which the Buhl Foundation sponsored, underwrote, and built as a demonstration to developers that they could make profits when building housing to sell to working-class families. The Buhl Foundation discovered that building expenses, even when the Depression deflated construction costs, inflated Chatham Village units beyond what workers could afford to pay. The foundation decided to rent rather than sell the units, and even then had to market them to entry-level white collar workers and highly skilled industrial workers rather than the typical factory employee.[8]

Many of the company towns constructed after 1914 incorporated design features championed by the town-planning movement under way among urban planners, architects, and landscape architects. This loose movement sometimes took the form of very specific organizations, such as the Regional Planning Association of America (RPAA), which Clarence S. Stein formed in New York City just after World War I. Stein's work with urban architecture, the settlement house movement, and federally sponsored housing for workers in World War I convinced him that good design could improve the lives of America's urban poor. The RPAA never had more than twenty members, but it shaped the way that professional planners and architects understood their significance, potential, and work.[9]

If urban and town planners embraced the humane purposes of the "new" town movement, industrial employers remained focused on their overall profits. They accepted some aspects of the garden city ideal in order to deter labor conflict, but no one ever confused the company town with a social service agency. In fact, even historians sympathetic to companies that built their workers' homes see the typical company town in the early twentieth century as roughly equivalent to the poor and working-class sections of the country's largest cities.[10] This sets a low bar for certain, as working-class housing in large urban areas offered little to uplift the lives of its residents.

Historians have been far more interested in exploring those "model" company towns that offered innovative, humane, and often enriching living conditions than they have been in explicating the dreary oppressiveness that characterized so many company towns. This may result in part from the difficulties that historians face in gathering information about the more exploitative towns. Arnold R. Alanen documents the paucity of accessible resources for researching mining communities in the Upper Midwest, in part because companies with contentious labor relations have not shared their records openly.[11] Few companies with model towns sought to hide them from the public gaze, however, and historians can locate sources about these much more readily.

The company town typically derived from the need to house workers at a large industrial or manufacturing site. Factories and mills located in or very close to urban centers typically did not have to build housing for their employees, as they could draw their workforces from nearby neighborhoods. But factories located outside of cities, often to be near natural resources or power sources, had to import their workers and then provide housing of some kind. At the peak, the United States had roughly twenty-five hundred such company towns.[12] Western Pennsylvanians most often encountered these company towns through the coal industry, which needed miners to live close enough to the rural mines to walk to work every day. Mining companies established "coal-patch" settlements near the mouths of mine shafts that extended underground for thousands of feet. A review of some of their common characteristics provides a look at the communities from which Norvelt's residents came in the 1930s, the limits of the "new" company town movement's influence on the coalfields of western Pennsylvania, and the model that Norvelt designers reacted against. For in many ways, coal patches dampened individualism, or the dignity of the individual, with their relentless regimentation of work and home life and the constant material deprivation that they imposed upon residents. Coal companies denied the economic security and dignity at the foundation of true volitional community through low wages and inadequate housing. The coal-patch design saw the miner as a machine part and his home as little more than a low-cost storage unit. Once the mines closed, those workers and families had fewer resources, and their suffering increased immensely.

Thomas Carter and Elizabeth Collins Cromley recommend "reading" houses the way literary critics read written texts.[13] Instead of analyzing plays and novels, though, students of vernacular architecture focus on the built environment in which people live out their lives—with a special emphasis on people's houses. These houses both reflect and shape the lives of those who live within their walls and visit their confines. Any such analysis requires a close reading of the floor plans, the building materials (or fabric), and the broader community in which the house sits. Borrowing some of the techniques from those who study material culture sheds important light on the lives of those who lived in Norvelt.

Perhaps the most significant point that such a study reveals is the great contrast between the coal-patch homes from which many of the Norvelt residents came and the houses into which they moved in Norvelt. The homes marked a substantial improvement in almost every measureable dimension—number of rooms, amenities, opportunities for privacy, comfort, and durability. Jim Davis recalled that when he moved his family into the community, "We thought we were in heaven. . . . I never had a place like this in my whole life—indoor bathroom, running water, furnace in the basement."[14] Mining companies sought to build the houses as efficiently as possible, with a minimum of amenities. In fact, the mining companies believed that the immigrant residents were so used to poor standards of living in their home countries that they did not need such amenities as indoor plumbing, central heat, or closets.[15] The houses that mining companies built and then leased to employees and their families were little more than small empty spaces of few rooms, constructed of cheap, low-grade materials. Hardy Green calls these coal-patch communities "Exploitationvilles" based upon their clear purpose of extracting the maximum work from employees at the lowest cost to the employer.[16] Westmoreland Homesteads resident Sarah Malnofsky recalled, "We'd never had a home of our own; lived in a company house with no water or indoor plumbing. We felt pretty lucky coming here."[17]

Coal-patch communities in western Pennsylvania bore little resemblance to the "new" towns that Clarence Stein helped to design in places like Radburn, New Jersey, and Pittsburgh's Chatham Village neighborhood. Mining companies did not hire architects or town planners to design their homes and towns. Instead they relied on company engineers, who, quite predictably, made efficiency their chief design goal. The streets invariably followed the grid pattern, and houses looked alike throughout each plan. The overriding impression that these communities left on their inhabitants was regimentation, discomfort, and gloom. Hardy Green reports that only 2 percent of Appalachia's mining towns included "such amenities as comfortable housing, recreation facilities, and well-laid-out streets and parks."[18]

Coal-patch houses afforded little comfort or privacy. The typical mining family lived in either a small detached home of four rooms or a semidetached house with another family on the other side of a central wall. Mining companies rarely built

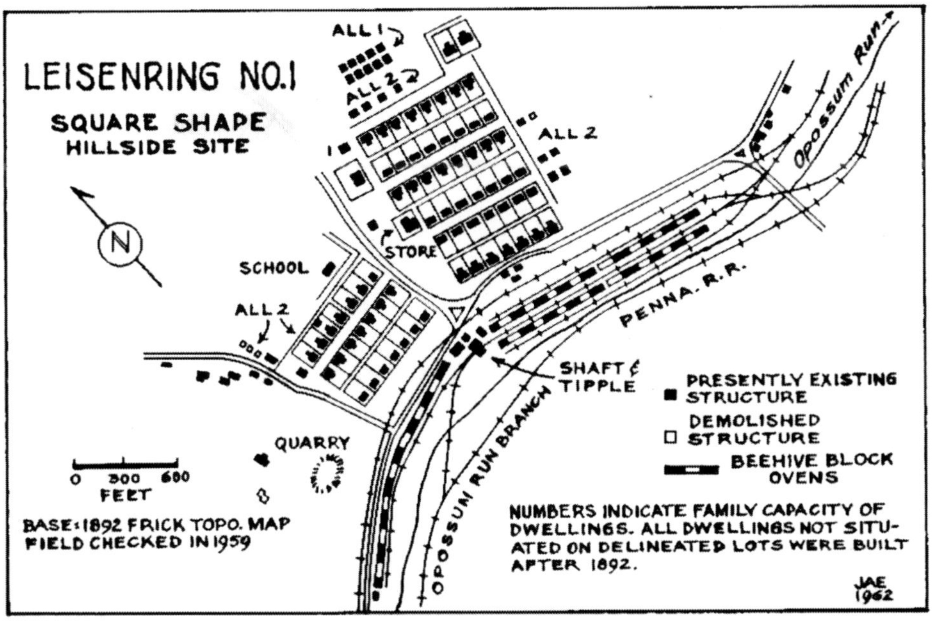

MAP 3 Typical coal patch. This map conveys the grid pattern for streets and houses in the Leisenring No. 1 patch. Note the location of the houses and the uniformity of the street pattern. John A. Enman Papers, Coal and Coke Heritage Center at Penn State Fayette, The Eberly Campus.

larger structures, such as the row houses ubiquitous in steel mill towns, for fear of fire spreading across multiple dwellings. The homes usually consisted of a kitchen and living room on the first floor and two bedrooms above.

The homes often had no furnace, sinks, tubs, or toilets. Families relied on the kitchen stove for heat in the winter, with all other rooms getting heat only through air passing through doors or up the stairwell. The homes had no insulation, which meant that the heat that the kitchen stove generated moved quickly through the walls and roof and out of the house. Ed Cibulas recalls how cold his house was in the Whitney coal patch, close by to Norvelt. The family huddled under thick blankets to try to stay warm through the night. He also recalls the discomfort winters posed for such rudimentary things as going to the bathroom. The patch houses had outhouses in the backyards, and Ed recalls that relieving himself in winter was no easy task. After dark most families used a chamber pot that they kept upstairs in one of the bedrooms. Each morning his mother emptied the pot in the outhouse.[19]

The houses were cold in the winter, hot in the summer, and covered in soot all year round.[20] One 1911 survey of coal-miner homes in southwestern Pennsylvania concluded that "[l]iving conditions, as a rule, are exceedingly insanitary. Toilets are in all cases dry, with ground vaults, and are often located near the dwellings. Some mining communities near the larger cities use the city water supply; others draw their water, which is usually filtered, from company reservoirs. In many cases the inhabitants of the villages depend upon the wells sunk at regular intervals. Wells or hydrants are placed about 200 yards apart, one for each ten or twelve families."[21] "Honey dippers," the only African Americans that many patch-community residents encountered in their regular routines, came at night to scoop out the privy vaults when they got full.[22]

David Day and Paul Campbell kept records of the conditions from which the original Westmoreland homesteaders came, and Campbell later used them in his 1940 master's thesis at the University of Pittsburgh. They reveal much about the residents' demographic characteristics and the conditions in which residents lived just prior to coming to Westmoreland Homesteads. Roughly two-thirds of the original settlers came from the coal patches in the area near Norvelt. One hundred and forty of the first 150 families (93 percent) relied on coal stoves to both cook and heat their homes. Only 16 percent had bathrooms in their homes. A surprisingly high percentage, 84, had some running water available in the home, but in many cases "it was not suitable for drinking or cooking purposes." Since only 16 percent had toilets, it is not clear how the families would have used such water—perhaps for cleaning.[23]

Patch houses were spartan and small, with less than seven hundred square feet of total living space for families that often consisted of husbands, wives, and more than a half dozen children.[24] The families who lived in these houses washed, cooked, and ate in the kitchen, where mothers toiled long hours preparing, cooking, and cleaning up from meals. The stove required regular attention to keep from going out, and burned coal that blanketed the house in a sooty film. Daughters assisted their mothers in these domestic chores so that they would be ready to take on their own homes when they married—often in their early teens.[25]

Many mining families took in boarders to provide housing for single men and to supplement the meager family earnings. This crowded even more people into the houses, created more cooking and cleaning for the mothers, and reduced the meager privacy even further.

One Westmoreland Homesteads resident recalled that before he moved to Norvelt he "used to live in a smelly, dirty, grubby company town—a mining patch. Oh, it was beautiful—I'm telling you. A smelly outhouse, a broken-down pump for water, single bedroom for all the family."[26] Economist Price Fishback concurs that western Pennsylvania coal miners lived in poor housing. After describing the small, cramped, poorly insulated, and rough conditions of Alabama mining patches, he notes that "housing in Pennsylvania was at this time considered inferior to Alabama housing, which was inferior to much of the housing in Midwestern and southwestern coal communities, where a significant number of miners owned their own homes."[27]

While the company town was organized around the factory, Norvelt's organizing imperative was the residential community. In this aspect Norvelt more resembled the "garden city" and "new town" ideals than the company town blueprint. Norvelt's overall layout reflects the tensions within the planned community movement. Planners valued design and architecture that both cultivated community

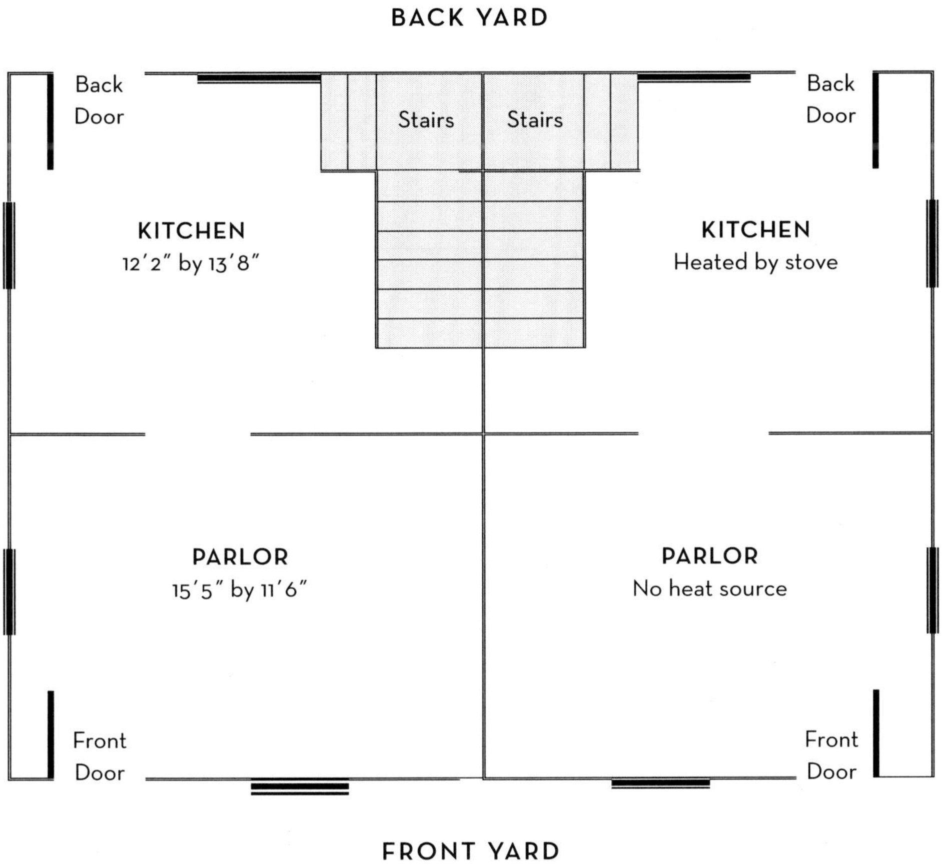

FIG. 36 First floor of a coal-patch house in western Pennsylvania. Note the absence of indoor plumbing, as there is no sink in the kitchen nor bathroom in the house. The only heat source in winter was the kitchen stove. Drawn by authors based on information from Mulrooney, *Legacy of Coal*.

bonds and privileged the role of green space, adaptation to existing topography, and efficiencies of scale in building structures. The constraints that cities posed forced planners to combine these seamlessly. The urban grid structure limited the options for green space and forced designers to maximize the shared and open areas within a narrow space. It pushed the houses to the front edge of plots and opened the block interiors to green space development. The common lawns and gardens lay between the homes, whose fronts faced the more pronouncedly public streets and whose rears lined the gardens. (This pushed architects to alter the rears of urban houses, to make them less kitchen "work space" extensions and more family relaxation areas.) While the limited space pushed the houses toward the periphery and each other in order to maximize green space, this location also made for efficient building. Builders could replicate Henry Ford's assembly line, only with building crews moving along rather than the houses themselves.[28]

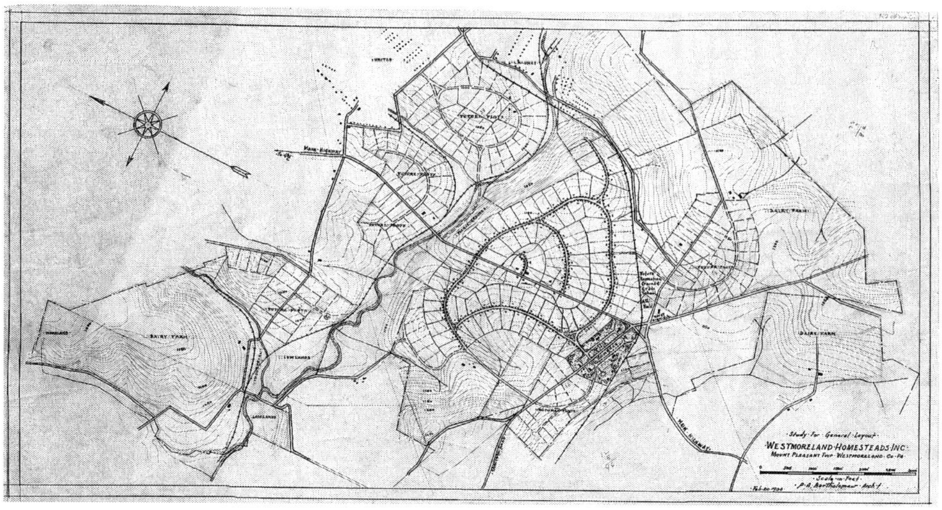

MAP 4 Norvelt plot map. This map shows the street layout and building location for a section of Westmoreland Homesteads. Note the extensive stretch of property behind the houses for each plot of land, while the houses themselves cluster along the streets. Westmoreland Homesteads plans, 1934. From the collection of the Westmoreland County Historical Society, Greensburg, Pennsylvania.

Suburban planners had more land with which to work, and they abandoned the urban grid structure almost immediately. In its place they put curvilinear streets that meandered through neighborhoods. But even they saw the street as an almost hyperpublic space in which private cars and service trucks would intrude regularly. They too designed neighborhoods to shield homes and "true" community development from the more pronouncedly public spaces that vehicles traversed. They turned homes to face each other across the green space and away from the streets that surrounded the homes. Clarence Stein and Henry Wright designed Radburn, New Jersey, so that the houses' front doors faced pedestrian walkways, lawns, gardens, and other homes, while the streets passed by the back doors.[29] Here too, and especially in Chatham Village, locating the houses close to the streets that served them made them efficient to build. The Buhl Foundation's decision to build attached row houses with shared walls and roofs increased the construction savings even more.

Both urban and suburban planners built on relatively finite space, with standard lot sizes measured in the hundreds of square feet. The residents who inhabited these model communities encountered each other regularly because they lived so close together. The planners' task was to create pleasant landscapes to host these inevitable encounters, and to offer peaceful respite from the even more intruding world that streets brought. Norvelt measured its lot sizes by the acre. The challenge in Norvelt was not marking off sufficient land to preserve green space for residents, but almost the opposite. How might a community with immense stretches of open area nurture social bonds between widely scattered neighbors?

Bartholomew's solution incorporated the same curvilinear street design that the RPAA favored, and extended individual plots in large rectangles from the street. He placed the houses very close to the streets, landing them near to the "public" world that the street represented and close to neighbors on either side. Each plot had a garage, grape arbor, vegetable garden plot, and chicken coop. Rather than these "service" areas and buildings facing the street, as did the service areas of homes in Radford, New Jersey, or Chatham Village, the house fronts in Norvelt faced the streets and shielded the working buildings from public view. Perhaps in a nod to the urban planners, though, Bartholomew placed the entrance doors on the houses' sides, facing neighbors' homes. This allowed savings on utility connections and construction and maximized neighbor interaction.

Bartholomew designed individual houses rather than row houses, a practice that favored individualism over communalism. The Chatham Village row house model had to be fresh in Bartholomew's mind as he contemplated the Westmoreland Homesteads design, but he also operated under constraints, offered as recommendations, imposed by the Architectural Unit of the Division of Subsistence Homesteads.[30] The homestead communities had to "demonstrate the practicability of home ownership through means of long-term loans which necessitate a small down payment or, in some projects, none at all. These housing demonstrations, located as they will be in the various sections of the country, will point the way, it is hoped, for private enterprise and other groups in providing better homes for low-income groups."[31] The Architectural Unit sought to produce houses in each of the homesteads that would serve as models for housing the poor with comfort and dignity that private developers might emulate. Just as the Buhl Foundation sought to keep construction costs down, so too did the DSH. But where this concern led the Buhl Foundation architects to shed early plans for free-standing houses in favor of attached dwelling units, and to abandon direct unit ownership in favor of rental agreements, the subsistence homesteads program had an added concern that militated against taking this path. External critics regularly accused it of undermining "individualism" in favor of a "collectivist" ideal, of subverting what many considered a bedrock American character trait. The program sought to demonstrate the cost-effectiveness of housing poor people without turning them into socialists. The houses had to reinforce the American disposition for property ownership and bolster individualism. As one writer to the *New York Times* put it in 1933, "'rugged individualism,' which some now scorn, held the heavy end of the burden in building up those genuine subsistence homesteads of [our frontier] past."[32] Free-standing homes better cultivated that value than attached units or apartments.

The houses might be free-standing and front the street, two characteristics that tended to work against communal values, but Bartholomew did seek in other ways to orient residents to communal interaction. Any neighborhood with comparably sized lots constructed today would inevitably set the houses far back on the plots, according each home owner an ample front as well as backyard. Even the Garden City, New York, suburban plan from the nineteenth century planned houses seventy-five feet back from the street.[33] Bartholomew placed Westmoreland Homesteads houses exactly forty feet from the street's edge, though, which placed residents in close proximity to their across-the-street neighbors. They did not share a common wall, but they traveled but a short distance to borrow a cup of sugar.

Interpreting Norvelt's Architecture and Cultural Landscape: The Norvelt Houses' Interiors

Paul Bartholomew designed five floor plans for Norvelt houses. They each shared a basic Cape Cod type, and they ranged in size from four rooms to six. Bartholomew identified each by a distinct number that ranged between 402 and 601.[34] These numbers were part of the DSH's overall numbering system, which encompassed houses from projects all over the country. The division published a book of drawings and floor plans designed to encourage private developers, or even individual families, to use as a resource when building their own houses. The 601 house plan came from Westmoreland Homesteads, but the 615 was for a New England project. The 402 was from Westmoreland Homesteads, but the 412 was from the deep South. Altogether the plan book contains thirty-two different plans. Each plan followed a few basic rules, which a close review of one of the Norvelt houses will make clear.

House 402

Each Norvelt house appears to be in the Cape Cod style, with a few potentially significant variations. The DSH directed that each house style should follow the basic architectural types in the host region. Phoenix houses were single-story adobe dwellings, for example. The Cape Cod was native to New England rather than western Pennsylvania, though, which would seem to break this directive. Paul Bartholomew maintained that the houses that he developed for Westmoreland Homesteads were "Pennsylvania farm houses." Most other commentators referred to them as Cape Cod designs, which they most resembled to lay observers. The DSH plan book called the 601 type a "New England Colonial of Cape Cod type," a designation that resonates with architectural historians. Americans had begun a colonial house revival in the 1920s, and the Cape Cod would become the most popular of all American house designs over the next half century.[35]

House type 402 is a relatively standard Cape Cod house with a kitchen, living room, and bathroom on the first floor, and two bedrooms with dormer windows on the second floor. The DSH directed that all houses be relatively small, "in order to keep within the required budget," and the 402 *is* small, especially when compared to houses built in the latter decades of the twentieth century or even to middle-class homes then being built in urban and suburban communities. It measures one thousand square feet of living space in the DSH plans, and even less in Bartholomew's more detailed blueprint drawings. But the typical western Pennsylvania coal-patch house was smaller still, topping out at about seven hundred square feet.[36] These small, economically efficient dwellings constituted a modest increase in size for the mining families. The 601 house, intended for families with four or more children, was more commodious, coming in at 20 percent larger than the standard mining-patch home.[37]

Even so, the DSH recognized that families might feel cramped within the walls. They asked architects to design the houses so that they "may be conveniently expanded without destroying the design of the original unit." Most Norvelt residents did expand their homes in the decades following World War II, once their purchase of the home freed them from federal proscriptions against modifications and their postwar prosperity made these expansions affordable.[38]

The DSH also prescribed that all of the designs make efficient use of space, and eschew such indulgences as areas that might be used "but a few hours weekly," such as dining rooms. Bartholomew's task was to combine the dining area with either the living room or kitchen. He chose to build kitchens large enough to accommodate tables for family meals. Though the loss of a dining room was no doubt a sacrifice for the typical family employing an architect's services, few coal-mining families had come from such relative luxury. Similarly, the DSH instructed architects to forgo formal living rooms, "too often reserved for extraordinary functions," in favor of ones that families would use regularly. Though formal living rooms might have been common among affluent families, coal-patch residents surely did not have them, and certainly did not reserve any room in their small homes for "formal" occasions.[39]

More significant to the Westmoreland Homesteads families coming from coal patches or working-class homes in industrial areas were instructions regarding privacy, air flow, and light. The DSH noted that it "considers of paramount importance proper bedroom accommodations for both adults and children, and access from the bedrooms to the bath without passing through other rooms."[40] Bartholomew hewed to these instructions in most cases. The 402 house, for example, followed the bathroom-accessibility model. It included a first-floor bathroom located off of a hallway that contained the staircase to both second-floor bedrooms. A resident could move from the bathroom to each bedroom without passing through the kitchen, living room, or other bedroom. (The 601 house did contain a room on the second floor designated as either a child's room or storage space that was accessible only through an attached larger bedroom.) The 402 also offered two separate bedrooms, one for parents and the other for children. Larger families could live in houses with up to four bedrooms.

The DSH also specified that "all kitchens, living rooms, as well as most bedrooms" be "provided with cross ventilation," as well as with "ample lighting."[41] The 402 house had fourteen windows to let in sunshine and light during the day, and each window was positioned to allow cross breezes to blow through even with

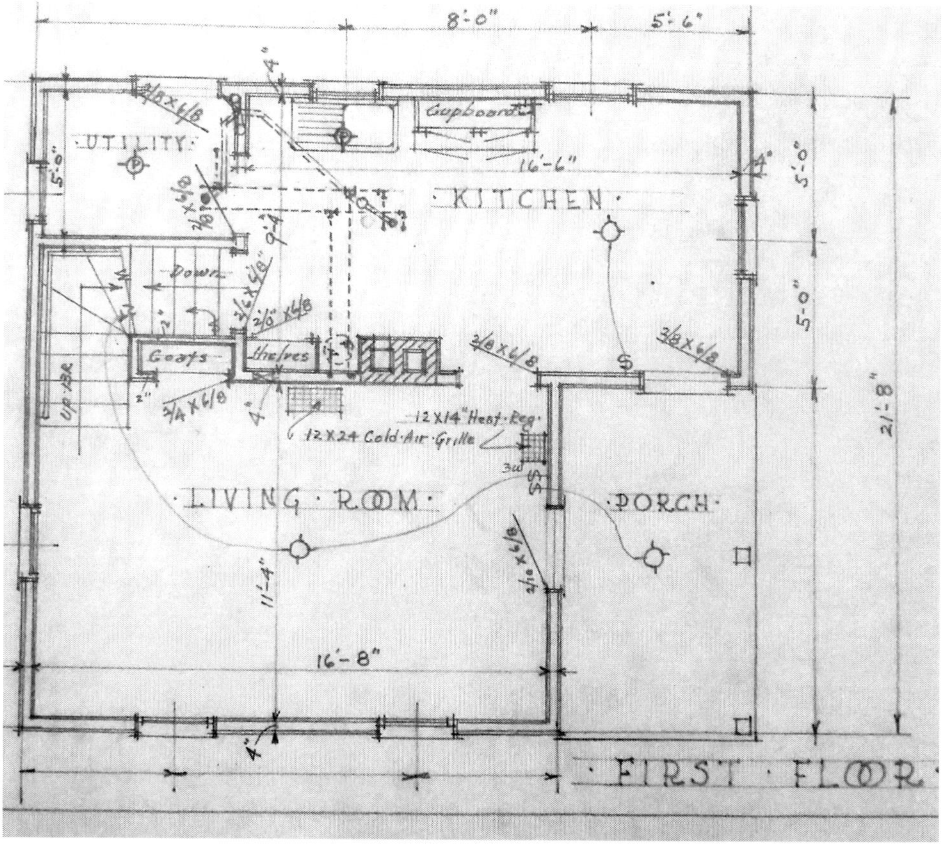

FIG. 37 House 402 first-floor plan. Architect Bartholomew's drawing of the first floor. National Archives and Records Administration, College Park, Maryland, folder (folio) 330-17-1-3-10.

the rooms' doors closed. The Westmoreland Homesteads resident had no trouble getting access to fresh air.

The houses addressed the lighting issue in another important way as well. For most of history, sunrise and sunset shaped people's lives dramatically. Darkness limited opportunities for work and leisure. This was especially so in western Pennsylvania, where the typical year brought only fifty-nine clear days. On most days throughout the year, heavy cloud cover kept the region pretty dark even before the sun set for the evening.[42] Candles, oil lamps, and even gas lamps had proven largely ineffective, dangerous, and expensive as means of illuminating homes. Though many urban areas began bringing electricity to homes and businesses in the 1880s and effectively transformed city life, rural America remained mostly dark for another half century. David Nye points out that the contrast between urban and rural America actually worsened in the 1930s as city dwellers used more and more electricity and "farmers continued to use outhouses, read by kerosene lamps, and cool themselves with palm-leaf fans."[43] The New Deal would eventually electrify farms, but in the early 1930s many rural Westmoreland County residents still

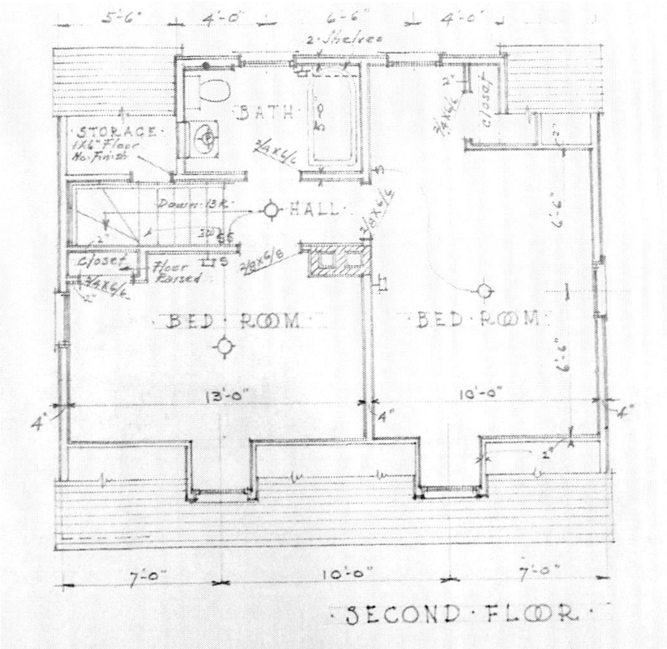

FIG. 38 House 402 second-floor plan. Architect Bartholomew's drawing of the second floor. National Archives and Records Administration, College Park, Maryland, folder (folio) 330-17-1-3-10.

FIG. 39 A children's bedroom in a Westmoreland Homesteads house. Library of Congress, Prints and Photographs Division, Washington, D.C., LC-USF33-000369-M5. Farm Security Administration/Office of War Information Collection. Photo: Carl Mydans.

lacked electricity. David Day noted that a third of Norvelt's initial residents had no electric lights in their homes before coming to Westmoreland Homesteads.[44]

Absent electricity, the means of lighting dark houses proved both dangerous and inadequate. Gaslights had become common in middle-class homes and urban streets, but they offered little illumination. Natural gas–powered streetlights had the power of twenty-five-watt bulbs, and lights in homes typically offered even less. Coal companies operating at remote patch communities did not run natural gas lines to workers' homes. Instead, residents relied on oil lamps that ran on kerosene—a highly flammable source.[45] The lack of good light shaped people's lives. Candles and oil lamps did not provide sufficient lighting for many of the kinds of activities that individuals and families take for granted today. Paul Freedman points out that "people who were not rich tried to get all their meals eaten before dark." It was simply too cumbersome to eat and clean up from meals in the little light available to working-class and farm families before light bulbs came on the scene. In fact, Freedman suggests that eating "way after dark because you could afford electric lights was a mark of high status, urbanity and class."[46] And families with electricity could not only eat later, but they could more easily "sew, read, whittle, or repair a broken tool."[47] If so, then moving to Westmoreland Homesteads conferred this status on its residents, a third of them for the first time.

Each room in Westmoreland Homesteads had plentiful windows to bring in sunlight, ceiling-mounted light fixtures (which Bartholomew designed himself), and outlets into which residents might plug in additional lamps. These sources made it possible for families to play board games, read, or stay up talking well into the night. For Norvelt women, electric lights and other appliances brought the mixed blessing of extending their workdays at both ends. Subsistence homestead officials saw the lengthened day as an opportunity to build the community spirit and fellow feeling that they prized so highly. They organized socials, community theater, and cooperative adult education classes in the evenings for residents. Darkness did not shut Norvelt down.

Bartholomew introduced design features not specified by the DSH. In the 402 house, he put an external porch off of the side of the living room that stretched ten feet toward the back of the house. On the opposite side of the house Bartholomew added a formal, enclosed side entry into the kitchen. One can see here a peculiar aspect of the Bartholomew designs. In the 402 house, as in two of the other four designs, the main entrance does not open on the front face of the house. A view of the house's front reveals no entry at all. More typically Cape Cod designs include a front door located at the center of the house's front. What might this mean?

Henry Glassie provided possible clues in his examination of vernacular housing in nineteenth-century Virginia. He noted a trend to moving the main entry from the side of the house facing the road to a side facing away from the road.[48] In the houses Glassie studied, the residents themselves designed their houses, and he saw the turning away from the road as reflecting a shift in their orientation toward the outside world. They became more private, more insular.

FIG. 40 This front view of the 501 house highlights the absence of a traditional front door, a feature shared by other house models in Norvelt. Library of Congress, Prints and Photographs Division, Washington, D.C., HABS PA, 65-NORV, 1-14.

Similarly, Clarence Stein and Henry Wright developed a plan for Radburn, New Jersey, that turned the front doors away from the street and toward green space and other houses. They wanted to relegate the car and delivery services that needed the streets to homes' rears and focus the houses' orientations to pedestrian traffic and each other. They sought to foster community development by orienting neighbors to communal spaces and each other. Wright also developed the site plans for Pittsburgh's Chatham Village, and here too the service entrances were turned to the road while the front doors faced communal grounds and neighbors.[49]

Norvelt residents did not design their homes, and so they did not choose to shield themselves from the street in this way. But the homes shaped their experience of the world, and this architectural feature put a strong premium on mediating their interaction with the public sphere. A side entrance, in each case covered by a porch roof, shielded an exiting resident from immediate contact with the public street and the elements. It also drew visitors into the home in stages. From the street they approached the house along a walk or the driveway, then entered the porch—open to the air on three sides but covered by a roof—and then finally turned sharply to enter into the living room itself (or, if they entered from the other side of the house, into the kitchen).

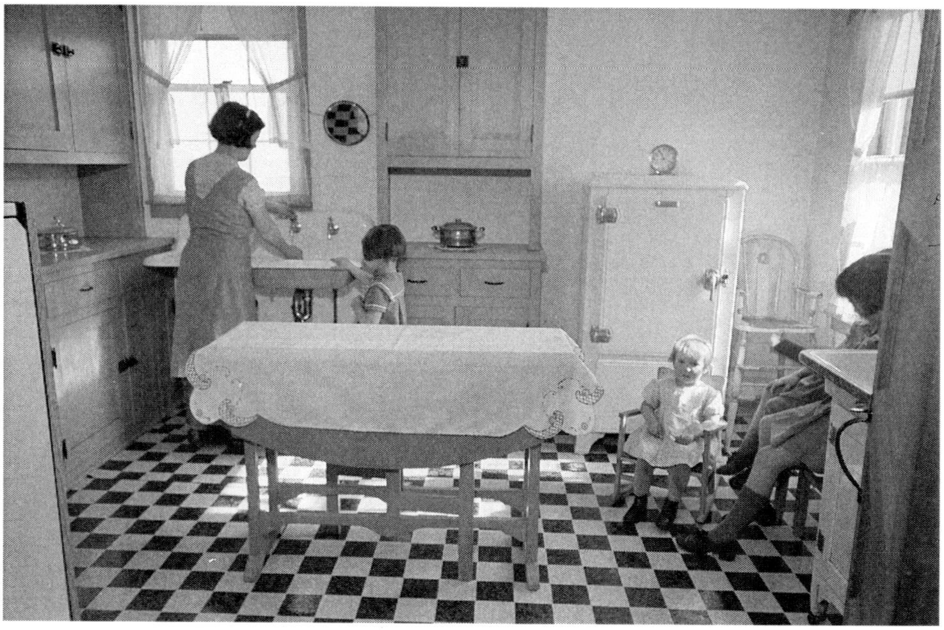

FIG. 41 A mother works in the kitchen with her four children. Note the space, the sunlight coming in, and the windows positioned to allow a cross breeze. Library of Congress, Prints and Photographs Division, Washington, D.C., LC-USF33-000366-M2. Farm Security Administration/Office of War Information Collection. Photo: Carl Mydans.

Residents of the 402 house had a heightened sense of privacy, of isolation. Though Norvelt was designed with strong community bonds as a central aim, this feature of the architectural plan militated against those ties in favor of privacy from that community. This might have been Bartholomew's response to the dislocating effects of the Great Depression. He shielded the residents from the outside world (the road) by moving the main entry way to the side (their own driveways).

Though Norvelt families came with little wealth, and therefore limited possessions, the houses provided storage space for personal items. Each bedroom contained an ample closet, and the living room had one as well. The house had a basement with a cold-storage room (for canned vegetables and fruits), and the kitchen came with cabinets and a completely enclosed separate entry room that could be used to store items as well. Each house also had a garage to store tools and, for some residents at least, a car. In this way the homes placed residents firmly in the rising American consumer culture. To be American meant to own things, even in the midst of the greatest economic collapse in the nation's history. Westmoreland homesteaders aspired to middle-class comforts, and their houses affirmed these aspirations, even when their current circumstances did not. Sarah Malnofsky recalls that her family moved everything they owned to Norvelt in a "small delivery truck."[50] They would have had plenty of room in their new house to distribute the furniture and ample closet space to store items they wanted to put away.

Many of the residents came from homes without indoor plumbing, and, when their homes did have plumbing, they did not often contain bathrooms with tubs and toilets. Each Norvelt home had one bathroom and a working kitchen sink. As discussed in chapter 3, Eleanor Roosevelt had insisted that houses in the first subsistence homestead community be equipped with indoor plumbing, even though it made each house more expensive and, as Harold Ickes pointed out, 80 percent of rural America did not have such amenities.[51] Alison K. Hoagland, in her history of the bathroom, suggests that its introduction "was probably the single greatest change to the architecture of middle- and working-class houses." It shaped many aspects of living: "women's work, servants' work, standards of cleanliness, perceptions of status, circulation patterns, design, and ideas of convenience."[52] The subsistence homesteads were to provide dignity to their residents, and indoor plumbing helped to reach this aim.

Indoor bathrooms represented a significant improvement over the outhouses that working-class families typically used. Norvelt included in each house a three-fixture bathroom, with a toilet, sink, and bathtub. Though these had become standard for middle-class homes in urban and suburban areas, they were still uncommon in the mining towns that spread across much of Appalachia and the Upper Midwest. Residents of company towns especially often had to petition to have toilets installed in their homes, and the houses' basic floor plans offered limited location options. Most ended up putting toilets in basements, open spaces with dirt floors and little light, accessible through trap doors in kitchen floors.[53]

Bartholomew's kitchen location also shaped the lives of Norvelt residents. Andrew Scott Dolkart points out in his study of the renovation of New York City townhouses in the early twentieth century that architects moved the kitchens from the houses' rears to the fronts, facing the street.[54] The kitchens had once been connected to the backyards for very practical purposes, to provide easy access for the food preparation that occurred in both the yard and kitchen. Newer and smaller kitchen appliances were largely responsible for the move to the front, as they allowed food preparation to take place without the need to use the yard. Almost all food-preparation activity could be contained within the one room. Once this was possible, people could locate their kitchens almost anywhere they preferred. Moving the kitchen to the front of the house also made the room serve as a buffer between the public street and the private lives of the townhouses' residents and their guests. The backyards ceased to be the work area of servants and instead became private garden retreats for residents. Dining rooms and living rooms that connected to the backyards severed the physical proximity to a public space that had become more heterogeneous. The uncontrollable streets penetrated less readily to the living spaces that residents most often inhabited.

Bartholomew also located his kitchens in the front of the houses, straddling a central divide that in most Cape Cod designs would have included a front door and central hall. Bartholomew's kitchen shared its orientation to the street with the living room, and the bathroom blocked direct access from the kitchen to the backyard. The backyard did not serve as a kitchen extension, as it did in the pre–kitchen appliance era for urban houses. In this way the Norvelt house was "modern." But at the same time, the homestead included a working garden, chicken coop, and grape arbor, which pulled the kitchen to the yard more powerfully than in any modern urban house. Bartholomew's design appears to anticipate the ambivalence that residents came to feel toward working the land. The bathroom severed the direct connection between kitchen and garden, and the side entry mediated that link. But the design did not embrace the more modern link between food source and kitchen, the grocery store. It located the driveway and garage on the opposite side of the house, forcing residents returning from the food store to travel through the living room with grocery bags or boxes rather than accessing the kitchen directly.

The Norvelt residents were thrilled to find the sinks, toilets, and tubs when they moved in. Edward Cibulas came to Norvelt from a coal-mining town and a home with an outhouse. He recalled, "When we lived in Whitney we had outside toilets and sometimes in the winter it was very cold out there, and when you had to go to the bathroom you moved very quick. What amazed me when I first moved to Norvelt was this commode. You went to the bathroom and flushed it. I stood there for five minutes watching the water going down. I couldn't believe that you could go to the bathroom in the house. That was amazing to me."[55] But even in the new indoor bathroom residents had to work quickly in the winter, as there was no heat source in the bathrooms of the 402 house plans.

Each house in Norvelt had a central furnace, but they did not have ductwork to each room in the house. The 402 contained heating grates in the living room and the hallway by the stairs on the first floor, and none at all on the second floor. The kitchen stove was to provide heat for that room, and the bathroom took its heat from the hallway if the bathroom door stayed open. Residents stayed warmer in winter than they had in patch houses whose only heat came from kitchen stoves, but they knew cold pretty well. Other Norvelt models had ducts leading to the second floor, and a more direct source of heat in the bedrooms as a result.

Both kitchens and bathrooms benefited from regular access to hot water in the winter months, as the coal furnaces also heated water for these two rooms. It is hard to overstate the benefits in cleanliness, sanitation, convenience, and comfort that hot water provided to residents. Unfortunately, this system did not work so well in warm months, when families did not run their furnaces. At these times many families had small water heaters attached to the furnace that they ran for a few hours each day. The heat that these water heaters generated did not overwhelm the houses, but they also limited access to hot water for cleaning and bathing to a few strategic hours daily.

Conclusion

Norvelt's domestic architecture contained the tensions between community and individualism that characterized the entire subsistence homestead program. Through opportunities for privacy, warmth, nutrition, and cleanliness that had been so elusive in patch communities, the houses afforded the kind of dignity commonly reserved for middle-class Americans. The extension of middle-class domestic realities to homesteaders raised their standard of living and nurtured a hope for the future that recently had seemed unattainable. Much of this coincided with prevailing ideals of individualism in American culture. In houses this meant opportunities for privacy, especially through separate bedrooms for parents and children, boys and girls. Even the commitment to independent, free-standing houses, as opposed to row houses or side-by-side duplexes, highlighted the family as an individual unit, separate from the community. This value extended outside as well. Individual garden plots as opposed to communal gardens downplayed cooperative ideals. Families grew their own carrots and tomatoes rather than on communal plots for all to share.

Individualism did not always trump communal values, however. For example, government officials who worried about preserving the houses' economic value forbade families from making any substantive change to the homes. Families could not build additions, move interior walls, alter the exterior appearance, or otherwise "individualize" the houses as homeowners do commonly—and as Norvelt residents did frequently once they owned their houses outright. At the same time, the common school, public spaces for organizations and group activities like the Mothers' Club, theater group, scouts, and athletic teams created space for community. These activities clustered around the "commons," a space set aside for communal activities near the road that runs through Norvelt. Community planners built the school, day care, Co-op Store, beauty salon, and barbershop here. Homesteaders reported a strong sense of local identity, that they felt connected to each other and their community.

Norvelt's very architectural and landscape design contained this tension between the two competing ideals of individualism and community, and residents necessarily experienced the struggle simply by living in the homes and under the rules imposed upon them. It is difficult to discern which, if either, value predominated, and it may be sufficient to note the competing ideals embedded in the very structures in which homesteaders lived out their lives.

One thing is clear, though. Norvelt was a far more desirable place to live than any of the nearby coal-patch towns from which it drew so many of its residents. This can be seen, ironically, in a report on health conditions in coal-mining communities just a few years after World War II ended. The U.S. Department of the Interior's Coal Mines Administration produced a *Medical Survey of the Bituminous-Coal Industry* in 1947 that highlights the contrast between the deplorable

FIG. 42 A, B Norvelt home in government publication. This example of a "privately owned home" from the 1947 *Medical Survey* of coal mining houses was used to support the benefits of private home ownership over company-owned coal-patch homes. The authors gave no evidence that they realized that the house in the top photo was built for Westmoreland Homesteads by the federal government. U.S. Coal Mines Administration, *A Medical Survey of the Bituminous-Coal Industry*.

conditions in many patch communities and the more healthful living situations in others. The survey ranges across West Virginia, Pennsylvania, Oklahoma, Kentucky, and other states. At one point it highlights the range of living conditions for miners in privately owned homes. It includes a photo of a miner's home with holes in the roof, a sagging front porch on which a double bed perches, and two forlorn-looking people in old clothes seeking shelter from an oppressive sun. The survey contrasts this grim photo with one of a well-appointed, freshly painted home with shutters, a well-tended lawn, grape arbor, and driveway. The caption identifies this house only as a privately owned home in Pennsylvania, and draws the conclusion that the houses represent the "striking contrasts" observable in "privately owned homes." The Pennsylvania house clearly led readers to understand that families in bituminous-coal country could live in relative comfort and dignity. The survey fails to note—perhaps because the authors did not realize—that the Norvelt model 402 house featured in the good half of the contrast resulted from a government program aimed at improving the lives of those who once lived as those featured in the desperate half of the photo did.[56]

Chapter Eight

Norvelt Today

The Evolution of a New Deal Community

Norvelters today venerate the cooperative ethos that infused the community's founding and early years. Traces of this spirit remain in the collective pride that Norvelters feel in their parents' and grandparents' joint efforts to build and sustain Westmoreland Homesteads and in the community's and its inhabitants' successes today. It can also be seen in community gatherings and undertakings, such as the celebration of the seventy-fifth anniversary, which we discuss below.

However, individualism dominates much of Norvelt, as it does most of the United States. One clear expression of the power of individualism is the transformation in Norvelt's political allegiances. Once a firm bastion of the Democratic Party, Norvelt began the slow but steady swing toward the Republican Party in the mid-1960s. In the 2008 and 2012 presidential elections, the majority of Norvelters voted for the Republican candidates over Barack Obama. In so doing, they abandoned the party that sponsored the founding of their community at a time when their parents or grandparents, like millions of Americans, lacked jobs, security, or much hope. They voted for the party least likely to support the kind of government intervention in the wake of the 2008 recession that proved so beneficial to their parents and grandparents three quarters of a century earlier. This chapter traces the evolution of Norvelt to explain how and why this change occurred.

Norvelt's Seventy-Fifth Anniversary

Before 5:00 P.M. on Friday, July 24, 2009, an enthusiastic crowd of Norvelters lined up outside Eleanor Roosevelt Hall (also the home of the Norvelt Volunteer Fire Department) to celebrate the seventy-fifth anniversary of the establishment of their community.[1] The banquet and dinner they looked forward to were part of a three-day-long series of festivities held to celebrate the diamond anniversary of the founding of Norvelt. Other anniversary activities included golf at the Norvelt Golf Course; a parade, booths, entertainment, and fireworks on the 25th; and a breakfast

FIG. 43 Sign outside Eleanor Roosevelt Hall, Norvelt Volunteer Fire Department, July 2009. Margaret Power's archive.

at Eleanor Roosevelt Hall, followed by a church service at Norvelt Union Church on the 26th. On Sunday afternoon, attendees chose between outdoor entertainment and historical presentations at the church. The church also housed a "temporary museum," which featured a special anniversary exhibit of memorabilia and artifacts from the homesteaders and their descendants.[2]

Although the banquet did not start until 5:30 P.M., the overflow crowd of Norvelters wanted to make sure they did not miss a moment of this special event, or the chance to greet friends and family members. The four hundred tickets for the dinner sold out quickly.[3] By all accounts, the anniversary was an unqualified success. The *Mount Pleasant Journal* carried a full page of color photographs of the celebration and noted that the events were "well-attended, with hundreds flocking" to partake in the festivities.[4]

The large and enthusiastic turnout at the various events offered vivid proof of the pride and self-confidence that current and former residents of the community had in their town and themselves. Hundreds of people came to the events, some of them from as far away as California. They welcomed the opportunity to pay tribute to their parents and grandparents, who were the ones who had built and maintained Norvelt. They were also eager to reconnect with family, neighbors, and friends to celebrate what they had built and who they had become. The gathering offered a snapshot of how Norvelters thought about themselves and their community in the new millennium and how both have evolved in the seventy-five-plus years since the New Deal settlement began.

Mary Bogot was born in Norvelt in 1938. She traveled twelve hours by train to join the celebration, which she praised effusively in her blog. Bogot concluded her blog entry by linking Norvelt's 2009 prosperity with its founding members. "The homes [in Norvelt] have been kept in pristine condition; many with additions; many with additional homes built by the sons and daughters of the first generation families. My father would have been so delighted to have been a party of this historical occasion that he was so involved in at its inception."[5]

Lee Speer, chief of the Norvelt Volunteer Fire Committee, a grandson of homesteaders, and chairman of the 75th Anniversary Committee, opened the program by asking people from the different sections of Norvelt to stand up in turn, which they did to enthusiastic applause.[6] Elected officials from both the Democratic and Republican parties offered remarks that clearly reflected their respective politics and how they used Norvelt's past to promote their current political agenda. The first speaker was a representative from Democratic U.S. congressman John Murtha's office who read the text "In Honor of Homesteading and the 75th Anniversary of Norvelt," which the congressman had entered into the *Congressional Record* on July 15, 2009. Congressman Murtha's remarks focused on Eleanor Roosevelt's "concern" following her visit to the "impoverished mining towns," where she had "witness[ed] first hand the severe poverty the families were enduring." She encouraged "[h]er husband . . . [to] establish[] the homesteading movement in the New Deal."[7] Tom Bayla, a Democratic Westmoreland county commissioner, extolled the original inhabitants as workers who had built Norvelt.

The Republican speakers included state senator Kim Ward and state representative Mike Reese. In contrast to the Democratic speakers, neither of them mentioned the New Deal or the Roosevelts. Instead, they lauded Norvelt as a great place to raise a family and attributed its success to the town's embrace of family values. Leaving aside the role that government, and a Democratic one at that, had played in establishing the community, the Republican narrative focused on what families had done to make their town work.

Just as homesteaders had embraced both the cooperative and individualist ethos in the 1930s and '40s, most Norvelters today combine the two narratives to explain their town's origins and successful development. They praise the New Deal and the Roosevelt administration, hold Eleanor Roosevelt in particularly high esteem, and extol the cooperative spirit of the homesteaders. On the other hand, they emphasize that the achievements of which their descendants are so proud today are due to the homesteaders' integrity and their willingness to work hard. Whichever construction of the town's past and present residents emphasize, Norvelters definitively agree that their community is a success.

The words of high school student Marie Emanuelle summarize the thoughts of many in Norvelt. She wrote the prize-winning essay in the contest sponsored by the Norvelt Volunteer Fire Department and the 75th Anniversary Celebration Committee "to write or draw about the history of Norvelt and what makes Norvelt special."[8] Her essay, "How Norvelt Began," concisely traces the origins of Norvelt and reflects what most, if not all, of the current inhabitants think of their community. "Today, in the year 2009, the town that was originally meant for people in the

Great Depression who could not afford a place to live has developed into a well running town. The small simply designed houses have grown and gotten updated through the years and the common buildings have grown also. Small businesses have also come up. Norvelt has changed from a small project to a large success that houses many residents to this day."[9]

The Deserving Poor

The seventy-odd years that have elapsed since the founding of Westmoreland Homesteads have produced significant changes in Norvelters' relationships to each other, their political attitudes, their standards of living, and even their understanding of their families' histories. When Westmoreland Homesteads began, the planners insisted, and many homesteaders believed, that they needed to work together in order to survive and prosper. This is not to say that family allegiances and individualism did not strain the cooperative ethos; they did. Nonetheless, two generations later, Lee Speer believes that originally "everybody got along and pulled together for a common goal." At the same time, he expressed concern that that same spirit no longer existed in Norvelt.[10]

None of the original adult homesteaders, the founding generation, is still alive. But many of their children and grandchildren draw on the founders' stories, especially their tales of deprivation and suffering in coal patches and neighboring towns in the years before Norvelt's establishment, to construct the history of their family and community as well as their own personal narratives. However, they do so in the context of the present, a radically different political and economic reality.

Hearing stories about suffering is not the same as experiencing it. The material reality of those who live in Norvelt today is far removed from that of their ancestors in the patch communities. The success of Norvelt has meant that the people who currently inhabit the community enjoy a higher standard of living than did their parents and grandparents. It appears that the improved economic well-being of many in Norvelt, along with a transformed national discourse on who the poor are, has contributed to generating a new understanding of poverty.

Many twenty-first-century Norvelters' concept of the poor, who or what causes poverty, and what constitutes the government's responsibility to the poor varies depending on whether they are referring to their own ancestors or those they imagine to be the current poor. Many perceive Norvelt's founding generation as the "deserving poor," while they consider the poor today to be unworthy of state support. Indeed, many in Norvelt contrast the work ethic that characterized the homesteader generation with the laziness that Norvelters impute to the nation's more recent poor.

It is not clear to what extent the association of poverty with African Americans shapes Norvelters' notions of who constitutes the deserving or undeserving poor. What is clear is that since the 1960s many white people in the United States have associated welfare with people of color, as a number of studies have shown and as we discuss below.[11]

A Profile of Norvelt in the Twenty-First Century

Before we discuss the political evolution of Norvelt, we offer a portrait of key economic, demographic, and social characteristics of the community in the first decades of the twenty-first century. Norvelt remains an unincorporated community in Mount Pleasant Township, Westmoreland County. It exudes an air of tranquility, well-being, respectability, self-confidence, and homogeneity. In 2010, 948 people lived in the community; of that number 940 or 99.4 percent identified themselves as white and only a handful saw themselves as being of another race. None identified as African American.[12]

As the Republican elected officials who spoke at the 75th Anniversary banquet emphasized, Norvelt is a (heterosexual) family-based community.[13] Of the 403 households in Norvelt, 309 are "family households." Most of the 94 non-family households consist of seniors (over sixty-five) living alone due, most likely, to the death of their spouse. Furthermore, of the total of 424 housing units, only 21 were vacant in 2010, and of this number only 1 was for rent.[14] Norvelt today is a community of people who live in family-owned homes, just as it was when it began.

Norvelt is not a racially diverse community today, nor has it been at any point in its history (see table 3). From its beginnings in the 1930s to today, Norvelt has been an overwhelmingly white community. As we pointed out in chapter 5, the original Norvelters were of European descent, with the single exception of the White family. The current inhabitants of Norvelt overwhelmingly hail from the same ethnic groups as the original homesteaders. In short, Norvelters are white, of European descent, and Christian.[15]

Although the living patterns and racial makeup have remained much the same since the community began, Norvelters' economic status has improved greatly. Early twenty-first-century Norvelters are not wealthy, but the desperate days of the 1930s lie far behind them. Today, most Norvelters are solidly middle class.[16] They fared better during the 2008 economic crisis than did many other Americans. For example, in 2009, 7.5 percent of Norvelt's residents lived in poverty, which compared favorably to the 12.5 percent of Pennsylvanians living below the poverty line and especially to the national rate of 16.7.[17]

People in Norvelt may or may not know all the fine points of their history, but they do know that their parents and grandparents, or in some cases their great-grandparents, were very poor. When they compare their standard of living today with that of their ancestors, they accurately conclude that theirs is substantially higher. For many in Norvelt, economic advancement, measured by the size of the home and the ability to purchase desirable cars and consumer goods, appears to be as important a yardstick for gauging family and community success as it is

TABLE 3 **Racial composition of Calumet/Norvelt, 1940–2010**

Year	Total population	White	Black	Latino/ Hispanic	Am Ind / Alaska Native	Asian	Two or more	Some other race
1940	1,305	1,298 (99.5%)	7 (0.5%)	0	0	0	0	0
1950	2,155	1,983 (99.4%)	13	0	0	0	0	0
1960	1,211	1,211 (100%)	0	0		0	0	0
1970	2,588	2,581 (99.7%)	4 (0.22%)			0		
1980	2,541							
1990	1,790	1785 (99.72%)	4 (.22%)	6		14	0	1
2000	1,682	1,672 (99.4%)	6 (.36%)	8	0	0	1	3
2010	942	942 (100%)						

in many other places. Their comfortable economic status, as compared to that of the homesteaders, indicates the degree to which the residents of Norvelt have progressed economically to achieve the American dream.

This is not to suggest that economic progress is the sole quality that Norvelters value. They place a high premium on their community and the sense of security and belonging that it offers them. As almost any Norvelter will state, "Norvelt was and is a great place to grow up in; it's a safe community."[18]

Catherine Bosich's father had been a miner in the nearby community of Mammoth when her family moved to Norvelt in 1937. She has lived there ever since. "I just love this place, I would never want to move any place else." After she married, she and her husband "built a home beside my mother's and so did my sister."[19]

Norvelt's volunteer fire department (housed in Eleanor Roosevelt Hall) serves as the community's social center and de facto governing body. Norvelt's post office, Union Church, Open Pantry Food Mart, gas station, insurance agency, funeral home, and heating and air-conditioning business (and gun dealer) all cluster nearby. So too do the pizzeria and the pharmacy, the local magistrate and the state representative's office. Norvelt's only sizable business, Jim Schmidt's Electro-Glass Products, employs forty-seven people to make precision glass products for the electronics industry.[20] The Norvelt Golf Club, the Norvelt Elementary School, and a sports field round out the main public facilities in the community.

Many of the original homesteaders of Norvelt lacked the means or opportunity to obtain higher degrees, or in some cases even a high school degree, but parents in Norvelt have always valued education. Mary Ann Seminary taught first grade at Norvelt Elementary School for thirty-four years. She considered Norvelt a "special place" to teach because she and the other teachers always had "such wonderful support from the parents."[21]

Despite the importance people in Norvelt place on education, Norvelt lags considerably behind the national average for college degrees. While 28 percent of all Americans older than twenty-five have a college degree, only 14 percent of Norvelt residents did as of 2013.[22]

Norvelters' Myth of Origins: Using the Past to Promote the Present

Norvelters take great pride in their community, a feeling they readily manifest to others. Lois Weyandt grew up in Norvelt, the daughter of homesteaders. Although she now lives in nearby Greensburg, she is actively engaged in preserving and promoting Norvelt's history. She worked hard, along with Earl Saville, to get the Pennsylvania Historical and Museum Commission to erect a historical marker in 2002 (see figure 44). The sign is located in front of the Norvelt Volunteer Fire Department (Eleanor Roosevelt Hall).

When Weyandt talks of Norvelt, she mingles her memories of growing up there with her sense of Norvelt today. She compares Norvelt to the other subsistence homesteads and concludes, "Norvelt was the most successful." Weyandt explains, "Norvelt, you could go out there today and the place is neat and tidy, and people take pride in their homes and they realize how they got them. So many people say they were given to us. They weren't given to us; we were given the opportunity to provide and work to keep that house and to pay for it in the work we did."[23]

Weyandt's comment, like the prize-winning essay by Marie Emanuelle and the blog entry by Mary Bogot, captures Norvelt's "mythic origin stories."[24] The term "myth" does not imply a made-up tale of how Norvelt began, but rather, how Norvelters tell the story of their own beginnings and use their past to explain their present.

When Norvelters talk about the founding of Norvelt, they stress that their parents and grandparents needed help, not because they were lazy, but because the economic devastation unleashed by the Depression made it impossible for them to survive without federal assistance. They wanted to work, but jobs did not exist. So many people were poor in the 1930s that poverty was neither something to be ashamed of nor used to gauge the worth of a person. As Lois Weyandt remarked, "Everybody was poor, nobody knew the difference."[25]

Doris Hiller, née Byers, moved to Norvelt with her parents in 1936 or 1937.[26] She points out that "they [the original homesteaders] were all poor, that's why they

FIG. 44 Earl Saville and Lois Weyandt unveil the Norvelt historical marker, September 8, 2002. The text reads, "Originally called Westmoreland Homesteads, Norvelt was established April 13, 1934, by the federal government as part of a New Deal homestead project. With 250 homes, Norvelt provided housing, work, and a community environment to unemployed workers and their families during the Great Depression. It was renamed 'Norvelt' in 1937 in honor of First Lady Eleanor Roosevelt and her interest in the project." Lois Weyandt personal collection.

were able to get a house."[27] Or, as Earl Saville remembers, "Our neighbor didn't have any more than what I had, and so we thought we're in the same boat. Of course, if we knew people that had something better than us, that would be different, but everybody was the same."[28]

Earl Saville lives in the same Norvelt house that his parents originally inhabited when they moved to Norvelt in September 1936. When asked what he thought of Franklin Delano Roosevelt, he said simply, "that's the savior." He, like most Norvelters, holds Eleanor Roosevelt in particularly high regard. "Actually, Mrs. Roosevelt was the one that was behind the whole thing, even though he [President

Roosevelt] was behind her of course. She saw that the people, especially in the coal-mining areas, this is all-coal-mining area, the way they were living so bad, [they] had hardly any food. She wanted to do something for them and she started this project. She wanted things done for the people that couldn't help themselves, because if the coal mines shut down, there was no other work around. People were living in squalor."[29]

Other Norvelters share Saville's thoughts on the Roosevelts. Doris Hiller was a young girl in the 1930s, yet she remembers very clearly that her mother had a very positive opinion of Eleanor Roosevelt. "She was the one who started [Norvelt] for people who didn't have anything."[30] Although today Hiller is a staunch Republican, she has only positive things to say about government intervention in the 1930s. The government started Norvelt to help people, "that's what it was for."[31] Lois Weyandt praises both the Roosevelts and the New Deal. "I think the New Deal as a program was a fantastic lifesaver for a lot of people. It really was. I think the New Deal was very advantageous for people who came up through the Depression. The mines had shut down, they were out of work, and it was very sad."[32]

In addition to being grateful to Eleanor Roosevelt and the Roosevelt administration, Norvelters attribute the community's success to their parents' and grandparents' work ethic and spirit of cooperation. As we showed in chapters 4 and 5, Norvelt was designed to offer a home and livelihood to people who were willing to work together with others to build the community. The process by which David Day, Paul Campbell, and other members of the original selection teams decided who was and who was not a good candidate for the Westmoreland Homesteads "experiment" resulted in the original homesteaders being a group of people who valued labor, understood the need for it, and did not shy away from it. Community managers sometimes evicted residents who passed the original selection process but failed to maintain the community's work or personal standards. As the children and grandchildren of the homesteaders told the authors, the community succeeded because the people who built it worked hard to make sure that it did. Further, the original homesteaders instilled in their descendants the belief that they, too, needed to work and work hard in order to succeed. Though critics at the time insisted, like critics today, that government support for projects such as Norvelt eroded the will to work, Norvelt homesteaders and their descendants put labor at the center of their personal value system.

Homesteader Dewey Honse mined Westmoreland County coal before an injury forced him to work as a constable and then for the WPA. His great-grandson, Jimmy Hontz (note the new spelling adopted after Dewey settled in Norvelt), attributed Norvelt's success to "the hard work and determination of the original homesteaders. Their work from the coal mines. Their hard work made them accomplish what they wanted to."[33]

Many Norvelters ground their success stories firmly on the bedrock of hard work. Material conditions, such as the size and condition of the homes in which current inhabitants of Norvelt and their children and grandchildren live, offer demonstrable proof of the community's success.

Almost all of the original Norvelt houses remain, but residents have renovated and expanded them, adding more rooms and amenities. Today, many houses in Norvelt have central air conditioning, wall-to-wall carpet, nice furniture, televisions, computers, microwaves, and the electronic equipment associated with twenty-first-century middle-class life in the United States. The houses are well cared for, the lawns manicured, and the interiors spic and span. Houses are freshly painted, and there are few signs of sloppy housekeeping.

Our Parents and Grandparents Were Poor but Deserving

The community's economic achievements confirm many residents' belief that the government chose the right people when it approved their parents' or grandparents' applications to move to Westmoreland Homesteads. The founding generation was "deserving" and "entitled." As Lee Speer, chairman of the Norvelt Seventy-Fifth Anniversary Committee, wrote, "The one thing that has made Norvelt what it is today is its people, and while similar government projects have come and gone, Westmoreland Homesteads is still thriving, and I don't see that changing anytime soon."[34]

However, this very sense of descending from the "deserving" poor can also erect barriers against and create distance from those who have not been as successful, based on the standards outlined above. When descendants of the original homesteaders define their parents and grandparents as the "deserving poor," they simultaneously and implicitly, perhaps symbolically and certainly consequentially, differentiate themselves from an unnamed "undeserving poor."

In 2008, Mike Reese defeated his Democratic opponent and became the first Republican to represent Norvelt in the state legislature since the community's founding. He contrasted President Obama's economic policies with those of President Franklin Delano Roosevelt when he claimed that Obama wanted to redistribute wealth without demanding that people work for it, in contrast to Roosevelt, who demanded that people work in return for government aid. According to Reese,

> To me it looks like the President [Obama] believes in the redistribution of wealth. . . . FDR said okay, look this is what the government is going to do, but this is what you have to do to benefit from this. You know, there was an agreement, a deal if you would, that the government is going to be there for you, we're going to do this, but you have to work to get it. It's not going to be free. It's not going to be a handout. There is going to be a commitment on both of our parts. I think that the current administration pushes that the government is going to take care of you. And that's it; which of course, when you get into these entitlement programs, it becomes a concern.[35]

Norvelters' support for Reese reflects a larger shift in the community's political alignments and votes that began in the mid-1960s. The following sections analyze the causes of this transformation.

The Political Evolution of Norvelt

From the 1930s through the 1950s, Norvelt was a Democratic Party bastion. In 1940, 414 people in Norvelt voted in the presidential elections. Of that number, 357 cast their ballots for Democrat Franklin Delano Roosevelt, while only 57 voted for Republican Wendell Wilkie. Voters in Norvelt supported Roosevelt at a much higher rate than did residents of the surrounding communities or Westmoreland County as a whole (see table 4).

A majority of Norvelters first supported a Republican presidential candidate, George H. W. Bush, in 2004 (see figure 45). Although President Bush received only six more votes than did John Kerry, this was the first time more Norvelters voted for a Republican than for a Democrat for president. A sharper change in party preference occurred in 2008, when 373 Norvelters (45.2 percent) supported Democrat Barack Obama and 452 (54.8 percent) voted for John McCain.[36]

The 2008 presidential election solidified the trend away from the Democrats that Norvelters first began to exhibit, however unevenly, in the mid-1960s. What caused the majority of residents in Norvelt, the New Deal community, whose origin and name link it to the Roosevelts and the Democratic Party, to vote for Republicans John McCain and Sarah Palin in 2008? For Earl Saville, the answer is an easy one. According to Saville, "there's a reason for that . . . a black president. I don't care if it's in Norvelt, if it's down in Poughkeepsie, New York, wherever. It's because discrimination is still here."[37]

Race, Politics, and Norvelt

The 2004 and 2008 elections represent a tipping point in how inhabitants of Norvelt voted. The once solidly Democratic community cast the majority of its votes for Republican candidates in both of those elections. As figure 45 illustrates, these elections confirm a trend that had been growing since the mid-1960s. In order to understand why a growing number of Norvelters support the Republican Party, this section explores the changing national discourse on poverty and suggests that these attitudes influenced voters in Norvelt.

The face of poverty in the United States shifted in the 1960s and beyond. From the Depression until the 1960s, poor whites, such as the parents and grandparents of most of the current inhabitants of Norvelt, represented the popular definition of what poverty looked like. Beginning in the 1960s, however, the public increasingly labeled black people as the embodiment of poverty. Concomitant with this change

TABLE 4 **Presidential election, November 5, 1940, Westmoreland County**

Community	Franklin D. Roosevelt (Democrat)	Wendell Wilkie (Republican)
Hecla	327 (73.3%)	119 (26.7%)
Mammoth	185 (53.3%)	162 (46.7%)
United	458 (77.5%)	133 (22.5%)
Westmoreland Homesteads (Norvelt)	357 (86.2%)	57 (13.8%)
Westmoreland County	64,567 (60%)	42,643 (40%)

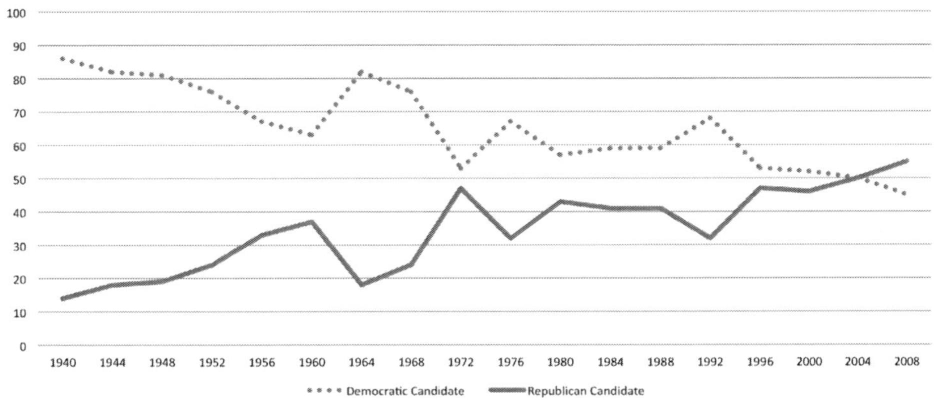

FIG. 45 Norvelt presidential election votes (percent), 1940–2008. Westmoreland County Courthouse, Greensburg, Pennsylvania. Records Management Office, Electoral Records, General Elections, 1940 through 2008, Westmoreland County.

came a shift in attitudes. Much of the white public attributed black poverty to personal laziness, not to ongoing structural problems. Since, according to this line of thought, blacks were responsible for their own poverty, they deserved neither sympathy nor government support.

Until the 1960s, no serious ideological or programmatic challenges threatened the hold New Deal politics and philosophy had on Americans.[38] This was because, in large part, the majority of Americans accepted the basic tenets of the New Deal and benefitted from its policies.[39] However, as Ian Haney López argues, this began to change during the 1964 presidential election, when Republican candidate Barry Goldwater used racial appeals to southern voters "to convince even the staunchest Democrats to abandon New Deal liberalism."[40] Goldwater's ability to do so resulted from southern whites' opposition to the civil rights movement and their implacable unwillingness to end entrenched segregation, inequality, and white supremacy. Before the civil rights movement, as Thomas and Mary Edsall show, many U.S. government programs had disproportionately benefitted white people, while many New Deal policies had most directly helped poor and working-class white people. As a result, up until the 1960s most white people strongly supported federal intervention and government programs.[41]

This support declined not just in the South but nationally, Thomas and Mary Edsall argue, following the passage of the 1964 Civil Rights Act, the federal statute that demanded an end to racial segregation, and the growing body of federal legislation that sought to address and correct poverty and inequality. These programs, which were most closely associated with the Democratic Party, necessitated a massive financial commitment to end, or at least weaken, the gross racial inequalities that defined the United States.[42] The focus of federal spending on programs that could potentially weaken if not eliminate black oppression on one hand and white supremacy on the other generated anger, resentment, and a change in party allegiance among a broad swath of the white population nationwide.

Doug McAdam and Karina Kloos argue that this resentment took the form of a "white backlash" in the deep South initially, but throughout most of the nation by the late 1960s. They point to the passage of the Civil Rights Act as pivotal in generating strong white voter disaffection from the Democratic Party. Joseph Lowndes traces the efforts of national politicians such as Nixon and Reagan to channel this widespread national white backlash into electoral victories on the national stage.[43]

Much of the white backlash was articulated as a concern over taxes. As Thomas and Mary Edsall write, "Taxes . . . have been used to drive home the cost to whites of federal programs that redistribute benefits to blacks and other minorities. . . . Race and taxes, on their own, have changed the votes of millions of once-Democratic men and women."[44]

Concomitant with many white people's reluctance to see their tax dollars finance programs that benefitted black people was the transformation in the former's perception of who was poor. In the 1960s, the public face of poverty decisively altered and became black. At the same time, the connection that many white people made between poverty, entitlement, and themselves weakened.

Daniel Patrick Moynihan's 1965 report, *The Negro Family*, contributed to linking welfare to blacks and generating public disapproval of federal support for the poor, especially when they were black and caught in the "tangle of pathology."[45] The report decried the high number of black families led by women: "Almost One-Fourth of Negro Families are Headed by Females." It proclaimed that the "Breakdown of Negro Family [leads to] a Startling Increase in Welfare Dependency." To further compound the problem, "Negro women not only have more children [than white women], but have them earlier," and these women are in families "with the least financial resources."[46]

The Moynihan report painted a decidedly negative portrait of African Americans in the United States, but it was hardly alone in its dismal depiction of blacks and their connection to welfare. In his study of how the media portrayed poverty in the United States over the course of forty years (from the 1950s to the 1990s),

Martin Gilens concludes that in the 1960s poverty became most visibly and closely associated with black people. Up until the mid-1960s, "poverty appeared overwhelmingly as a 'white problem' in the national news media."[47] In fact, as he points out, the "dominant image was of the white rural poor in Appalachia."[48] Gilens's study shows that between 1965 and 1967, media images of the poor became racialized black, and, as they did, the poor became increasingly defined as undeserving.

The idea that the poor were no longer deserving since they and the programs that supported them were wasteful, inefficient, and abused, as the depictions Gilens discusses suggested, coincided with the increased association of poverty with blacks. In short, the deserving white poor of the Depression had become transformed into the lazy black welfare chiselers of the 1960s and beyond.[49]

Few comments have epitomized more crudely the idea that blacks, specifically black women, are too lazy to work yet sufficiently devious to rip off the welfare system than Ronald Reagan's oft-repeated "welfare queen." The welfare queen, according to Reagan, lived on the south side of Chicago and "has 80 names, 30 addresses, 12 Social Security cards. . . . She's got Medicaid, getting food stamps and she is collecting welfare under each of her names. Her tax-free cash income alone is over $150,000."[50] The term was so powerful and enduring that it "has succeeded in imprinting stereotypical racial and gender images in the minds of many Americans."[51]

A significant number of Norvelters appear to share these assumptions about poverty, race, and entitlement, as the interviews cited above illustrate. They distinguish their parents and grandparents from the poor today. They assume that the first homesteaders were part of the deserving poor. Since their impoverished condition was not of their making, it was only fair and just that the federal government should step in and help them. Certainly, government support allowed the original homesteaders to get back on their feet and progress. However, Norvelters largely conclude, the homesteaders' willingness to work, and work hard, made Norvelt the success it is today.

But what about government aid today? Or during the height of the economic crisis? According to some Norvelters, recipients of government aid who continue in poverty lack the commitment to work that the homesteaders and their descendants had and have. Thus, they are not the deserving poor and, as a result, are not entitled to receive government support. And, some ask, why should their hard-earned money go to pay taxes to finance those who choose not to work? Doris Hiller's mother escorted Eleanor Roosevelt around Westmoreland Homesteads when the first lady visited the community in 1937. In 2009, Margaret Power asked Hiller if she thought government intervention could help overcome the economic crisis that had engulfed the country. Hiller said, "Everybody [today] wants something for nothing, because the government will give it to them. Well, we couldn't get that, we had to earn it. They're too easy on them now. I'm glad I was born when I was."[52]

It is difficult to determine when, to what extent, and why the ideas outlined above about who is deserving and who is not developed in Norvelt. What is clear is that Norvelters' understanding of their ancestors' strong work ethic has possibly made them susceptible to a discursive tradition that links contemporary poverty and race and ends up blaming today's victims of poverty for their condition. In recent times, the media and some political campaigns' construction and conflation of crime, drugs, and people of color have served to deepen racial fault lines in the United States.[53] In order to assess to what extent attitudes toward race may have influenced how people in Norvelt voted, the next section examines the 2008 presidential election in Westmoreland County.

The 2008 Presidential Election in Norvelt and Westmoreland County

On April 6, 2008, candidate Barack Obama spoke at a fundraiser in the upscale Pacific Heights neighborhood of San Francisco. The crowd consisted of well-off, cosmopolitan liberals. In an attempt to explain why many in "small-town Pennsylvania" supported Republican candidates, Obama said,

> You go into these small towns in Pennsylvania and, like a lot of small towns in the Midwest, the jobs have been gone now for 25 years and nothing's replaced them. And they fell through the Clinton administration, and the Bush administration, and each successive administration has said that somehow these communities are going to regenerate and they have not. And it's not surprising then they get bitter, they cling to guns or religion or antipathy toward people who aren't like them or anti-immigrant sentiment or anti-trade sentiment as a way to explain their frustrations.[54]

While it is not clear how people at the Obama fundraiser responded to the comment, Republicans in southwestern Pennsylvania attempted to use it to their advantage. Elaine Gowaty formerly chaired the Republican Party of Westmoreland County. Her father was a coal miner, a member of the United Mine Workers of America, and a life-long Democrat. In the 1980s, she decided that she liked Ronald Reagan's philosophy and switched parties.

When asked what she thought of Obama's comments about Pennsylvania, she said, "everybody [in the Republican Party office] was mad . . . because we don't cling to our guns and our religion." But Gowaty does hold both closely. She pointed out that "we care about what's going on in our community. I mean I'm pro-gun but I don't really have a gun. It's not that I have to have a gun, but I definitely want anyone who is a legal citizen who doesn't have a, you know, history or record to have a gun. I mean everyone should be able to have a gun."[55] Gowaty added, "We are very religious. I'm Catholic. I go to Mass every Sunday, which is, that's how my mom was, you went to Mass, that's what you were supposed to do and I still do that so religion is very important to me."[56] Perhaps she interpreted Obama's comment as a criticism of people who turn to guns and religion to overcome their sense of marginalization. She, on the other hand, sees guns and religion as cultural practices that define and reflect middle America. Bearing arms is a constitutional right, therefore mainstream, while her religious beliefs are traditional American values, learned from her mother.

Barack Obama lost in Westmoreland County and in Norvelt, for reasons that probably have very little to do with his comment. John McCain received 57.8 percent of the Westmoreland County vote to Obama's 41.1 percent. The results from the 2008 Democratic presidential primary and election suggest that race contributed to Obama's loss.

In the presidential primaries, Hillary Clinton received 69.2 percent of the vote in Westmoreland County, while Obama only got 30.8 percent.[57] John Boyle's experiences in the election offer evidence that at least some white Democrats in Westmoreland County rejected Barack Obama due to his race.[58] Boyle grew up in Greensburg, the Westmoreland County seat, in a strongly Democratic Party family. An attorney, he worked as an aide to U.S. congressman John Murtha in his district office in western Pennsylvania from 1990 to 1997.[59] He ran for Pennsylvania state representative from the 57th District in 2008 and lost to Republican Tim Krieger, who garnered 51.7 percent of the vote.[60] The fact that Boyle lost the seat in what had long been a Democratic stronghold was surprising; the factors that contributed to his defeat reveal much about how race affects how white people in Westmoreland County vote.

During the primary election, John Boyle went door to door in Westmoreland County to talk to potential voters and get their support for his candidacy. He remembers that some of them asked him if he allied with Hillary Clinton . . . or "that nigger." As Boyle sees it, many Democratic Party voters in Westmoreland County felt "racial hatred" toward Obama and did not want a black man to be president of the United States. Boyle believes that opposition to Obama for president contributed to his own loss, since many white people in Westmoreland County did not want to vote for a candidate from the party that chose a black man as its presidential candidate.[61]

A recent study by Seth Stephens-Davidowitz explores the impact that race had on the 2008 and 2012 elections; it corroborates Boyle's conclusions. Stephens-Davidowitz points out that surveys frequently fail to uncover prejudice since many people are unwilling to reveal racist attitudes in them. To avoid the ambiguities and inaccuracies of direct questioning, Stephens-Davidowitz determined the number of Google search queries using "racially-charged language" that occurred in an area.[62] He then compared the number to the amount of votes Barack Obama received to determine if race influenced voters' choice of candidates.[63] Stephens-Davidowitz concludes that race mattered and "prejudice cost Obama 4.2 percentage points of the national popular vote in 2008 and 4.0 percentage points in 2012."[64]

Stephens-Davidowitz ranks the fifty U.S. states based on how many racially charged searches residents in them conduct. Pennsylvania comes in third from the top, behind West Virginia and Louisiana.[65] Of direct relevance to this study is Stephens-Davidowitz's finding that the highest number of searches in the state using derogatory terms to refer to blacks occurred in western Pennsylvania.[66]

The media have also contributed to the ideological and political shift that has taken place in Westmoreland County in general and Norvelt in particular.[67] The county's largest newspaper, the *Greensburg Tribune-Review*, is an influential voice in favor of conservative candidates and politics. In 1969, Richard Mellon Scaife purchased the *Greensburg Tribune-Review*.[68] He subsequently bought six small weeklies in the area and launched the Pittsburgh edition of the *Tribune-Review*. While the newspapers retain their local names, they are now all part of the Tribune-Review Publishing Company. As part of his work to promote conservative thinking and politicians, Richard Mellon Scaife has poured an estimated $312 million into the newspapers since 1992.[69]

The money appears to have served at least part of its purpose. According to Jeff Simmons, circulation director of the *Tribune-Review*, sales of the Mellon Scaife papers grew from 85,379 on Sunday and 52,177 during the week in 1992 to 202,230 on Sunday and 188,405 Monday to Friday in 2012.[70] As of 2012, the *Greensburg Tribune-Review* had 55,000 subscriptions for the daily paper and 95,000 for the Sunday edition.[71] The paper reaches throughout and beyond Westmoreland County. Somewhere between two and three hundred households in Norvelt, a sizable number, subscribe to the paper.[72] These numbers suggest that a significant percentage of the population is both influenced by and agrees with the extremely conservative political perspective Richard Mellon Scaife promoted through his publishing industry.[73]

Arthur Boyle, who has lived most of his life in Westmoreland County, believes that the *Tribune Review* has had a significant impact on the attitudes of people in the area. As he said, referring to the *Tribune Review*, "that newspaper is rabidly Republican and anti-Democrat. It is pro-Republican 365 days out of the year and, in a sustained manner, keeps hammering away the Republican position." This, Boyle thinks, has contributed to declining support for the Democratic Party in Westmoreland County.[74]

On the day following the 2008 presidential election, the *Tribune Review* published an editorial titled "Obama Wins. **America Loses.**" Referring to the newly elected president as Barack *Hussein* Obama (emphasis added), it predicted that Obama's promised changes would be "ugly" and his presidency would be "dangerous for all." The editorial ended on a dour and alarming note. "It is customary to wish an incoming president the best of luck. But it's the American people on whom we bestow that wish today. For they'll need all the luck that can be mustered to weather what one can only hope will be a one-term anomaly."[75]

The November 2011 Elections in Westmoreland County

The 2008 election was not a flash in the pan. Despite the fact that there were a hundred and twenty-nine thousand registered Democrats in Westmoreland

County and only eighty thousand Republicans, the Republican leadership sought to continue the 2008 political upsurge.[76] To do so, it sought and obtained the endorsement of the very active and locally influential Tea Party. Republicans worked very hard to mobilize voters dissatisfied with the Obama presidency. Its goal for the November 2011 elections was to do "what no GOP candidates have done in more than 60 years—win a majority in Westmoreland County on the board of commissioners."[77]

By midnight on November 9, 2011, the day of the election, it was clear that the Republican Party had surpassed its goal. They not only won the majority in the three-member board of commissioners, they also gained control of all five county offices.[78] As Mike Reese, who represents Norvelt, commented, "The Republicans took control of the courthouse for the first time in a very long time!"[79] As the lead article in the *Tribune-Review* noted, "nearly 60 years of [Democratic] domination at the courthouse ended with a historic takeover of the county offices."[80]

Conclusion

This chapter discusses the significant political realignment that has occurred in Norvelt over the last five decades. It seeks to explain why a solidly New Deal, pro–Democratic Party community now votes, in its majority, for the Republican Party. We suggest that many of the changes that have occurred in Norvelt mirror political transformations that have taken place in the United States at large over the last fifty years. The primary factor is that since the 1960s an increasing number of white Democrats have switched parties and now vote with the Republican Party, a trend that the majority of Norvelters has followed. Ian Haney López argues in *Dog Whistle Politics* that the key explanation for this shift is "an open secret: Republicans rely on racial entreaties to help win elections."[81] When Ronald Reagan denounced welfare queens, Americans knew he was referring to black women, even though he never mentioned race. When Lois Weyandt describes Norvelt as "safe," or Catherine Bosich contrasts Norvelt to Pittsburgh, where "[a]ll you hear . . . is shooting," it seems likely they are comparing the security of all-white Norvelt to the insecurity produced, in their minds, by dangerous, gun-toting blacks in Pittsburgh.

In the minds of many in Norvelt, the belief that the role of the government in the 1930s was to support the deserving poor, their grandparents and parents, has been replaced by one that decries the use of their tax dollars to maintain lazy welfare cheats, that is, blacks, the undeserving poor. Yet this shift in political allegiances has not been an easy one for many in Norvelt. Almost 70 percent of Norvelters continue to register as Democrats. Their identity as Norvelters is integrally tied to their community and the history of Norvelt, as the outpouring of support for the seventy-fifth anniversary attests. The origins, the very name "Norvelt," are irrevocably linked to the Roosevelts, the New Deal, and the Democratic Party. To define oneself as a Republican would represent a rejection of their past and the homesteaders, their parents, grandparents, and great-grandparents. It would also require a degree of ingratitude that runs counter to the basic values many in Norvelt cherish.

Yet times, conditions, and consciousnesses have changed. Norvelters' material reality today is far different from that of the homesteaders, as are their politics and position in society. The majority of them may not firmly identify themselves as Republicans, but that is the party for which they cast their ballot.

Conclusion

Did Norvelt Succeed?

Federal support for the poor and the unemployed was much more controversial in the 1930s than it is today. In this book, we have told the story of how the federal government, faced with the devastating human toll the Depression created, confronted by mass and increasingly radical protests, and pushed by concerned individuals like Eleanor Roosevelt, Clarence Pickett, and David Day and scores of politicians and administrators, implemented a specific New Deal program.

We decided to write about Norvelt because we think that it was and remains a success story, albeit a little-known and unrecognized one. It is an example of how government programs and intervention positively transformed people's lives. Is Norvelt a model that the U.S. government should follow today? Would such a project work today? Given the radically different political, social, and economic climates of the 1930s and the 2010s, providing a definitive answer is not possible. However, we do think that the story of Norvelt offers a significant and, in today's world, innovative approach to dealing with some of the economic and social problems that plague the United States. We hope that those concerned with finding solutions to some of our nation's key economic and social issues, such as unemployment and underemployment or homelessness, to give but a few examples, have found our discussion of Norvelt, the daring social experiment that turned out to be a success, stimulating and suggestive.

Today's debates and discourse regarding the role of government echo those that Norvelt's development engendered in the 1930s. The subsistence homestead program provoked strong responses from contemporary supporters and critics, who reached no consensus on its success or failure. Supporters saw it as a prototype for a new way of living in times of severe and prolonged economic crisis. Its material comfort, its cooperative and mutually supportive communities, its embodiment of the emerging belief that citizens' welfare mattered to the national government, offered dignity and hope to people buckling under the Depression's hardships. Most homesteaders obtained the security that eluded so many in Depression-era America. Critics, on the other hand, saw in these homesteads a great threat to U.S.

civic and economic traditions. They worried about the rise of socialism and the decline of the American character, and they argued that the communities would never pay for themselves.

Judgments about subsistence homesteads started before residents dug the first foundations and continued through the program's lifetime. As we noted in chapter 5, the *Pennsylvania Review* deemed Westmoreland Homesteads to be a great success as early as 1937 because its residents found "themselves substantially better off than most of their former co-sufferers. They live in clean, healthy surroundings. They live in houses for which they pay amazingly low rental."[1] But Charles Loomis, writing in the *American Sociological Review* three years later, determined that residents in homestead projects did not really take to growing their own food, the cooperative enterprises did not turn profits, and residents wanted to own their own homes outright. He determined that the problem lay with efforts to direct and control local communities from a centralized Washington, D.C., bureaucracy, and that "regimentation resulting from bureaucratic control is more apt to destroy communities than it is to revitalize them."[2]

Most discussions on the viability and significance of the homesteads centered on Arthurdale, the flagship subsistence homestead project located in West Virginia. Indeed, *Harper's Magazine*'s Millard Millburn Rice considered Arthurdale to be representative of all homestead projects. Although he conceded that it "raised the standard of living comfort for most [residents] above anything they have previously enjoyed," he determined that the program did not succeed. It lacked the "pioneer spirit" and the "slow and natural growth" of locally driven communities. Most importantly, it reaffirmed for Rice the "belief still strong that men must find their own places in life; must work out the solution of their own problems; must do this by a process of adjustment and readjustment rather than suddenly—with sympathetic help, if necessary, from those more fortunate, but without their dictation."[3] Rice did not so much "measure" Arthurdale's success or failure as characterize the reasons for what he considered its self-evident inadequacies. When he visited Arthurdale, he did not find rampant crime, substandard housing, discordant neighborly relations, or deep enmity within the community. Instead, he found the exact opposite. But he noted the persisting economic hardship, the struggles with efficiency in the construction process, and tensions between federal administrators and the local community, and judged the whole program—every subsistence homestead community—to have failed.

Paul Johnson published his expanded study of nine subsistence homesteads the following year and found more to praise than did Rice. He completed supervising and writing a study that Russell Lord had begun on behalf of the Department of Agriculture, a kind of "official" assessment of subsistence homesteads after half a decade of existence. Johnson concluded that each community differed too substantially from the others for broadly applicable conclusions to be drawn. But he did venture that planners had moved forward with the program based on a fundamentally flawed expectation, and that this flaw undermined the program's success. None of the nine communities was able to attract or initiate industrial work sufficient to move relief-dependent families off the rolls. Each community expected the subsistence gardens to reduce the need for wages by half, but not altogether. Residents had to have some source of income in order to pay rents, provide for household needs, and buy the food that the gardens could not provide. On average, subsistence homestead households needed $100 each month in order to survive, and many families did not earn this amount. Johnson thought that more modest houses on smaller plots would cost less to build and maintain, and therefore might allow economic success for families that earned less than $100. However he acknowledged that the families in every community improved their standard of living, that they benefited from and cherished their new homes and yards—places with "land to dig in, to have trees, grass, flowers, small vegetable gardens, possibly poultry, possibly even space for a cow—above all elbow room and a wholesome and healthy place to rear children." The families wanted the lives that the homesteads provided, and Johnson recommended that the nation invest in a broader but scaled-down version of the model once World War II came to an end.[4]

The debate changed over the seventy-five years since the programs began until it settled primarily on questions of national impact, efficacy, and efficiency. Critics found the program wanting because it did not transform the way Americans lived and worked throughout the nation. Thus, William Leuchtenburg, who looked upon the New Deal favorably overall, found the subsistence homestead program to be a failure because it did not generate a large-scale migration out of cities to beyond the suburbs.

> Although the leaders of the movement believed they were affording people the opportunity to escape the evils of a vulgar industrial society, the subsistence homesteads which proved most successful were precisely those, such as El Monte near Los Angeles and Longview in the Columbia River valley, which quickly took on the character of any suburban subdivision. As soon as the pall of the early depression years lifted, people hurried to get back into the "real" world of the bustling city streets. Ostensibly experimental and utopian, the subsistence homesteads movement soon seemed rather a quest for an ark of refuge, an indication of the despair of the early thirties.[5]

Kevin Cahill used a similar metric and found that the program failed in that it "did not lead to the decentralization of the nation's industrial sector."[6] Robert M. Carriker, who found the specific communities that he studied to be successful, noted that homesteads overall "failed in their mission to bring about a mass movement toward part-time farming and reduced wage employment."[7] C. J. Maloney, on the other hand, faulted the program because it succeeded too well. In his view, "to read of America before the New Deal is not so much to read of another time but of another country altogether. Arthurdale was the tipping point—every American born after its birth knows nothing of life in a republic."[8]

Those who studied specific communities intensely found them to have been successful, though. Thus, Robert Carriker saw the overall program's failures, but insisted that the homesteads in the west succeeded.[9] Kevin Cahill deemed the national initiative to have failed, but also pointed out that "the homestead [Arthurdale] significantly increased the living conditions of the homesteaders and gave them an opportunity to own a home. Equally important, was the improved diet and health of the homesteaders that was evident at least at Arthurdale, Tygart Valley and even Red House."[10] Paul Conkin concluded that the broad group of New Deal communities that included subsistence homestead projects succeeded in one significant goal: "For each dollar expended, the communities represented more tangible, enduring achievements than most other relief expenditures."[11] Clarence Pickett reported in his memoir that "altogether on the material side the homesteads have been more successful than the most hopeful prophet could have predicted. In fact, three out of the four communities with which I was personally associated have returned a modest profit to the government on its investment."[12] Blanche Wiesen Cook characterizes Eleanor Roosevelt's efforts in Arthurdale as the building of a "model community." Cook's comments on how people in Arthurdale assess their homestead experience mirror those of current-day Norvelters: "Today, every family tells virtually the same story: We worked together, we danced together, and we learned together."[13]

Homesteaders themselves saw only success. Earl Saville reflected back on his decades of living in Norvelt and concluded, "What happened here showed that it works if the government steps in and helps a group of stranded people who want to go on to help themselves. And we did."[14] Ward Beckwith, who lived in Norvelt while he served as community manager, observed that Norvelt's "improved environment" and "adequate healthy and happy living conditions" helped to restore "to our body politic a cohesive group of active, useful citizens who in their individual characters, personalities, and varied abilities, represent a cross section of the better elements constituting the American people."[15]

The evidence from Norvelt belies the conclusion of so many academics, even those sympathetic to the New Deal, who found failure in the subsistence homestead program. Ward Beckwith and Earl Saville reached far more prescient judgments based on their "lived" examination of the community. They understood that Norvelt leveraged the homesteaders' capacity to create new lives of dignity for themselves, their children, and their grandchildren. The example of Norvelt, which met with much skepticism and sharp resistance in the beginning and through much its history, shows that in hard times of economic crisis and desperation, bold projects that offer people work, dignity, community, and hope have been and can be imagined, planned, and attempted. And they can succeed.

APPENDIX: INTERVIEWEES

Bartolomeo, Margaret LaPenta
Bilik, Ed
Bosich, Catherine
Boyle, Arthur
Boyle, John
Brown, Sarah
Cibulus, Ed
Cotter, Bill
Davis, Carol
Dupey, Peter
Gowaty, Elaine
Herm, Lisa
Hiller, Doris
Hontz, Jimmy
Hutter, Timothy
Karwatsky, Charles
Lukas, Francis
Lulich, Mary Mae
Reese, Mike
Saville, Earl
Schmidt, Jim
Seminary, Mary Ann
Simmons, Jeff
Solo, Len
Speer, Lee
Thomas, Jane Schlingman
Trumka, Rich
Vahaly, Virginia
Weyandt, Lois
Wolk, Valeria
Zaksek, Andrew

NOTES

Introduction

1. Ruth Love, "Reflections of a Homesteader," *Greensburg Tribune Review*, October 27, 1985, B6.
2. Ibid.
3. Norvelt was originally called Westmoreland Homesteads. In 1937, the community agreed to change the name of the community to Norvelt in honor of Eleanor Roosevelt. To avoid confusion, we generally refer to the community as it was known at the time under discussion.
4. The term "homesteader" refers to the original inhabitants of Westmoreland Homesteads.
5. Schlesinger, *The Age of Roosevelt*.
6. Leuchtenburg, *Roosevelt and the New Deal*, xii.
7. Bernstein, "The New Deal"; Biles, *A New Deal*, 2–4; Badger, *The New Deal*, 4–5.
8. Kennedy, *Freedom from Fear*.
9. See, for example, Rauchway, *The Great Depression*, 5; Watkins, *The Great Depression*, 348.
10. See, as examples, Shlaes, *The Forgotten Man*; Powell, *FDR's Folly*; Rosen, *Roosevelt*; Smiley, *Rethinking the Great Depression*.
11. Bateman, Hirai, and Marcuzzo, *The Return to Keynes*.
12. Rohatyn, *Bold Endeavors*, chaps. 7 and 8.
13. Hiltzik, *Colossus*, xiii.
14. Hiltzik, *The New Deal*. Despite his enthusiastic support for most of Roosevelt's New Deal, he found the subsistence homestead program, especially as exemplified by the project in Arthurdale, West Virginia, to be a failed experiment.
15. Stuart, "Constructing Identity."
16. Taylor, *American-Made*, 2.
17. Leighninger, *Long-Range Public Investment*.
18. Smith, *Building New Deal Liberalism*, 4.
19. Field, *A Great Leap Forward*, 1–4.
20. Lind, *Land of Promise*.
21. Conkin, *Tomorrow a New World*, 331.
22. Grattan, "The Vine-Covered Factory Worker," 69.
23. Harding, "The Record of Subsistence Homesteads," 409.
24. See, for example, Maloney, *Back to the Land*; Rice, "Footnote on Arthurdale," 411–19; Leuchtenburgh, *Roosevelt and*

the New Deal, 136; Badger, *The New Deal*, 240; Hiltzik, *The New Deal*.

25. Ghirardo, *Building New Communities*, 186–87.
26. Robert M. Carriker, *Urban Farming in the West*, 166.
27. Garvey, "The Duluth Homesteads," 2–16.
28. Hargis, *Crossville Chronicle*.
29. Wiesen Cook, *Eleanor Roosevelt*, vol. 2, 151–52.
30. Celebrated young adult author Jack Gantos set his 2012 Newbery Award–winning novel *Dead End in Norvelt* in Norvelt, where he had spent a number of his childhood years.
31. Linda Shopes's discussion of oral history and local history focuses on Pennsylvania. She notes, "If there is a single theme running through the interviews, it is the importance of 'hard work' in the shaping of a person's life and identity." Shopes, "Oral History," 594.
32. Mechling, "Oral Evidence and the History," 580–81.
33. Thelen, "Memory and American History," 1122.
34. Carol Davis, interview with authors, Norvelt, Pa., November 11, 2011. Davis added, "I had a Catholic boyfriend but I had to sneak to see him. I wasn't allowed to see him."
35. Earl Saville preserved copies of the *Homestead Informer*, which he generously allowed us to use.
36. U.S. Bureau of the Census, Census 1940, Statistical Abstract.
37. Rebecca S. Kraus, e-mail message to Margaret Power, May 30, 2012.

Chapter 1

1. Despite numerous strikes, miners did not successfully unionize until 1933, when miners and coke workers throughout the region joined the United Mine Workers of America. See Yankovich, "The Rise of the United Mine Workers," 117; Sheppard, *Cloud by Day*, 110. The term "patch" is commonly used to designate a small piece of land, but we have not been able to determine the origins of the term as it relates to mining communities.
2. At least one contemporary observer of mining communities in southwestern Pennsylvania would dispute this image of solidarity. "'Community' is quite completely a misnomer for non-union mining camps (and almost for many union towns). The towns are visibly split along racial lines; there are generally 'American' and 'foreigner' sections and in the latter 'hunky' streets, or 'wop' or 'slavish.' . . . Racial divisions admittedly were fostered by the coal companies; 'it keeps the men from getting together;' or as a miner at Jerome complained, 'there's no sociability in a non-union town.' . . . Normally suspicion between the racial groups is the non-union rule." See Blankenhorn, *The Strike for Union*, 49. Jerome was a coal-mining town in Somerset County, Pennsylvania.
3. For a discussion of the early nineteenth-century economic transformation, see Charles Sellers, *The Market Revolution*; and Heilbroner and Singer, *The Economic Transformation*. Emma Lapsansky focuses on economic developments in Pennsylvania in "Building Democratic Communities." DiCiccio, *Coal and Coke*, 31, 7. For a history of coal in Pennsylvania, see 4–29. By 1902, the United States produced more coal than any other country in the world, surpassing

Great Britain. Harris, *Keystone of Democracy*, 105.

4. Warren, *Wealth, Waste, and Alienation*, xv–xvi.
5. Miller, "Connellsville Beehive Coke," 144. As Miller noted, the coal had "a carbon content of 57 to 60 per cent, volatile matter 30 to 35 per cent, ash content less than 8 per cent, and sulphur under 1 per cent. . . . Because of its lack of impurities the Pittsburgh coal needed no preparation, such as washing, before it was coked." Brestensky Hovanec, and Skomra, *Patch/Work Voices*, 28–30. For a good description of how the beehive oven functioned, see Enman, "Connellsville Coke," 15. Elaine H. De Frank, e-mail communication, July 28, 2011.
6. Fitch, "The Process of Making," 240; Miller, "Connellsville Beehive Coke," 145–46.
7. Miller, "Connellsville Beehive Coke," 147.
8. Standiford, *Meet You in Hell*, chap. 5.
9. For an analysis of the impact that coke manufacturing had on Overton, see Sandow, "The Impact of Coking." The coke industry replaced the production of whiskey, which had been the village's first economic activity. Reinert, "Historic Shoaf"; Sandow, "The Impact of Coking"; Warren, *Wealth, Waste, and Alienation*, 56, 210; Harvey, *Henry Clay Frick*, 78. As a result of the deal, Carnegie "paid about eighteen cents less per ton . . . than did his competitors," which saved him fifty thousand dollars in 1885. Standiford, *Meet You in Hell*, 60; "Mr. Carnegie's Representative," *New York Times*, July 12, 1892; "Henry C. Frick Dies; Leaves Art to City," *New York Times*, December 3, 1919. In 2010 dollars, that sum would equal roughly $936,000,000.
10. Margaret LaPenta Bartolomeo, interview with Elaine H. De Frank, Coal and Coke Heritage Archives, University of Pennsylvania, Fayetteville Campus, January 19, 1999. During the 1891 strike, Frick sent a telegram to a local mine manager saying, "I would throw those huns [Hungarians] out of the houses the moment their time is up, without any ceremony." His refusal to accept the demands of the Homestead workers in 1892 led to the defeat of organized labor in the mills for decades. See Harris, *Keystone of Democracy*, 108–14; Warren, *Wealth, Waste, and Alienation*, 92; Nasaw, *Andrew Carnegie*, 390–91; Harvey, *Henry Clay Frick*, 108. As cited in Warren, *Wealth, Waste, and Alienation*, 88–96.
11. Hovanec, "Southwestern Pennsylvania's Coal," 60. See Lauck, "The Bituminous Coal Miner." Lauck worked for the U.S. Immigration Commission and was in charge of general industrial investigation. This report is based on his study of the region and analysis of data related to the mine and coke industry and laborers. Also see Hovanec, "Southwestern Pennsylvania's Coal," 56–58; Warren, *Wealth, Waste, and Alienation*, 212. That would be roughly 5.5 million in 2013 dollars. That same year, Frick wrote to Andrew Carnegie, crowing that the "Union Supply Company [the name of the company stores] has this day declared a dividend of 100 percent, your share being $31,914.00. It is earning at the rate of 350 percent per annum on its capital at present. Has made almost $2 million dollars on its capital of $75,000 since its formation in 1882." For a description of Frick, Mellon, and Carnegie as philanthropists, see Cannadine, "Andrew

Mellon," 20. For information on the Frick Collection in New York City, see http://www.frick.org/.

12. Bartolomeo, interview.
13. U.S. Bureau of the Census, *Historical Statistics*, 591; Lauck, "The Bituminous Coal Miner," 35.
14. Morawska, *For Bread with Butter*, 25. She notes that peasants became increasingly "open to new experiences," came to believe that they could "actively advance [their] own goals," and accepted "quantitative bases for acquiring and distributing rewards," which encouraged them to seek more gainful employment elsewhere (23–24, 39).
15. Metheny, *From the Miners' Doublehouse*, 83; Thernstrom, *Harvard Encyclopedia*, 928, 790.
16. Daniels, *Coming to America*, 188; Thernstrom, *Harvard Encyclopedia*, 547; 551.
17. Hereafter referred to as the Dillingham Report, for Senator William Dillingham, chair of the United States Immigration Commission, which was created in 1907 to study the "subject of immigration." The commission published a forty-one-volume report, which recommended, among other things, that immigrants "unable to read or write in some language" be excluded, as well as those who "have no intention of becoming American citizens" but only seek to make enough money to "return permanently to their home country." The volume on miners based its information on a representative study of miners. *Reports of the Immigration Commission* (Dillingham Report), vol. 5, 47–48. As Linda Joyce Brown notes, "the extensiveness of the Commission's Investigation—which was completed over a period of three years and cost about one million dollars –appears indicative of the growing anxiety about immigration in the period immediately before World War I." *The Literature of Immigration*, 1, 6; Lauck, "The Bituminous Coal Miner," 35; Metheny, *From the Miners' Doublehouse*, 79.
18. For a discussion of anti-Catholic sentiment prior to the Civil War directed against the Irish, see Dinnerstein, *Natives and Strangers*, 97–99.
19. Dillingham Report, vol. 1, 42–44, 335; Thernstrom, *Harvard Encyclopedia*, 720, 927–28; and Morawska, *For Bread with Butter*, 23–25.
20. Dillingham Report, vol. 1, 42–44.
21. Ibid., vol. 6, 487. A higher percentage of these workers received more than two dollars a day than white, native born of native fathers did, since the former had extensive mining experience. This wage differential remained unchanged in 1911. In that year, "native Americans," which meant those born in the United States of northern European ancestry, earned $2.17 a day, while southern and eastern Europeans earned roughly $2.00 a day, except for Romanians, who only received $1.85 a day. Lauck, "The Bituminous Coal Miner," 45.
22. Roediger, *The Wages of Whiteness*, 179. As a girl growing up in Greensburg, Westmoreland County, Pennsylvania, in the 1960s, Margaret Power remembers her mother and aunt (both Protestant descendants of Scots) referred to Italians as having "olive skin" or being "swarthy." Schrag, *Not Fit for Our Society*, 111–13.
23. Lauck, "The Bituminous Coal Miner," 36.
24. Maclean, "Life in the Pennsylvania Coal Fields," 347.

25. Leiserson, "Labor Conditions in the Mines," 94.
26. Jenkins, *Hoods and Shirts*, 66.
27. Blee points out a similar reality in her account of the Klan in Indiana in the 1920s. Blee, *Women and the Klan*.
28. Ibid., 12–16. Dinnerstein labeled the Klan from 1915 to 1925 as "one of the most powerful anti-Catholic, as well as antiforeign, organizations in the history of the country," *Natives and Strangers*, 186; "Johnston Immigration Act Kills the Ku Klux Klan," *Daily Courier*, September 4, 1924.
29. For a vivid and detailed description of KKK activities in western Pennsylvania, particularly their attacks on Catholic immigrants and the immigrants' efforts to oppose them, see Craig, *The Ku Klux Klan*, 11; Jenkins, *Hoods and Shirts*, 70–71.
30. Peter Dupey, interview with Elaine H. De Frank, Coal and Coke Heritage Archives, University of Pennsylvania, Fayetteville Campus, December 8, 1995. Dupey did not say who he saw limping around, but he did say that the grand wizard of the Klan lived in Peanut, Westmoreland County.
31. In 1935, the federal government passed the Guffey-Snyder Bituminous Coal Conservation Act, which, among other provisions, authorized workers' collective bargaining rights and established a maximum number of work hours. See DiCiccio, *Coal and Coke*, 183. Miners told Metheny that their long-time suspicions that operators underweighed their cars were confirmed when a union representative finally was able to observe the weighing process directly. The average weight of cars in one mine rose two hundred pounds right away. (Operators paid miners by the ton of coal produced, adjusted somewhat for the quality of the coal in the car.) Metheny, *From the Miners' Doublehouse*, 113.
32. Andrew Zaksek, interview with Elaine H. De Frank, Coal and Coke Heritage Center Archives, University of Pennsylvania, Fayetteville Campus, February 3, 1995.
33. Dupey, interview.
34. "Women Must Not Work on the Coke Yards in the Future," *Connellsville Courier*, July 17, 1885; Charles Karwatsky, interview with Elaine H. De Frank, Coal and Coke Heritage Archives, University of Pennsylvania, Fayetteville Campus, January 1, 1999.
35. Ed Bilik, interview with Margaret Power, Norvelt, Pennsylvania, June 24, 2011.
36. Women, by and large, did not work in the mines until 1973. For a history of women and mining see Moore, *Women in the Mines*. They did, however, work in the coke ovens, helping their husbands or fathers. For a discussion of this see Karwatsky, interview.
37. P. Nyden, "Miners for Democracy," 46. He drew the term from Kerr and Siegel, "The Interindustry Propensity to Strike," 189–91.
38. Brophy, *A Miner's Life*, 29–30.
39. Bilik, interview.
40. Ibid.
41. Hovanec, *Common Lives of Uncommon Strength*, 17; Warren, *Wealth, Waste, and Alienation*, 198.
42. "The Company Store," *Connellsville Courier*, June 21, 1889.
43. Metheny notes that most miners were convinced that the prices of products in the company stores "were deliberately inflated." *From the Miners' Doublehouse*, 67; Dillingham Report, vol. 6, 325–27; Warren, *Wealth, Waste, and Alienation*, 214.

44. Francis Lukas, interview with Margaret Power, Latrobe, Pennsylvania, February 15, 2009.
45. Brestensky, Hovanec, and Skomra, *Patch/Work Voices*, 47; Dillingham Report, vol. 6, 327. Not everyone had a negative impression of the store. Elaine H. De Frank, e-mail communication with Margaret Power, July 27, 2011. Viola Ryan was born in 1904 in Washington County in southwest Pennsylvania. She remembers that "[during the Depression] the company store did see that you had a little bit of something to eat. And it was really better than what a lot of people think it was. They talk about the store not being good to you, but it was; it seemed that any time miners were out of work or there was sickness in the family, the company store would carry you over and give you anything you had to have." See Brestensky, Hovanec, and Skomra, *Patch/Work Voices*, 49.
46. Green, *The Company Town*, 70. Metheny, *From the Miners' Doublehouse*, 73.
47. Kessler-Harris, "The Organization of Negroes," 257. Wright, *The Negro in Pennsylvania*, 71; Lewis, *Black Coal Miners*, 191.
48. Shalloo, *Private Police*, 59; Rich Trumka, interview with Margaret Power, Chicago, August 15, 2011; Sheppard, *The Story of Coal*, chap. 10. Bilik remembers that when the Iron and Coal Police were walking through the patch, his parents would not let him go outside and he did his best to avoid them. Bilik, interview. For a discussion of solidarity among miners, see P. Nyden, "Miners for Democracy," 41.
49. P. Nyden, "Miners for Democracy," 33; Harris, *Keystone of Democracy*, 114–15; Montgomery, *Fall of the House of Labor*, 339.
50. Trumka, interview.
51. Montgomery, *Fall of the House of Labor*, 333.
52. Margaret would like to thank Rosemary Feurer, who pointed out the connections between the UMWA and the Knights of Labor: "the UMWA position on race was derived from the Knights of Labor." E-mail communication, December 28, 2011. For a discussion of race and the Knights of Labor see, Kessler, "The Organization of Negroes"; for a critical examination of the failure of the Knights to match practice with their stated policies on race, see Foner et al., "Knights of Labor"; Fox, *United We Stand*, 39; Trumka, interview.
53. L. Nyden, "Black Miners in Western Pennsylvania," 70; P. Nyden, "Miners for Democracy," 34; Barnum, *The Negro in the Bituminous Coal Mining Industry*, 15, 21.
54. Wright, *The Negro in Pennsylvania*, 95.
55. In 1931, Harry Haywood, a black member of the Communist Party, went to the Pittsburgh area to work with the National Miners Union to organize a strike. For a description of his experiences as "the leader of a mass of white miners with strong racial prejudices," see *Black Bolshevik*, chap. 13; L. Nyden, "Black Miners in Western Pennsylvania," 74.
56. Willis, "A Tribute to the Black Miners." We thank Raymond P. Washlaski, the historian and editor of the Virtual Museum of Coal Mining in Western Pennsylvania, for calling this document to our attention. His website, http://patheoldminer.rootsweb.ancestry.com/, is an excellent source of information on mining, miners, and patch communities in western

Pennsylvania. For similar stories, see P. Nyden, "Miners for Democracy," 773.

57. Montgomery, *Fall of the House of Labor*, 337.
58. Mary Mae Lulich, interview by Pamela Lehning, Coal and Coke Heritage Archives, University of Pennsylvania, Fayetteville Campus, 1977; Hovanec, *Common Lives of*, 206; Montgomery, *Fall of the House of Labor*, 337.
59. Lulich, interview.
60. Hovanec, *Common Lives of Uncommon Strength*, 206; Montgomery, *Fall of the House of Labor*, 338.
61. Palmer and O'Neill, *Report on the Miners' Strike*, 9–10. Neill was the commissioner of labor.
62. Ibid., 56–57, 15, 58. "Story of Atrocities," *Wellsboro (Pa.) Gazette*, June 8, 1911, 4.
63. Palmer and O'Neill, *Report on the Miners' Strike*, 59, 63–64.
64. Steeley, "They Sang Their Way," 30–31; Palmer and O'Neill, *Report on the Miners' Strike*, 18.

Chapter 2

1. David Kennedy notes that more shares of stock changed hands on October 29, 1929, than any previous day in the market's history and any subsequent day until the late 1960s. *Freedom from Fear*, 38.
2. McElvaine, *The Great Depression*, 35–37; Rauchway, *The Great Depression*, 12–13; Badger, *The New Deal*, 15.
3. Rasmus, *Epic Recession*, 175.
4. Field, *A Great Leap Forward*, 2.
5. McElvaine, *The Great Depression*, 37–41; Parrish, *Anxious Decades*, 218.
6. McElvaine, *The Great Depression*, 37–39.
7. Ibid., 38; Piketty and Saez, "Income Inequality," 1–39, as cited in Krugman, *Conscience of a Liberal*, 16.
8. Schlesinger, *The Age of Roosevelt: The Crisis of the Old Order*, 159–60; Edsforth, *The New Deal*, 21.
9. McElvaine, *The Great Depression*, 40–41. See also Hyman, *Borrow*, 55.
10. Lind, *Land of Promise*, 261.
11. McElvaine, *The Great Depression*, 75.
12. A word of caution is in order here. Unemployment statistics during the Great Depression were not collected scientifically, and likely underreport the actual percentages in any given year. No national or international standards existed for collecting the data through most of the period, and efforts to do so were sporadic and seriously flawed. For a full discussion of this problem, see Garraty, *Unemployment in History*, chap. 9.
13. Edsforth, *The New Deal*, 47, 77; Mintz and Kellogg, *Domestic Revolutions*, 134.
14. Edsforth, *The New Deal*, 79.
15. Biles, *A New Deal*, 11.
16. One way that the New Deal addressed this directly was with the Home Owners Loan Corporation (HOLC), which guaranteed loans and spread payments across twenty years rather than the existing standard of five or ten—thus reducing risk for banks and monthly payments for homeowners. Jackson, *Crabgrass Frontier*, 197.
17. Elmer B. Dillinger to Clarence E. Pickett, 1933, Record Group 96, Oversize Files, Westmoreland Homestead, National Archives and Records Administration (NARA); Clarence E. Pickett to Elmer B. Dillinger, December 13, 1933, RG 96, Oversize Files, Westmoreland Homestead, NARA.
18. Roughly five thousand banks collapsed by 1933. Badger, *The New Deal*,

239; Mintz and Kellogg, *Domestic Revolutions*, 135; Kennedy, *Freedom from Fear*, 162–63.
19. Crouse, *The Homeless Transient*, 48.
20. Leuchtenburg, *Roosevelt and the New Deal*, 1, 3.
21. Mintz and Kellogg, *Domestic Revolutions*, 136.
22. Berg, *All You Can Eat*, 60. It is difficult for historians to measure hunger in past societies, as the complexity of measuring hunger in the United States over even the most recent three decades indicates. Peter Eisinger identifies four separate ways of measuring hunger in *Toward an End to Hunger in America*, 23–35.
23. Levine, *School Lunch Politics*, 41.
24. Kennedy, *Freedom from Fear*, 170.
25. Lowitt and Beasley, *One Third of a Nation*, 19–20.
26. Ibid., 20.
27. Quoted in Patterson, *America's Struggle Against Poverty*, 38.
28. Letter from Mrs. I. H., Lawndale, California, to Franklin D. Roosevelt, in McElvaine, *Down and Out in the Great Depression*, 57–58.
29. Edsforth, *The New Deal*, 52.
30. Biles, *A New Deal*, 13.
31. Watkins, *The Great Depression*, 64.
32. Johnson, "Culture."
33. "New March of Idle to Be Made on Capitol; Priest Will Lead Anti-Communist Parade," *New York Times*, January 3, 1932.
34. Homeless people throughout the country constructed residential enclaves out of discarded building materials, boxes, scraps of metal, and cloth, and named these "Hoovervilles" to highlight their suffering and President Hoover's opposition to offering assistance. "Father Cox's Army Starts for Capital," *New York Times*, January 6, 1932.
35. During the 1928 presidential campaign, opponents of Al Smith's candidacy insisted that his Catholicism disqualified him from leading a democratic nation. J. Heineman, *A Catholic New Deal*, 15–22.
36. Smithfield Street housed the offices of Pittsburgh's financial elite. Ibid., 25; "Father Cox Says Idle Will Form Third Party and He 'May Run'; 55,000 Cheer at Pittsburgh," *New York Times*, January 17, 1932.
37. Watkins, *The Great Depression*, 79–80; Badger, *The New Deal*, 17.
38. McElvaine, *The Great Depression*, 92.
39. Levenstein, *Paradox of Plenty*, 60–66.
40. DiCiccio, *Coal and Coke in Pennsylvania*, 137; Coleman, *Men and Coal*, 96.
41. Scheler, "Technological Unemployment," 21.
42. Morris, *Plight*, 7–8.
43. Lamb, "Second Session," 51.
44. Morris, *Plight*, 8–13.
45. DiCiccio, *Coal and Coke in Pennsylvania*, 169.
46. Samuel Gompers, president of the American Federation of Labor, issued a statement in which he calculated that in 1921 "the coal miners of the United States worked an average of 113 days. The average wages for the last twelve months were $750 in round numbers. "Washington Waits Strike Emergency," *New York Times*, April 1, 1922.
47. Lubin, *Miners' Wages*, 214–15.
48. "Connelsville [*sic*] Mines Bar Foreign Labor," *New York Times*, August 20, 1922.
49. U.S. Coal Commission, press release, September 22, 1923, 7; Mulroney, *A Legacy of Coal*, 26; "Claim Big Victory in Non-Union Mines," *New York Times*, April 7, 1922.

50. "Big Association Groups Slow to Accept Cleveland Pact," *Coal Age* 22, no. 8 (1922): 298.
51. "Claim Big Victory in Non-Union Mines," *New York Times*, April 7, 1922, 1, 3; "Union Organizers Claim 5000 More Non-Union Miners," *New York Times*, April 10, 1922, 1, 3.
52. Blankenhorn, *The Strike for Union*, 147–53; Harris and Blatz, *Keystone of Democracy*, 171; Dubofsky and Van Tine, *John L. Lewis*, 67, 68.
53. According to Alan Singer, the Communists concluded this based on miners' history of militant struggle and their dissatisfaction with the UMWA leadership, particularly that of John L. Lewis. See Singer, "Communists and Coal Miners," 132–33; Ottanelli, *Communist Party*, 21; Howard, "The National Miners Union," 92; Nyden, "Black Miners in Western Pennsylvania," 87. In a reflection of the CPUSA's politics, the NMU organized special sections for youth and women and a department for "Negroes." Ibid., 88. After she graduated from Smith College, Lauren Gilfillan lived in a patch community in southwestern Pennsylvania. Her memoirs describe the abject poverty of the mining families as well as the organizing efforts of the Communists. See Gilfillan, *I Went to Pit College*.
54. "Labor Disputes are Increasing," *New York Times*, July 29, 1931.
55. Nyden, "Miners for Democracy," 93.
56. Foster, *Pages from a Worker's Life*, 179.
57. Klehr, *The Heyday of American Communism*, 44.
58. Foster, *Pages from a Worker's Life*, 180.
59. "Communist Foster Takes Leadership of Strike," *Connellsville Daily Courier*, July 14, 1931.
60. "8,000 in Hunger March," *New York Times*, July 1, 1931.
61. Both organizations were so popular that twenty-five thousand miners joined the NMU and one thousand people joined the CPUSA during the strike, albeit for a short time. Klehr, *Heyday of American Communism*, 44.
62. Coal operators' refusal to settle with the NMU contributed to the 1935 dissolution of the union. The NMU urged its members to join the UMWA, which many of them did. For a positive assessment of the impact that the NMU had on the UMWA, particularly on its opposition to racism within the union, see Nyden, "Miners for Democracy," 99–101.
63. Ottanelli, *Communist Party in the United States*, 27; Nyden, "Miners for Democracy," 95–96.
64. United States Coal Commission, Washington, D.C., press release, September 22, 1923; Abbott, "Improvement in Rural Public Relief," 187.
65. Golay, *America 1933*, 57.
66. Baker et al., "Relief Needs and Conditions," 596–600.
67. "14,694 Unemployed in Westmoreland," *Pittsburgh Press*, February 15, 1931, 7.
68. "14,694 in County Unemployed, Represents Total of 19 Percent of 73,577 Employees," *Jeannette Daily News Dispatch*, February 13, 1931, 1, 8.
69. "Over Two Million Spent on Relief in County," *Greensburg Daily Tribune*, December 27, 1933, 1, 8; DiCiccio, *Coal and Coke in Pennsylvania*, 154.
70. Baker et al., "Relief Needs and Conditions," 601.
71. "Governor Pinchot's Message, November 10, 1931," in Baker et al., "Relief Needs and Conditions," 606.
72. "Davis Condemns Activities of Government in Business," *Pittsburgh Press*, March 30, 1932, 4; These reports came from Lorena Hickok in letters

that she sent to Harry Hopkins in 1933. They can be found in Lowitt and Beasley, *One Third of a Nation*, 11; Dunham, "Pennsylvania and Unemployment Relief," 246–47.

73. Baker et al., "Relief Needs and Conditions," 607; Terkel, *Hard Times*, 196.
74. Henry W. Francis, "Report, Morgantown, West Virginia, November 18, 1934," box 66, Hopkins Papers, Franklin Delano Roosevelt Library, Hyde Park, N.Y., http://newdeal.feri.org/hopkins/hop10.htm, accessed June 27, 2011.
75. Ibid.

Chapter 3

1. McElvaine, *The Great Depression*, 56.
2. See especially Shlaes, *The Forgotten Man.*
3. Kennedy, *Freedom from Fear*, 84–85. By the summer of 1932, the RFC had also begun to loan money to states to use for unemployment relief, which made it a source of funds for something approaching direct relief—a modification of Hoover's strong resistance to such aid. See Arthur Dunham, "Pennsylvania and Unemployment Relief," 252–55, for a discussion of the RFC loans to Pennsylvania's relief efforts.
4. Kennedy, *Freedom from Fear*, 84–85.
5. Alan Lawson, *A Commonwealth of Hope.*
6. Purdy, "The Roberts Court v. America," 47.
7. Van Hise, *Concentration and Control.*
8. Moley, *After Seven Years*, 184.
9. Ibid.
10. Lawson, *A Commonwealth of Hope*, 83.
11. Leuchtenburg, *Roosevelt and the New Deal*, 56–57.
12. Adam Cohen, *Nothing to Fear*, 243.
13. Dubovsky and Dulles, *Labor in America*, 245.
14. Smith, *Redeeming the Time*, 449.
15. Leuchtenburg, *Roosevelt and the New Deal*, 57; Badger, *FDR*, 95–96.
16. Watkins, *The Hungry Years*, 341.
17. Ibid., 344.
18. Domhoff and Webber, *Class and Power*, 90. Net farm income fell also, from $9.6 billion to $4.5 billion over the same period. Hiltzik, *The New Deal*, 96. Gross farm income fell even more dramatically.
19. Hiltzik, *The New Deal*, 96.
20. Watkins, *The Hungry Years*, 345.
21. Joseph Stiglitz sees the decline in the agricultural sector, especially the efficiency-driven decline in jobs there, to be the main cause of the Great Depression. Stiglitz, "The Book of Jobs."
22. Kern, "The Bankhead Experiment," 367.
23. McElvaine, *The Great Depression*, 148.
24. Leaving acres untilled turned out to be an imperfect way to reduce output, at least in cotton farming. New methods and fertilizers allowed cotton farmers to plant rows closer together, so that even with reduced acres, cotton farmers in 1934 were able to produce more cotton than they had in 1933. Senator John Bankhead introduced legislation to limit each farmer's output rather than the acres that he tilled.
25. Rauchway, *The Great Depression*, 77.
26. Cohen, *Nothing to Fear*, 145.
27. Schlesinger, *The Age of Roosevelt: The Coming of the New Deal*, 41.
28. McElvaine, *The Great Depression*, 149.
29. Cohen, *Nothing to Fear*, 144.
30. Edsforth, *The New Deal*, 176.
31. Ibid., 174.
32. Cooley, "John Hollis Bankhead II."

33. Ibid.
34. "Historical Note, Collection 2100—M. L. Wilson Papers, 1913–1970," Montana State University Library, www.lib.montana.edu/collect/spcoll/findaid/2100.html, accessed December 26, 2011.
35. Robert M. Carriker relates that Wilson's departure was semivoluntary, that he left when Ickes wrested control of the DSH and demanded centralized control. *Urban Farming in the West*, 30.
36. Wilson, "The Place of Subsistence Homesteads," 73–75. Wilson later authored an article published in the *New York Times* that mirrored many of the arguments he made in the journal article, but reached far more readers. M. L. Wilson, "Government Testing Value of Subsistence Homesteads," *New York Times*, February 11, 1934.
37. Wilson, "The Place of Subsistence Homesteads," 74–75. Wilson also saw the substantial movement to the suburbs as a reflection of the same impulse that drew Americans back to family farmsteads, and so included that migration in his evidence of a re-embrace of farm living.
38. Wilson, "The Place of Subsistence Homesteads," 77.
39. Ibid., 79.
40. Ibid., 81.
41. Ibid., 74, 81.
42. Pickett, *For More than Bread*, 19–22.
43. The generally accepted position was that three hundred thousand coal miners were out of work, and that roughly two hundred thousand would never work as coal miners again. "A Program for the Redistribution of Unemployed Coal Miners," Coal Relief Sections, Subsistence Homesteads, General 1933 file, General Administration 1933 Coal Relief Section (Projects—Cambria & Clearfield Counties, PA) to (Projects—Lincoln County, WV) box, American Friends Service Committee Archives (AFSCA).
44. The four communities were Arthurdale and Tygert Valley in West Virginia, Cumberland Homestead in Tennessee, and Westmoreland Homesteads (Norvelt) in Pennsylvania.
45. Clarence E. Pickett to "Friend," September 16, 1933, Coal Relief Section, Subsistence Homesteads, Westmoreland, Pa., 1933, General file, General Administration 1933, Coal Relief Section (Projects—Cambria and Clearfield Counties, PA) to (Lincoln County, WV) box, AFSCA.
46. Pickett, *For More than Bread*, 62.
47. Pickett, "The Social Significance," 478.
48. Clarence E. Pickett, "CEP's Journal, Nov. 1933 to Dec 1935," box 30, Clarence Pickett's Journal, 1912–1936 (Jan.–June), Clarence Pickett Papers, AFSCA.
49. Cook, *Eleanor Roosevelt*, vol. 2, 131–32; Lowitt and Beasley, *One Third of a Nation*, 20.
50. Cook, *Eleanor Roosevelt*, vol. 2, 132.
51. O'Farrell, *She Was One of Us*, 48.
52. Roosevelt's column quoted in Cook, *Eleanor Roosevelt*, vol. 2, 132.
53. For an extended examination of Louis Howe's relationship with the Roosevelts, see Fenster, *FDR's Shadow*.
54. Pickett, *For More than Bread*, 45.
55. Cook, *Eleanor Roosevelt*, vol. 2, 135.
56. Wilson, "Government Testing Value of Subsistence Homesteads"; Cook, *Eleanor Roosevelt*, vol. 2, 135–36.

Chapter 4

1. "Home Project Officers Named," *Greensburg Daily Tribune*, January 10,

1934, 7. In addition to Homer Morris, the board members named were Kenneth H. Bair of Greensburg, president; Ruben Barnhart of Mt. Pleasant, vice president; Mrs. John Barclay of Greensburg, secretary; and John A. Robertshaw of Greensburg, treasurer.

2. "News of the Day," *Greensburg Daily Tribune*, January 11, 1934, 4.
3. "Homestead Project Gets $276,000 from Government," *Greensburg Daily Tribune*, January 17, 1934, 1.
4. "Homestead Management Ready to Receive First Applications," *Greensburg Daily Tribune*, January 17, 1934, 1, 8. Adjoining counties include Armstrong, Indiana, Cambria, Somerset, Fayette, Washington, Allegheny, and Butler.
5. Campbell, "Westmoreland Homesteads," 36. Note that the term "rurban" was coined to emphasize the combined rural and urban character of the planned homestead communities. Paul Campbell offers an insider's perspective through his master's thesis because he served as Day's assistant in Westmoreland Homesteads' early years.
6. "Management Ready," *Greensburg Daily Tribune*, 1, 8.
7. Timothy Hutter, interview with authors, June 14 and June 19, 2012. Hutter, Minerd's grandson, now retired, was an educator in the Greater Latrobe school system.
8. Ibid.
9. Clarence Pickett to William Beaver, Correspondence with the General Public to which individual replies were made, 1933–1935, RG 96, box 2, file Beau to Beg, National Archives and Record Administration (NARA).
10. *Homestead Informer*, October 18, 1935, 5, and November 15, 1935, 3. The *Informer* was the community newspaper/newsletter for the Westmoreland Homesteads project and was published at two-week intervals by the project management from August 8, 1935, to July 15, 1937. *Informer* copies provided courtesy of Carol Davis and Lois Weyandt, formerly of Norvelt, and Earl Saville and Virginia Speer, current Norvelt residents. All four individuals are the children of original homesteaders.
11. Campbell, "Westmoreland Homesteads," 36.
12. "Management Ready," *Greensburg Daily Tribune*, January 17, 1934, 8.
13. "Russian Type Collective Farm Planned Here," *Greensburg Daily Tribune*, February 3, 1934, 7; Campbell, "Westmoreland Homesteads," 38.
14. Campbell, "Westmoreland Homesteads," 37. The final ratio tilted toward area residents who had not worked in the mines.
15. "2 Manufacturing Plants Seek Homestead Sites," *Greensburg Daily Tribune*, March 8, 1934, 1.
16. "Memo from Homer L. Morris to Charles E. Pynchon regarding Homesteads for stranded and permanently displaced workers December 28, 1934," General Correspondence 1935–1942, RG 96, box 17, file 183, NARA.
17. Campbell, "Westmoreland Homesteads," 39, 37.
18. "Construction of Homes Starts Soon in State," *Olean (N.Y.) Times-Herald*, June 14, 1934.
19. Matthew M. Baker to President Roosevelt, July 10, 1934, RG 96, box 2, file Baker to Bard, NARA.
20. Campbell, "Westmoreland Homesteads," 37–38.
21. "Population & Family Size of Homestead Families, May 15, 1935," General Correspondence 1935–1942,

Resettlement Administration, Management Division, Subsistence Homestead Unit, RG 96, box 17, file RP-183 Reports (General) Oct. 1934 thru May 1935, NARA.

22. "Applications and Acceptances, Home Completions and Occupancies, & Occupant Population, March 1, 1937," RG 96, box 30, file RP-500-RP-505-04, NARA.
23. David Day to Clarence Pickett, September 2, 1933, Coal Relief Section 1933 file, box General Administration 1933, Subsistence Homesteads General, American Friends Service Committee Archives (AFSCA).
24. "Program of Eventual Use of Cooperative Association," Coal Relief Section 1934 file, General Administration 1934 box, Subsistence Homesteads Westmoreland, Pa. correspondence, n.d., AFSCA.
25. Campbell, "Westmoreland Homesteads," 71; William (Bill) Byerly to AFSC staff members, January 13, 1935, Social-Industrial Section 1935 Coal Area file, General Files 1935 Social-Industrial Section Volunteer Placement to Work Camps box, Subsistence Homesteads Westmoreland, Pa., AFSCA.
26. "Program of Eventual Use of Cooperative Association," n.d., AFSC.
27. Federal Emergency Relief Administration Grant (hereinafter FERA Grant), "Training Program—Subsistence Homestead," "Application for Grant from Self-Help and Barter Exchange Funds of Federal Emergency Relief Administration for Westmoreland Homesteaders' Cooperative Association," February 10, 1934, Coal Relief Section 1934 file, General Administration 1934 Coal Relief Section box, Subsistence Homesteads Westmoreland, Pa. General (n.d.), AFSCA. FERA was the Roosevelt administration's relief agency before the creation of the Works Progress Administration. The grant was awarded on March 15, 1934. "Ruddock Quits as Chairman of Relief Board," *Indiana (Pa.) Evening Gazette*, March 16, 1934, 1.
28. S. Howard Pennell to David Day, April 2, 1934; Day to Pennell, May 10, 1934, AFSCA; Day to Pennell, June 21, 1934, and June 13, 1934, Coal Relief Section 1934 file, General Administration 1934 Coal Relief Section box, Subsistence Homesteads Westmoreland, Pa. Correspondence, AFSCA.
29. S. Howard Pennell to David Day, June 29, 1934, Coal Relief Section 1934 file, General Administration 1934 Coal Relief Section file, Subsistence Homesteads Westmoreland, Pa. Correspondence, AFSCA.
30. David Day to S. Howard Pennell, February 11, 1934, AFSCA; Pennell to Day (telegram), February 13, 1934, Coal Relief Section 1934 file, General Administration 1934 Coal Relief Section—Subsistence Homesteads box, Subsistence Homesteads Westmoreland, Pa. Correspondence, AFSCA.
31. Ruth Love, "Reflections of a Homesteader," *Greensburg Tribune-Review*, October 27, 1985, B6.
32. Circular No. 1, *General Information Concerning the Purposes and Policies of the Division of Subsistence Homesteads*, United States Department of the Interior, Division of Subsistence Homesteads, November 15, 1933, 8, Coal Relief Section 1933 Subsistence Homesteads General file, General Administration 1933 box, AFSCA.
33. S. Howard Pennell to David Day, March 15, 1934, AFSCA; Day to Pennell, March 17, 1934, Coal Relief Section 1934 file, General Administration

1934 Coal Relief Section—Subsistence Homesteads box, Subsistence Homesteads Westmoreland, Pa. Correspondence, AFSCA.

34. Day to Elizabeth Marsh, May 29,1934, Coal Relief Section 1934 Subsistence Homesteads file, General Administration 1934 Coal Relief Section box, Westmoreland County, Pa. Correspondence, NARA. Articles of Association of the Westmoreland Homesteaders' Cooperative Association, March 19, 1935, RG 96, file Charters & By-Laws, box 460, NARA.
35. Quakers did not favor formally led, spirited Congregational praying and singing. Instead, "friends" joined quietly until the spirit moved one or another to offer thoughts on a subject.
36. Campbell, "Westmoreland Homesteads," 88. Campbell's master's thesis offers an insider's perspective because he served as Day's assistant in Westmoreland Homesteads' early years.
37. Ibid., 88, 89; "Group Study Clubs," *Homestead Informer*, March 4, 1937; *Homestead Informer*, February 19, 1936, 113.
38. "Suggested Outline for Study Groups," *Homestead Informer*, May 12, 1937, 1. Ironically, even some residents who worked in the cooperative dairy bought their milk from local farmers. It is likely the lingering resentments about dependence on coal-patch company stores, which also charged higher prices for necessary items, informed these transactions.
39. Ruth Schwartz Cowan shows how new technological devices raised expectations for women and resulted, ironically, in an increased workload. We did not find this to be the case in Norvelt, however, in large part because life in the patch community had been so demanding for women and the administration encouraged women to participate in the life of the community. See Cowan, *More Work for Mothers*.
40. Beckwith, "Westmoreland Homesteads," 3–4, copy provided by Earl Saville; Catherine Boisch, interview with Margaret Power, Norvelt, June 30, 2012; "Norvelt Mothers Club Holds 12th Birthday," *Greensburg Daily Tribune*, March 1, 1947; "Norvelt Couple Honored on 50th Anniversary," *Greensburg Daily Tribune*, January 6, 1953.
41. Beckwith, "Westmoreland Homesteads," 8; the *Homestead Informer* announced times and places where the various clubs would meet and notes from the meetings; "Norvelt Women Are Hostesses," *Greensburg Daily Tribune*, January 23, 1950; "Card Party at Norvelt," *Greensburg Daily Tribune*, May 4, 1942; *Homestead Informer*, January 27, 1937, 5.
42. Hoagland and Mulrooney, *Norvelt and Penn-Craft*, 42, and "Norvelt Mother's Club," pamphlet from the personal archives of Virginia Vahaly; Schimizzi and Wolk, *Norvelt*, 58; "Norvelt Mothers Club Holds 12th Birthday," *Greensburg Daily Tribune*, March 1, 1947, 2; *Homestead Informer*, May 24, 1937, 1.
43. *Norvelt Mother's Club* (pamphlet).
44. "Mrs. Plummer Hostess to Norvelt Club," *Greensburg Daily Tribune*, July 19, 1938, 2.
45. *Homestead Informer*, fragment from Earl Saville's personal collection, probably April 1, 1936.
46. Ibid.
47. *Homestead Informer*, January 27, 1937, 8. The Ladies Bible Class met monthly, and membership, apparently, was open only to Protestant women; *Homestead Informer*, May 24,

1937, 8; *Homestead Informer*, July 15, 1937, 4; *Homestead Informer*, May 3, 1937, 5; *Homestead Informer*, June 13, 1937, 5–6; *Homestead Informer*, June 13, 1937, 7; Virginia Vahaly, interview.

48. *Homestead Informer*, February 3, 1937, 2.
49. *Homestead Informer*, February 3, 1937, 8; *Homestead Informer*, April 15, 1937, 3; *Homestead Informer*, June 13, 1937, 7; *Homestead Informer*, July 15, 1937, 4.
50. *Homestead Informer*, May 24, 1937, 8.
51. NARA, "Proposed Plan for Medical Care—Westmoreland Homesteads, Resettlement Administration Project" (n.d.), RG 96, file Gen. Misc., box 459, NARA.
52. Ibid.
53. F. D. Mott to R. C. Williams (FSA Medical Director), October 19, 1937, RG 96, file Gen. Misc., box 459, NARA.
54. "Homesteaders," *Homestead Informer*, June 29, 1937; J. C. Haering to D. M. Warren, March 18, 1937, RG 96, file Gen. Misc., box 459, NARA; "Well Baby Clinic," *Homestead Informer*, February 3, 1937; Alma Walker, "Well Baby Clinic," *Homestead Informer*, February 3, 1937, 2.
55. The Burial Fund, which required a one-time only payment of $1.00, had 145 members in 1940. Campbell, "Westmoreland Homesteads," 82.
56. Irene Dull, "Health Club," *Homestead Informer*, July 15, 1937.
57. F. D. Mott to R. C. Williams (FSA Medical Director), October 19, 1937, RG 96, file Gen. Misc., box 459, box 459, NARA.
58. Ibid.
59. *Homestead Informer*, January 27, 1937; *Homestead Informer*, May 24, 1937, 9; Alma Walker, "Toxoid Treatment Complete," *Homestead Informer*, May 24, 1937, 10; "X Ray Pictures," *Homestead Informer*, June 13, 1937, 6; Alma Walker, "Many Operations," *Homestead Informer*, June 13, 1937, 5.
60. David Warren to Dr. R. C. Williams (Farm Security Administration), September 9, 1937, Medical (Cooperatives), RG 96, Box 459, file Gen Misc., NARA.
61. F. D. Mott, M.D., to Dr. F. J. Pyle, June 28, 1938, RG 96, file Gen. Misc., box 459, NARA.
62. F. D. Mott, M.D., to H. Ellis White, President, Health Club, June 28, 1938, RG 96, file Gen. Misc., box 459, NARA.
63. Campbell, "Westmoreland Homesteads," 82.
64. William Crawford, "Solid Front," *Homestead Informer*, January 27, 1937, 6.
65. Minutes of the Board of Directors Meeting in Special Session, October 14 1937, copy provided by Earl Saville; William Craig, "Change of Cooperative to Westmoreland Community Enterprises, Inc.," *Homestead Informer*, April 1, 1937, 11.
66. The ostensible reason for switching from the WHCA to Westmoreland Enterprises, Inc. was that the federal government had lent substantial money to the WHCA to fund the construction and early operating costs of the Co-op Store, dairy lunch, barber and beauty shop, dairy farm, and poultry farm with a forty-year repayment schedule. The WHCA had only a thirty-year charter from the State of Pennsylvania, and the federal government wanted an entity that would extend for the entire length of the repayment. "Suggested Outline for Study Groups," special supplement to the *Homestead Informer*, May 12, 1937, 1–2.

67. Campbell, "Westmoreland Homesteads," 55.
68. Minutes of Meetings, WHCA, RG 96, file FSA & Predecessor Agencies, box 460, NARA.
69. Ibid.; RG 96, file 590-042 Stores and Markets, Cooperatives, box 459, NARA.
70. "Suggested Outline for Study Groups," 1–2.
71. Ibid; "Five Families Ordered to Move from Homestead at Greensburg," *Titusville Herald*, September 2, 1937, 1, 5.
72. Joseph Haering, "Important: Your General Store," *Homestead Informer*, June 13, 1937, 2.
73. "Extraordinary Store Opening," *Homestead Informer*, June 29, 1937, 3.
74. Joseph Haering, "Barber Shop Secures 100% Rating," *Homestead Informer*, July 15, 1937, 11; Joseph Haering, "General Store," *Homestead Informer*, July 15, 1937, 11.
75. Joseph Haering, "Important Information," *Homestead Informer*, July 15, 1937, 1.
76. Minutes of the Board of Directors Meeting in Special Session, October 14, 1937.
77. "Minutes of the Board of Directors Regular Meeting," *Homestead Informer*, October 4, 1937.
78. Ibid.
79. Report of the Board of Directors, Westmoreland Homesteads Cooperative Association, *Homestead Informer*, October 18, 1936, 6.
80. Franklin D. Roosevelt: "Executive Order 7041—Transferring Subsistence Homesteads Activities to the Resettlement Administration," May 15, 1935. In Gerhard Peters and John T. Woolley, *The American Presidency Project*, http://www.presidency.ucsb.edu/ws/?pid=15059. Also, Memorandum: Report of the Division of Subsistence Homesteads for the National Emergency Council, Charles E. Pynchon, General Manager, Division of Subsistence Homesteads to Rexford Tugwell, Administrator, Resettlement Administration, May 24, 1935. RG 96, file RP183 General, box 17, May 1935–August 1935, NARA.
81. Sherwood Jones, memo, May 29, 1935, RG 96, file 590-0101, box 455, NARA; Beckwith, "Westmoreland Homesteads," 6.
82. Cohen, *Nothing to Fear*, 289, 14; Heilbroner and Singer, *The Economic Transformation*, 281.
83. Campbell, "Westmoreland Homesteads," 40. The cooperative purchased another 140 acres in 1937. Plans (Cooperatives) SH-PA, RG 96, file 590-0201-3, box 457, NARA.
84. Beckwith, "Westmoreland Homestead," 4.
85. M. L. Wilson to Harold Ickes, May 1, 1935, RG 96, file 590-02 Industrial Industry Plans, box 457, NARA; Sherwood Jones to L. L. Baxter (memo), May 29, 1935, RG 9, file Plans 590-0101, box 455, NARA.
86. Campbell, "Westmoreland Homesteads," 56. It used the remaining money to establish the following businesses: the general store, $17,000; the barber and beauty shop, $3,350; the dairy lunch; $4,000; the trade center building; $46,500 for capitalization and $338,875 "as working capital to establish the various enterprises."
87. Hatching Egg Contract Between Westmoreland Homesteads Cooperative Association and Pennsylvania Farms Hatchery, May 8, 1936, RG 96, file 7, box 457, NARA.
88. Ed Cibulas, interview with authors, Norvelt, Pa., November 14, 2011.

89. "Baby Chicks or Peeps," *Homestead Informer*, April 1, 1936, 5.
90. "1,200 Shade Trees Now Being Planted at Homestead Site," *Mount Pleasant Journal*, May 8, 1936, 1.
91. "Homestead Calendar," *Homestead Informer*, March 18, 1936, 235; "About Chickens," *Homestead Informer*, March 4, 1937, 6. These measures are required because "the shell of an egg is primarily composed of lime . . . and contains pores through which the chick must breathe if it is to hatch. Water . . . fills up the pores making it impossible for a chick to live long enough to get out of the shell."
92. W. C. Sterrett, "Narrative Farm Department Report," June 1, 1936, RG 96, Box 455, file Plans 590-0101, NARA.
93. Ibid.; David Warren to Major Walker (memo), October 13, 1937, file 3, Poultry Finance (Budgets, etc.) 1937, box 457, NARA.
94. "Slickers," *Homestead Informer*, April 1, 1937, 11.
95. "Chicken Notes," *Homestead Informer*, June 13, 1937, 4.
96. "Poultry Accounts Receivable," September 27, 1937, RG 96, file 3, Poultry Finance (Budgets, etc.) 1937, box 457, NARA.
97. J. C. Haering, "Poultry Information," *Homestead Informer*, June 24, 1936, 6–7.
98. David Day, *Homestead Informer*, March 18, 1936, as quoted in Campbell, "Westmoreland Homesteads," 54.

Chapter 5

1. Conkin, *Tomorrow a New World*, 116–18.
2. Ibid., 212.
3. Banfield, *Government Project*, 128.
4. The nearby *Greensburg Daily Tribune*, for example, published the following editorial comment before the 1938 election: "Westmoreland county is traditionally Republican. In the middle nineties the Republicans took over all county offices and gave a good account of its stewardship until 1932 inroads began on the part of the New Deal. IT HAS BEEN SORRY DAYS FOR THIS COUNTY SINCE THAT TIME." *Greensburg Daily Tribune*, November 7, 1938, 1.
5. Taylor and Gold, "San Francisco and the General Strike; "Depression Era: 1930s"; Kennedy, *Freedom from Fear*, 288–322; Leuchtenburg, *Roosevelt and the New Deal*, 239–43.
6. "Homesteaders Angry over U.S. Ban on Hunting," *Greensburg Daily Tribune*, November 30, 1938, 1.
7. "County Homesteaders Ask U.S. to Oust Manager," *Greensburg Daily Tribune*, June 8, 1935, 5.
8. Len Solo, interview with Michael Cary, Norvelt, Pa., July 18, 2013.
9. Campbell, "Westmoreland Homesteads," 21–22.
10. W. C. Farson, "New Deal's Subsistence Homestead Plan Fails to Attract New Industries to Westmoreland," *Pittsburgh Post-Gazette*, October 16, 1935, 6.
11. "Homesteaders Will Receive Pay Increases" *Greensburg Daily Tribune*, June 8, 1935, 1.
12. "Credit Hour Liquidation" (memo), Division of Subsistence Homesteads, MA-940, August 28, 1935; Campbell, "Westmoreland Homesteads," RG 96, file 21-22, box 17, National Archives and Records Administration (NARA).
13. "Homesteaders Will Receive Pay Increase," *Greensburg Daily Tribune*, June 11, 1935, 1, 8.

14. Farson, "Plan Fails," 6. The new wage rates were as follows: masons and plasterers, $0.90 an hour; carpenters and plumbers, $0.80 per hour; experienced handymen, $0.65 per hour; and unskilled labor, $0.50 per hour.
15. Farson, "Plan Fails," 6.
16. "News of the Day," *Greensburg Daily Tribune*, June 14, 1935, 4.
17. M. L. Wilson to Professor William V. Dennis, RG 96, file Dea to Dunk, folder Dea to Den, box 9, NARA.
18. Rodney Dutcher, "Behind the Scenes in Washington," *Huntingdon (Pa.) Daily News*, June 11, 1935, 4.
19. David Lawrence, "Homestead Scheme Listed by Lawrence as New Deal Flop," *Daily Courier*, June 22, 1935, 4.
20. "Unhappy Apollo," *Uniontown Morning Herald*, September 13, 1935.
21. "Publishers 2 Districts Meet Here," *Greensburg Daily Tribune*, October 14, 1935, 1.
22. Farson, "Plan Fails," 6.
23. Resettlement Administration internal memo, "Delays in Payroll," October 26, 1935, RG 96, file MA-940, box 17, NARA; "Report on Delays Between Management Division and the Various Service Divisions," Resettlement Administration, August 28, 1935, RG 96, file MA-940, box 17, NARA.
24. David Day, monthly manager's report for October 1936, cited in Campbell, "Westmoreland Homesteads," 83.
25. NARA, J. O. Walker to E. E. Agger, October 9, 1936, RG 96, file 18301 "General," box 20, NARA.
26. *Homestead Informer*, October 14, 1936, 8.
27. "Day Dismissed as Managing Head of Homestead Project," *Mount Pleasant Journal*, 1. Rexford Tugwell, head of the Resettlement Administration, resigned three days earlier.
28. Conkin, *Tomorrow a New World*, 185.
29. Pickett, journal entry, November 21, 1936.
30. Pickett, journal entry, November 28, 1936.
31. Campbell, "Westmoreland Homesteads," 83.
32. Cooperative Notes, *Homestead Informer*, December 9, 1936, 4, 6.
33. Earl Saville, conversation with Mike Carey, Norvelt, Pa., June 4, 2013.
34. David Warren, "Save Your Co-op Sales Slips" and "Education—Adult School," *Homestead Informer*, December 9, 1936, 9.
35. David Warren, "Notice to Cooperative Employees," *Homestead Informer*, December 9, 1936, 11.
36. David Warren, "General Letter to All Homesteaders," *Homestead Informer*, June 29, 1937, 1–2.
37. "Manager Using 'Whip' Charges Homesteaders," *Monessen Daily Independent*, August 31, 1937, 1, and "Soviet Experiment in Westmoreland County Boils Over," *Clearfield Progress*, September 1, 1937, 1, 10.
38. "Homesteaders Rap Managers," *Pittsburgh Press*, September 1, 1937, 4.
39. Ibid.; "Soviet Experiment in Westmoreland County," 1; "Five Families Ordered to 'Move from Homestead at Greensburg," *Titusville Herald*, September 2, 1937, 2.
40. "Homesteaders Protest Eviction of Five Families," *Greensburg Daily Tribune*, September 1, 1937, 1.
41. Ibid.
42. Ibid.
43. "Homesteaders Battle Eviction Orders of Gov't," *Monessen Daily Independent*, September 2, 1937, 1.
44. "We the People of the Homesteads," 6.
45. "Two Homestead Families Evicted," *Connellsville Daily Courier*, September 7, 1937, 8.

46. "Neighbors Shelter Evicted Families," *Indiana (Pa.) Evening Gazette*, September 4, 1937, 2; "Homesteaders Protest Eviction," 1.
47. "Two Homesteads Families Evicted," *Connellsville Daily Courier*, September 7, 1937, 8, and "Homesteader Gives Cause of Eviction," *Titusville Herald*, September 3, 1937, 7.
48. "We the People of the Homesteads," 6.
49. Campbell, "Westmoreland Homesteads," 85; "Homesteads: A Significant Milestone in Human Betterment Grows in the Old Coal Lands of Westmoreland," *Bulletin Index*, November 4, 1937.
50. "U.S. Is Asked to Pay Homestead Taxes, *Monessen Daily Independent*, September 8, 1937, 1.
51. Campbell, "Westmoreland Homesteads," 84.
52. "We the People of the Homesteads," 7.
53. Ibid.
54. Ibid., 6–7.
55. Campbell, "Westmoreland Homesteads," 82–83.
56. Ibid., 84.
57. Ibid., 86.
58. Ibid., 85.
59. "Spending at Norvelt Needs Probing Homesteader Says," *Greensburg Daily Tribune*, December 1, 1938, 10.
60. Ibid.
61. "David Warren Quits as Westmoreland Homesteads Head," *Connellsville Daily Courier*, February 11, 1938, 6.
62. Campbell, "Westmoreland Homesteads," 87.
63. Ibid., 85–86.
64. "Homesteaders Angry over U.S. Ban on Hunting."
65. "Spending at Norvelt Needs Probing Homesteader Says," *Greensburg Daily Tribune*, December 1, 1938, 10.
66. Major John G. Walker, Director, Resettlement Division, Farm Security Administration, to Mr. Frank Klosky, May 29, 1940, quoted in "Homesteads Head Reports on Relief Situation," *Greensburg Daily Tribune*, September 7, 1940, 5.
67. Letter to the editor, *Greensburg Daily Tribune*, September 4, 1940, quoted in "Homesteads Head Reports on Relief Situation," *Greensburg Daily Tribune*, September 87, 1940, 5.
68. "Aver Norvelt Group Afoul of Hatch Act," *Greensburg Daily Tribune*, November 20, 1940, 1, 11.
69. "Homesteads Head Reports on Relief Situation," *Greensburg Daily Tribune*, September 7, 1940, 5.
70. Major John G. Walker to Mr. Frank Klosky.
71. Earl Saville, Lois Weyandt, Virginia Vahaly, and Betty Sue Mondock are among current and former Norvelt residents who remember much about growing up in Norvelt in the 1930s and 1940s, but nothing about the Protective Association.
72. Chauncey White worked at a service station in Greensburg, Pennsylvania, a job he kept until his retirement. Helen White did not work outside the home. U.S. Bureau of the Census, Census 1940, Statistical Abstract; Sarah Brown, phone interview with Margaret Power, Denver, Colorado, January 1, 2012.
73. E. B. Johnson to John P. Davis, March 30, 1935, RG 96, file Croo thru Day, box 8, NARA.
74. John P. Davis to E. B. Johnson, April 4, 1935, RG 96, file Croo thru Day, box 8, NARA.
75. General Manager, Division of Subsistence Homesteads, to John P. Davis, April 6, 1933, RG 96, file Croo thru Day, box 8, NARA.
76. David Day, quoted in "Homestead Management," *Greensburg Daily*

Tribune, 1, 8; David Day, "To All Homesteaders," letter to Westmoreland Homestead selected homesteaders, March 20, 1935. Personal copy of Carol Davis.

77. Campbell, "Westmoreland Homesteads," 49.
78. Brown, interview; "Norvelt's First Black Settler Leaves Behind Quite a Legacy," *Greensburg Tribune Review*, November 15, 1988, A1.
79. Day, "To All Homesteaders."
80. Ibid.
81. *Homestead Informer*, January 27, 1937, 1, 2, 12; *Homestead Informer*, February 18, 1937, 2; Sarah Brown, interview.
82. Brown, interview.
83. "Norvelt's First Black Settler."
84. Earl Saville, interview with Margaret Power, December 27, 2009, Norvelt.
85. Sarah Brown, interview.
86. Carol Davis, interview with authors.

Chapter 6

1. "President's Wife Conducts Party on Homesteads Tour," *Greensburg Daily Tribune*, May 21, 1937.
2. "President's Wife." Arthurdale, and by extension the entire New Deal, generated a significant amount of protest. As Blanche Wiesen Cook points out, "For some, the New Deal had now become a 'communist plot,' led by ER and epitomized by Arthurdale." Cook, *Eleanor Roosevelt*, vol. 2, 143.
3. Elinor Morgenthau had previously visited Arthurdale with ER. Eleanor Roosevelt, *This I Remember*, 138; "President's Wife"; "Wife of President Greeted by Throng on Homestead Trip," *Mount Pleasant Journal*, May 21, 1937; "Mrs. Roosevelt Visits Westmoreland," *Homestead Informer*, May 24, 1937.
4. "President's Wife"; "Mrs. Roosevelt Visits Westmoreland."
5. "President's Wife"; "Mrs. Roosevelt Visits Westmoreland."
6. Ruth Love, "Reflections of a Homesteader," *Greensburg Tribune-Review*, October 17, 1985.
7. Ibid.
8. "Mrs. Roosevelt Visits Westmoreland."
9. Ibid.
10. "Wife of President Greeted."
11. "President's Wife."
12. "Mrs. Roosevelt Visits Westmoreland."
13. "Reflections of a Homesteader."
14. "President's Wife."
15. Eleanor Roosevelt, My Day, May 24, 1937.
16. Al Haering, "Naming the Homesteads," *Homestead Informer*, April 29, 1936, 10; *Homestead Informer*, May 27, 1936, 9; *Homestead Informer*, June 10, 1936, 5; *Homestead Informer*, June 24, 1936, 11.
17. Schimizzi, "Eleanor Roosevelt," 6; *Homestead Informer*, July 8, 1936, 9; "Garment Factory Workers Strike Against Themselves," *Pittsburgh Press*, January 10, 1938.
18. H. Ellis White, "The Flag," *Homestead Informer*, July 15, 1937, 7–8.
19. Ibid., 8.
20. Circular No. 1, *General Information Concerning the Purposes and Policies of the Division of Subsistence Homesteads*, United States Department of the Interior, Division of Subsistence Homesteads, November 15, 1933, 8, American Friends Service Committee Archives (AFSCA).
21. Axel H. Oxholm to Frank Fritts and Clarence E. Pickett, April 6, 1934, RG 96, file 590-0201 Plans (Cooperatives), box 457, NARA; Clarence Pickett to

Philip M. Glick, April 18, 1934, RG 96, file 590-02 Industrial (Industrial) SH-PA-3, box 457, NARA; Campbell, "Westmoreland Homesteads," 19.

22. Axel H. Oxholm to Frank Fritts and Clarence E. Pickett, April 6, 1934.
23. The National Archives contains correspondence regarding at least nine other ventures with which David Day entered negotiations. But none had sufficient capital or viable plans attractive enough to win approval from DSH managers in Washington. Record Group 96 in NARA contains much correspondence regarding such proposals. See letters between Homer Morris and Charles A. Carpenter, August–October 1934, file 590-0221—Electrical Appliances (Cooperatives), box 457, regarding a proposal for a factory to build radios; correspondence between David Day and Leroy Peterson concerning a proposal for a needle factory, file 590-02 Industrial (Industrial), box 457; proposals regarding a steel company in that same folder; correspondence between David Day and Homer Morris, file 590-0215 Stone (Mining and Quarrying—Industrial—Coops) SH-PA-3, box 457; regarding a concrete manufacturing plant, and similar proposals in boxes 457, 458, and 459.
24. Leroy Peterson to David Day and David Warren to Major J. O. Walker, RG 96, file Garment Factories, FSA & Predecessor Agencies, 1935–1940, box 458, NARA.
25. Memorandum for Mr. R. W. Hudgens, file AD-SI-PA-3-300, Westmoreland Homesteads 1940–1941, box 458, NARA.
26. Ibid.
27. "U.S. Pants Factory Closed by Strike," *Joplin (Mo.) Globe*, October 8, 1938.
28. James T. Go to Mr. Baldwin, February 12, 1941, RG 96, file AD-SI-PA-3-300, Westmoreland Homesteads 1940–1941, folder Farm Security Administration & Predecessor Agencies, Project Records 1935–1940, box 455,Pennsylvania PA-3, NARA.
29. Ibid.
30. "Plant Burns at Norvelt," *Uniontown Evening Standard*, March 16, 1966.
31. Ibid.; James T. Go to Mr. Baldwin, February 12, 1941.
32. "Plant Burns at Norvelt." Klee Oppenheimer, the president of Washington Manufacturing Company, was simultaneously the treasurer of the Amco Athletic Apparel Corporation.
33. "25 Contracts Let on Pants for Army," *New York Times*, October 11, 1940. The army contracted with twenty-five different manufacturers to produce 361,232 pairs of trousers.
34. "Norvelt to Make Athletic Uniforms," *Connellsville Daily Courier*, February 21, 1948.
35. Klee Oppenheimer to C. B. Bryan, August 7, 1939, RG 96, file Garment Factories, box 458, NARA.
36. "Homesteads Factory Strike Situation Unchanged," *Greensburg Daily Tribune*, October 8, 1938.
37. In a checkoff system, the employer deducted a portion of the workers' wages to pay union dues or initiation fees, which guaranteed the union received money.
38. "Homesteads Factory Strike Situation Unchanged." According to press reports from the time, management fired Mr. Honse because he "let people into the factory at night."
39. Ibid.
40. Ibid.
41. "Plan Session over Strike," *Greensburg Daily Tribune*, November 10, 1938.

42. Strikers Win Fight at Government Plant," *Reading Eagle*, November 16, 1938.
43. "Strikers at Norvelt Win," *Greensburg Daily Tribune*, November 15, 1938. We have not been able to determine how or if his case was settled.
44. The sections of the 1940 Census that cover Norvelt can be found at http://1940census.archives.gov/.
45. "Clothing Workers Union Marks Jubilee," *Connellsville Daily Courier*, June 16, 1964.
46. "Norvelt Workers Favor Union Shop," *Connellsville Daily Courier*, May 18, 1948.
47. "Norvelt to Make Athletic Uniforms."
48. Frank L. Kluckhohn, "Subsistence Homestead Idea Spreading," *New York Times*, December 19, 1934.
49. Lawson, *City Bountiful*, xv.
50. Ibid. 148.
51. Ibid., 145; "State to Increase Gardens for Needy," *New York Times*, April 9, 1934. The state estimated that in 1933 the gardens cost $217,000 but produced $1,100,864 worth of food—a significant savings over providing food relief through market mechanisms.
52. Lowitt and Beasley, *One Third of a Nation*, 14, 17.
53. Shortly after the community's seventy-fifth anniversary, Norvelt began to connect the homes to a common sewer system.
54. Paul Campbell, "I Kept the Pig in the Parlor," *Homestead Informer*, March 4, 1937, 43.
55. Valoria Wolk, interview with authors, Norvelt, Pa., November 11, 2011.
56. Campbell, "Westmoreland Homesteads," 41.
57. W. L. Funkhouser, Garden Notes, *Homestead Informer*, March 4, 1937, April 15, 1937, May 3, 1937, June 29, 1937.
58. Harding, "The Record of the Subsistence Homesteads,"102.
59. Loomis, "Rebuilding American Community Life," 314.
60. Beckwith, "Westmoreland Homesteads," 9.
61. Campbell, "Westmoreland Homesteads," 69.
62. Carol Davis, interview with authors, Norvelt, Pa., November 11, 2011; Ed Cibulas, interview with authors, Greensburg, Pa., November 14, 2011; Jane Schlingman Thomas, interview with authors, Greensburg, Pa., November 14, 2011. This seems curious in light of the strong emphasis on "victory gardens" during World War II, but it also provides strong testimony to the rigors that substantial gardening entailed.
63. Campbell, "Westmoreland Homesteads," 42.
64. Ibid., 46.
65. Millard Milburn Rice, "Footnote on Arthurdale," *Harper's Magazine*, March 1940, 414.
66. Carol Davis recalled that neighbors sometimes gardened complementarily, with one family growing a lot of one fruit or vegetable and sharing it with a neighbor who in turn shared with them. She recalls that her neighbors had a lot of strawberries that often reached her family's table. Davis, interview.
67. "Norvelt Offered to Homesteaders for $542,314," *Connellsville Daily Courier*, June 16, 1944, 5; "Here Goes Another One," *Monessen Daily Independent*, July 5, 1944; "U.S. Selling Norbelt [*sic*] Dairy Project, New Deal 'Flop' Loses 1 1/2 Million," *Pittsburgh Sun-Telegraph*, July 18, 1944, 16; "Loss in Sale

of Homesteads," *Pittsburgh Sun-Telegraph*, August 8, 1944, 15.

68. "Taxpayers Lose Two Million by Experiment at Norvelt," *Connellsville Daily Courier*, December 12, 1945, 10.
69. "Housing: Utopia in Westmoreland," *Bulletin Index*, December 1945.
70. Resettlement Administration (FSA), Subsistence Homesteads, Westmoreland Homestead, PA file, RG 96, NARA.
71. "Here Goes Another One," *Monessen Daily Independent*, July 5, 1944.
72. "Norvelt Tenants Have Chance to Buy Homes," *Greensburg Daily Tribune*, September 10, 1943, 11.
73. "Norvelt Offered to Homesteaders for $542,314."
74. "Norvelt Residents File to Incorporate, Norvelt Committee to Conduct Sale of 251 Buildings," *Connellsville Daily Courier*, August 28, 1944, 1. The members were J. Watson Sisley, president; Lois Stouffer, secretary; Herbert Smith, treasurer and president of the Norvelt Activities Council, Mrs. Byers, Clarence Blackburn, Victor King, and William Baker.
75. J. Watson Sisley to All Homestead Residents, Westmoreland Homesteads, PA file, RG 96, NARA.
76. "Homesteaders Want to Deal with Government," *Connellsville Daily Courier*, March 5, 1945, 2.
77. The new board consisted of Victor King, president; Andrew Evancho, secretary; James H. Reaney, treasurer; Frank Klosky; and Fred Eicholtz. "Homesteaders to Buy Property," *Connellsville Daily Courier*, December 6, 1945, 1.
78. "Here Goes Another One"; "Norvelt Offered to Homesteaders for $542,314."
79. "Norvelt Residents Purchase Homes," *Greensburg Daily Tribune*, January 22, 1946, 1.
80. "Homesteaders to Buy Property."

Chapter 7

1. Alderfer, *The Ephrata Commune*; Reiber, *Old Economy Village*. Ephrata did not accept families, but Old Economy combined religious and economic enterprise successfully, and accommodated families.
2. Crawford, *Building the Workingman's Paradise*, 2, 3, 43.
3. Ibid., 43. Historians of both Vandergrift and Gary corroborate Crawford's interpretation of this interim period in company town history. Mosher, *Capital's Utopia*, 7; O'Hara, *Gary*, 7.
4. Howard first published his work in 1898 as *Tomorrow: A Peaceful Path to Real Reform*. But it gained classic status in its later edition. Howard, *Garden Cities of To-Morrow*.
5. Howard, *Garden Cities of To-Morrow*, 52, 53.
6. Bamberg, *Chatham Village*, 30. The two garden cities were Letchworth and Welwyn, England.
7. Ibid., 34.
8. Ibid., 60–65.
9. Ibid., 12, 13; Gillette, *Civitas by Design*, 7.
10. Reps, *The Making of Urban American*, 414, 420. Reps sees coal-patch communities in Pennsylvania and West Virginia as especially crude economic entities of exploitation. Fishback, *Soft Coal, Hard Choices*. Fishback argues that miners' frequent moves from one patch to another prevented mining companies from exploiting workers with low wages and poor living conditions. James Allen argues that

while many companies exploited their worker-residents, "owners of many company towns actually had the interests of their employees at heart" when operating company stores and houses. Allen, *The Company Town*, x.

11. John Garner focused both his book-length work and a 1971 article about company towns on those that offered models for others to emulate, rather than upon those that exploited their workforce. Garner, "Leclaire, Illinois." See also Spann, *Hopedale*. Even Hardy Green's chapter on "Exploitation-ville" in his work on company towns focuses more on workplace struggles and unionization battles in coal towns than on life in the patches themselves. Green, *The Company Town*, 3; Garner, *The Model Company Town*; Alanen, "Documenting." Karen Bescherer Metheny does focus on a Pennsylvania coal-patch company town in her work. She offers an innovative study, but must extrapolate a great deal from meager sources and archeological work that generated only a few clues as to mining families' lives. Metheny, *From the Miners' Doublehouse*.
12. Green, *The Company Town*, 3; Garner, *The Model Company Town*, 1.
13. Carter and Cromley, *Invitation to Vernacular Architecture*
14. Bob Stearns, "Norvelt . . . Eleanor Would Be Proud," *Pittsburgh Press*, October 28, 1979.
15. Mulrooney, *A Legacy of Coal*, 23; DiCiccio, *Coal and Coke in Pennsylvania*. 90.
16. Green, *The Company Town*; see especially chap. 3.
17. Stearns, "Norvelt . . . Eleanor Would Be Proud."
18. Green, *The Company Town*, 64.
19. Ed Cibulas, interview with authors, Greensburg, Pa., November 14, 2011.
20. Williams, *Coal Dust in Their Blood*, 55–57. Williams notes that houses began to include kitchen sinks and even furnaces as the century progressed, but observed that "the rooms were small, the construction was cheap, the walls were generally thin and the insulation was poor."
21. Lauck, "The Bituminous Coal Miner."
22. Cibulas, interview.
23. Campbell, "Westmoreland Homesteads," 39–41.
24. Michael Haines reports that miners' wives in eastern Pennsylvania *averaged* eight births in 1900. Haines, "Fertility, Marriage, and Occupation," as cited in Mintz and Kellogg, *Domestic Revolutions*, 103.
25. Bartoletti, *Growing Up in Coal Country*, 74.
26. "We the People of the Homesteads," 6.
27. Fishback, *Soft Coal, Hard Choices*, 153.
28. Dolkart, *The Row House Reborn*, 87–91.
29. Bamberg, *Chatham Village*, 47–52.
30. Angelique Bamberg argues that "[i]n the 1930s, every architect and planner with access to professional publications knew of its existence through detailed articles, plans, and photographs. Its large-scale planning, grouped housing, car-free courtyards, and greenbelt supplied the very vocabulary of residential site design during the Great Depression." Bamberg, *Chatham Village*, 142.
31. *Homestead Houses*.
32. W. H. Johnson, "Farms Held Lacking in Self-Sufficiency, Subsistence Homesteads Seen in Need of 'Rugged Individualism' if They Are to Succeed," *New York Times*, November 19, 1933.
33. Jackson, *Crabgrass Frontier*, 83.
34. The house style numbers were as follows: 402 (two bedrooms), 501 (three

bedrooms), 502R (three bedrooms plus a utility room), 503R (three bedrooms, no utility room), and 601 (four bedrooms plus a utility room).

35. *Homestead Houses*, 3; McAlester and McAlester, *A Field Guide to American Houses*, 322; and Gottfried and Jennings, *American Vernacular Architecture*, 137–58.
36. The coal-patch house measurements come from drawings in Mulrooney, *A Legacy of Coal*, 77, and Standard 8 Room Double Tenement House Patch/Work Voices, Coal & Coke Heritage Project, Penn State Fayette Campus. Karen Bescherer Metheny determined that the typical unit in Helvetia, Pennsylvania was larger, at approximately 900 square feet. Metheny, *From the Miners' Doublehouse*, 182.
37. Alison Hoagland and Margaret Mulrooney measure the Norvelt houses to be between 750 and 835 square feet of interior space. *Norvelt and Penn-Craft, Pennsylvania*, 29–30.
38. *Homestead Houses*, 11.
39. Ibid.
40. Ibid.
41. Ibid.
42. The figure of fifty-nine clear days comes from the National Climatic Data Center in Asheville, North Carolina. Brett Yasko published a slightly humorous challenge to that figure in the *Pittsburgh Post-Gazette* that he based upon counting the days during which the sun shone through for at least part of the day in 2006. But even he recorded only 145 days of at least partial sunshine, leaving 217 days of cloudiness—rendering the region cloudy 60 percent of the time. "The Real Number of Sunny Days in Pittsburgh Is 145, Not 59," *Pittsburgh Post-Gazette*, January 7, 2007.
43. Nye, *Electrifying America*, 287–89, 303.
44. Campbell, "Westmoreland Homesteads," 40.
45. Bryson, *At Home*, 114–15.
46. Freedman, quoted in Anneli Rufus, "Our Eating Habits Are Being Undermined by Modern Lifestyles and Corporate Conniving, but Is That Necessarily Bad?," *Pittsburgh Post-Gazette*, October 16, 2011.
47. Nye, *Electrifying America*, 304.
48. Glassie, *Folk Housing in Middle Virginia*, 190–92.
49. Bamberg, *Chatham Village*, 48–49, 76–77.
50. Stearns, "Norvelt . . . Eleanor Would Be Proud."
51. Cook, *Eleanor Roosevelt*, vol. 2, 135. Harold Ickes recorded in his diary that Franklin Roosevelt agreed that spending on such things as bathrooms was extravagant, but he deferred to Eleanor on the issue. See also Schlesinger, *The Coming of the New Deal*, 366.
52. Hoagland, "Introducing the Bathroom," 15.
53. Ibid., 16, 28–30.
54. Dolkart, *The Row House Reborn*, 87–91.
55. Quoted in Steeley, "Westmoreland Homesteads," 8.
56. U.S. Coal Mines Administration, *A Medical Survey*, 38.

Chapter 8

1. "Norvelters" refers to those whose families were among the original homesteaders and currently inhabit the community as well as those who have moved away.

2. Area newspapers publicized the celebration. See "New Deal's Norvelt Homestead Offered Help, Hope to Families," *Pittsburgh Tribune-Review*, June 14, 2009; "Old Neighbors to Gather for Norvelt Reunion," *Pittsburgh Tribune-Review*, July 13, 2009; "Norvelt 75th Anniversary Plan Moving Along," *Daily Courier*, July 13, 2009.
3. Unless otherwise noted, this section is based on notes taken by Margaret Power during the weekend.
4. "Norvelt Celebrates 75 Years," *Mount Pleasant Journal*, August 6, 2009, 14. Mount Pleasant is a borough of about five thousand residents roughly five miles from Norvelt; many teenagers from Norvelt attend high school in Mount Pleasant.
5. Mary K. Bogot, "Norvelt's 75th Anniversary," *My Family Journals*, August 7, 2009, http://myfamilyjournals.blogspot.com/2009/08/norvelts-75th-anniversary.html, accessed June 3, 2012.
6. A committee of local residents began meeting to plan the weekend celebration in 2008. Other committee members included Carol Davis, Earl Saville, Lois Weyandt, Tracey Surma, Virginia (Boytim) Vahaly and her sister Betty Mondock, Pete Maida, Ed Ungvarsk, Valeria "Vee" Wolk and her daughters Sandy Wolk Schimizzi and Anita Wolk Foriska, Gerry and Virginia Speer, Ed Bilik, Megan Bilik-Defazio, District Judge Roger Eckels, and Joe Kennedy, all of whose respective parents were original homesteaders, and coauthor Michael Cary.
7. John P. Murtha, "In Honor of Homesteading and the 75th Anniversary of Norvelt," *Congressional Record*, July 15, 2009, E1792.
8. Cary, *75 Years of Homesteading*, 54.
9. Ibid., 55.
10. Lee Speer, interview with Margaret Power, Norvelt, November 9, 2011.
11. For two excellent studies of public perceptions and misperceptions of who constitutes the "undeserving poor," see Katz, *The Undeserving Poor*, and Gilens, *Why Americans Hate Welfare*, especially chap. 3.
12. U.S. Census Bureau, Census 2010, Profile of General Population and Housing Characteristics. The numbers do not add up because some people identify themselves as Latino or Asian or as belonging to two or more races. The figures reflect only the population of Norvelt, not the combined numbers for Calumet and Norvelt, which is what earlier censuses used.
13. However, not everyone living in Norvelt is heterosexual. According to one long-time resident of Norvelt, a lesbian lives in the community. Anonymous, interview with Margaret Power, Norvelt, Pa., November 13, 2011.
14. U.S. Census Bureau, "Community Facts."
15. According to the 2010 Census, the U.S. population was 72.4 percent white, 12.6 percent Black or African American, 0.9 percent American Indian and Alaska Native, 4.8 percent Asian, 0.2 percent Native Hawaiian and Other Pacific Islander, 6.2 percent Some Other Race, 2.9 percent Two or More Races, and 16.3 percent Hispanic or Latino. U.S. Bureau of the Census, State and County Quick Facts.
16. The median household income for Calumet/Norvelt in 2009 was $49,047; the median household income for Pennsylvania that year was $49,520. The census data on Calumet and Norvelt were combined until 2010. For more information

on Calumet, see "Calumet-Norvelt, Pennsylvania," http://www.city-data.com/city/Calumet-Norvelt-Pennsylvania.html.

17. "New Numbers of Just How Many Americans Are Living in Poverty."
18. Lois Weyandt, phone interview with Margaret Power, Greensburg, Pa., July 28, 2012.
19. Catherine Bosich, phone interview with Margaret Power, Norvelt, Pa., June 30, 2012.
20. Jim Schmidt, interview with Margaret Power, Norvelt, Pa., November 9, 2011.
21. Mary Ann Seminary, phone interview with Margaret Power, Greensburg, Pa., June 25, 2009.
22. Alex Richards, "Census Data Show Rise in College Degrees, but Also in Racial Gaps in Education," *Chronicle of Higher Education*, January 23, 2011.
23. Weyandt, interview.
24. We adapt Miranda Joseph's discussion of national formation to describe how people in Norvelt construct their past. Joseph, *Against the Romance of Community*, xx. Joseph describes how "national formations" draw on stories to "restore some imagined historical community as timeless."
25. Weyandt, interview.
26. Hiller could not remember the exact date.
27. Doris Hiller, interview with Margaret Power, Greensburg, Pa., January 15, 2009.
28. Earl Saville, interview with Margaret Power, Norvelt, Pa., December 27, 2009.
29. Saville, interview.
30. Hiller, interview.
31. Ibid.
32. Weyandt, interview.
33. Jimmy Hontz, interview with Margaret Power, Norvelt, Pa., July 24, 2009.
34. Lee Speer, "Letter to Dear Friends and Neighbors," in Cary, *75 Years of Homesteading*.
35. Mike Reese, interview with Margaret Power, Norvelt, Pa., November 9, 2011.
36. General Election, November 2008, Westmoreland County, Westmoreland County Courthouse, Records Management.
37. Saville, interview.
38. These policies did not go unchallenged. Friedrich Hayek, the free market economist, launched a frontal attack on state intervention in the economy in *Road to Serfdom* in 1946. See Durham and Power, "Transnational Conservatism."
39. Poor white people generally received more advantages than did blacks from the New Deal programs. As Adolph Reed writes, "In reality, the New Deal was both racially discriminatory and a boon to many black Americans. Blacks benefited relatively less than whites from many social policy initiatives." Reed, "Race and the New Deal Coalition."
40. López, *Dog Whistle Politics*, 22.
41. Thomas and Mary Edsall note that this support was not limited to the North nor to immigrant populations; it was very strong among white southerners. "Although hostile to blacks, poor southern whites in the pre–civil rights period were among the nation's most liberal constituencies on non-racial economic issues, supportive of government intervention on behalf of full employment, improved education, and low-cost medical care. Only Jews and blacks were more left than they." Edsall and Edsall, *Chain Reaction*, 41.
42. One stark example of this is that Republican senator and presidential

candidate Barry Goldwater refused to sign the 1964 Civil Rights Act, which President Lyndon Baines Johnson had pushed through Congress.

43. McAdam and Kloos, *Deeply Divided*, 109–20; Lowndes, *From the New Deal to the New Right*, 106–39.
44. Edsall and Edsall, *Chain Reaction*, 4.
45. This is the title of chapter 4 of Moynihan, *The Negro Family*, 29. See also, 9.
46. Ibid., 12, 25, 27.
47. Gilens makes clear that the focus on poor whites did not reflect the actual state of poverty in which millions of blacks lived. Rather, it corresponded to the fact that "black poverty was ignored by white society throughout most of our history." Gilens, "How the Poor Became Black," 101.
48. Ibid., 102. AFDC, which began in 1935, was part of the larger body of Social Security legislation passed during the Roosevelt administration. See Kessler-Harris, *In Pursuit of Equality*, 66.
49. Gilens, 103, 113; Alesina, Glaeser, and Sacerdote reach the same conclusion in their study of American resistance to economic policies that redistribute wealth and income to the poor. "Why Doesn't the United States Have a European-Style Welfare State?," 4.
50. "'Welfare Queen' Becomes Issue in Reagan Campaign," *New York Times*, February 28, 1976. Kaaryn Gustafson conducted an investigation to determine if there really was a "welfare queen." She concluded that there were, in fact, three women who gamed the welfare system. Reagan "merged the identities of all three and exaggerated the abuses." Gustafson noted, "It's totally false that these women typified welfare recipients." John Blake, "Return of the 'Welfare Queen,'" *CNN*, January 23, 2012, http://www.cnn.com/2012/01/23/politics/weflare-queen/index.html, accessed June 8, 2012.
51. Gilliam, "The 'Welfare Queen' Experiment," 2.
52. Hiller, interview.
53. See, for example, Anderson, *Crime and the Politics*; Peffley, Shields, and Williams, "The Intersection of Race."
54. Fowler, "Obama: No Surprise."
55. Elaine Gowaty, interview with Margaret Power, Greensburg, Pa., March 11, 2011.
56. Ibid.
57. 2008 Primary Election, Elections Information, Pennsylvania Department of State, http://www.electionreturns.state.pa.us/Default.aspx?EID=17&ESTID=1&CID=2354&OID=0&CDID=0&PID=0&DISTID=0&IsSpecial=0#President of the United States, accessed July 27, 2015.
58. Race was not the only issue at play. Some Democrats preferred Hillary Clinton because they wanted a woman president.
59. John Boyle, interview with Margaret Power, Latrobe, Pa., March 10, 2011.
60. 2008 Primary Election, Elections Information.
61. Boyle, interview.
62. He searched for the use of the word "nigger."
63. Stephens-Davidowitz, "The Effects of Racial Animus," 26.
64. Ibid., 27.
65. Ibid., 38.
66. Ibid., 27.
67. For a study of the impact that Fox News has had on electoral outcomes, see DellaVigna and Kaplan, "The Fox News Effect."
68. Robert G. Kaiser, "Money, Family Name Shaped Scaife," *Washington Post*, May 3, 1999; Michael Joseph

Gross, "A Vast Right-Wing Hypocrisy," *Vanity Fair*, February 2008.

69. Much of the information on Mellon's financial commitments to his publishing industry emerged during the sensational divorce proceedings between him and his wife, "Ritchie" Mellon. Dennis B. Roddy, "Millions up for Grab in Scaife Divorce Fight," *Pittsburgh Post-Gazette*, March 17, 2012.
70. Jeff Simmons, phone interview with Margaret Power, Greensburg, Pa., June 14, 2012. Lisa Herm of the *Pittsburgh Post-Gazette* quoted much lower figures for the *Greensburg Tribune-Review*. According to her, the Sunday circulation is eighty-seven thousand and the daily figure is fifty-three thousand. Lisa Herm, phone interview with Margaret Power, Pittsburgh, June 14, 2012.
71. Bill Cotter, phone interview with Margaret Power, Greensburg, Pa., June 20, 2012.
72. Simmons, interview.
73. The Institute for Policy Studies' online publication *Right Web* lists the various right-wing institutions, foundations, causes, and individuals that Richard Mellon Scaife has supported. See "Mellon Scaife, Richard," http://rightweb.irc-online.org/profile/Scaife_Richard_Mellon.
74. Arthur Boyle, interview with Margaret Power, Laughlington, Pa., March 13, 2011.
75. *Tribune-Review*, November 5, 2008.
76. Rich Cholodofsky, "GOP Chair Elaine Gowaty Wants to Build on Successes," *Tribune-Review*, May 17, 2010.
77. Rich Cholodofsky, "GOP Aims for November Win in Westmoreland," *Tribune-Review*, May 18, 2011.
78. The five offices are treasurer, controller, register of wills, recorder of deeds, and sheriff. Rich Cholodofsky, "'Good Candidates,' Voter Anger Lead to Republican Sweep," *Tribune-Review*, November 10, 2011.
79. Mike Reese, interview with Margaret Power.
80. Cholodofsky, "'Good Candidates.'"
81. López, *Dog Whistle Politics*, 1.

Conclusion

1. "We the People of the Homesteads."
2. Loomis, "Rebuilding American Community Life," 318.
3. Rice, "Footnote on Arthurdale," 419.
4. Lord and Johnson, *A Place on Earth*, 180–84.
5. Leuchtenburg, *Roosevelt and the New Deal*, 135–36.
6. Cahill, "Fertilizing the Weeds," 133.
7. Carriker, *Urban Farming in the West*, 160.
8. Maloney, *Back to the Land*, 4.
9. Carriker, *Urban Farming in the West*, 3–4.
10. Cahill, "Fertilizing the Weeds," 169.
11. Conkin, *Tomorrow a New World*, 331.
12. Pickett, *For More than Bread*, 63.
13. Cook, *Eleanor Roosevelt*, vol. 2, 152. She also notes that "one issue that haunted ER" regarding Arthurdale was "the subject of race."
14. Ginny Kopas, "Norvelt: A '30s Experiment in Socialism," *Pittsburgh Post-Gazette*, September 11, 2002.
15. Beckwith, "Westmoreland Homesteads."

BIBLIOGRAPHY

Newspapers, Periodicals, Encyclopedias

Connellsville Daily Courier, 1885–1948.
Daily Courier, 1924–48, 2002, 2009.
Encyclopedia of Alabama.
Greensburg Tribune Review, 1934–40.
Mount Pleasant Journal, 2002, 2009.
New York Times, 1892–1947, 1976.
Pennsylvania in Review, 1937.
Pittsburgh Post-Gazette, 1935, 2007, 2011.
Pittsburgh Press, 1931–32.
Pittsburgh Tribune Review, 2008, 2009.
Wellsboro (Pa.) Gazette, 1911.

Archival Sources

Beckwith, Ward. "Westmoreland Homesteads After Five Years of Growth." November 20, 1940. From the private collection of Edward M. Bilik, Norvelt, Pennsylvania.

Farm Security Administration / Office of War Information Black-and-White Negatives, Library of Congress.

Hopkins Papers. Franklin Delano Roosevelt Library, Hyde Park, N.Y. http://newdeal.feri.org/hopkins/hop10.htm. Accessed June 27, 2011.

"Patch/Work Voices." Coal & Coke Heritage Project, Pennsylvania State University, Fayette, Fayette, Pa.

Pickett, Clarence E. "CEP's Journal, Nov. 1933 to Dec 1935." Box 30, Clarence Pickett's Journal, 1912–1936 (Jan.–June), Clarence Pickett Papers, American Friends Service Center Archives, Philadelphia, Pa.

———. Clarence Pickett Papers. American Friends Service Committee Archives, Philadelphia, Pa.

"A Program for the Redistribution of Unemployed Coal Miners." Coal Relief Sections, Subsistence Homesteads, General 1933 file, General Administration 1933 Coal Relief Section (Projects—Cambria & Clearfield Counties, PA) to (Projects—Lincoln County, WV) box, American Friends Service Committee Archives (AFSCA).*Reports of the Immigration Commission*. 41 vols. Washington, D.C.: Government Printing Office, 1911. Reprint, New York: Arno Press, 1970.

M. L. Wilson Papers, 1913–1970. Montana State University Library, Bozeman, Mon.

Secondary Sources

Abbott, Grace. "Improvement in Rural Public Relief: The Lesson of the Coal-Mining Communities." *Social Service Review* 6, no. 2 (1932): 183–222.

Alanen, Arnold R. "Documenting the Physical and Social Characteristics of Mining and Resource-Based Communities." *Bulletin of the Association for Preservation Technology* 11, no. 4 (1979): 49–68.

Alderfer, E. G. *The Ephrata Commune: An Early American Counterculture*. Pittsburgh: University of Pittsburgh Press, 1985.

Alesina, Alberto, Edward Glaeser, and Bruce Sacerdote. "Why Doesn't the United States Have a European-Style Welfare System?" Working Paper 8524, National Bureau of Economic Research, October 2001.

Allen, Frederick Lewis. *Since Yesterday: The 1930s in America, September 3, 1929–September 3, 1939*. New York: Harper and Row, 1939.

Allen, James B. *The Company Town in the American West*. Norman: University of Oklahoma Press, 1966.

Allen, Leslie Herbert. *Industrial Housing Problems*. Boston: Aberthaw Construction Co., 1917.

Allitt, Patrick. *The Conservatives: Ideas and Personalities Throughout American History*. New Haven: Yale University Press, 2009.

Alter, Jonathon. *The Defining Moment: FDR's Hundred Days and the Triumph of Hope*. New York: Simon and Schuster, 2006.

Anderson, David C. *Crime and the Politics of Justice: How the Willie Horton Story Changed America*. New York: Random House, 1995.

Arnold, Joseph L. *The New Deal in the Suburbs: A History of the Greenbelt Town Program, 1933–1954*. Columbus: Ohio State University Press, 1971.

Badger, Anthony J. *FDR: The First Hundred Days*. New York: Hill and Wang, 2008.

———. *The New Deal: The Depression Years, 1933–1940*. Chicago: Ivan R. Dee, 1989.

Baker, Horace Forbes, John L. Hanna, Arthur Dunham, Edwin D. Solenberger, Jacob Billikopf, Helen Glenn Tyson, and J. Prentice Murphy. "Relief Needs and Conditions in Pennsylvania, August, 1931." *Social Services Review* 5, no. 4 (1931): 596–600.

Bamberg, Angelique. *Chatham Village: Pittsburgh's Garden City*. Pittsburgh: University of Pittsburgh Press, 2011.

Banfield, Edward C. *Government Project*. Glencoe, Ill.: Free Press, 1951.

Barnum, Darold T. *The Negro in the Bituminous Coal Mining Industry*. The Racial Policies of American Industry, Report No. 14. Philadelphia: Industrial Research Unit, Wharton School of Finance and Commerce, University of Pennsylvania, 1970.

Bartoletti, Susan Campbell. *Growing Up in Coal Country*. Boston: Houghton Mifflin, 1996.

Bateman, Bradley, Toshiaki Hirai, and Maria Cristina Marcuzzo, eds. *The Return to Keynes*. Cambridge,

Mass.: Belknap Press of Harvard University Press, 2010.

Baxandall, Rosalyn, and Elizabeth Ewen. *Picture Windows: How the Suburbs Happened*. New York: Basic Books, 2000.

Berg, Joel. *All You Can Eat: How Hungry Is America?* New York: Seven Stories Press, 2008.

Bernstein, Barton J. "The New Deal: The Conservative Achievements of Liberal Reform." In *Towards a New Past: Dissenting Essays in American History*, edited by Barton J. Bernstein, 263–88. New York: Random House, 1967.

"Big Association Groups Slow to Accept Cleveland Pact." *Coal Age* 22, no. 8 (1922): 298.

Biles, Roger. *A New Deal for the American People*. DeKalb: Northern Illinois University Press, 1991.

Blake, John. "Return of the 'Welfare Queen.'" CNN, January 23, 2012. http://www.cnn.com/2012/01/23/politics/weflare-queen/index.html. Accessed June 8, 2012.

Blankenhorn, Heber. *The Strike for Union*. New York: H. W. Wilson, 1924.

Blaszczyk, Regina Lee. *American Consumer Society, 1865–2005*. Wheeling, Ill.: Harland Davidson, 2009.

Blee, Kathleen M. *Women and the Klan: Racism and Gender in the 1920s*. Berkeley: University of California Press, 1991.

Borsodi, Ralph. "Subsistence Homesteads: President Roosevelt's New Land and Population Policy." *Survey Graphic: Magazine of Social Interpretation* 23, no. 1 (1934): 11.

Brands, H. W. *Traitor to His Class: The Privileged Life and Radical Presidency of Franklin Delano Roosevelt*. New York: Doubleday, 2008.

Brendon, Piers. *The Dark Valley: A Panorama of the 1930s*. New York: Vintage Books, 2000.

Brestensky, Dennis F., ed. *The Early Coke Worker*. Connellsville, Pa.: Connellsville Printing Co., 1994.

Brestensky, Dennis F., Evelyn A. Hovanec, and Albert N. Skomra. *Patch/Work Voices. The Culture and Lore of Mining People*. Pittsburgh: University of Pittsburgh Press, 1991.

Brinkley, Alan. *Franklin Delano Roosevelt*. New York: Oxford University Press, 2010.

Brophy, John. *A Miner's Life*. Madison: University of Wisconsin Press, 1964.

Brown, Linda Joyce. *The Literature of Immigration and Racial Formation: Becoming White, Becoming Other, Becoming American in the Late Progressive Era*. New York: Routledge, 2004.

Bryson, Bill. *At Home: A Short History of Private Life*. New York: Doubleday, 2010.

Buckley, Cheryl. "Modernity, Tradition, and the Design of the 'Industrial Village' of Dormanstown, 1917–1923." *Journal of Design History* 23, no. 1 (2010): 21–41.

Burness, Tad. *The Vintage House Book: Classic American Homes, 1880–1980*. Iola, Wis.: Krause, 2003.

Burns, James MacGregor. *Roosevelt: The Lion and the Fox, 1882–1940*. New York: Harcourt, Brace, 1956. Reprint, San Diego: Harcourt, Brace, Jovanovich, 1984.

Cahill, Kevin J. "Fertilizing the Weeds: The New Deal's Rural Poverty Program in West Virginia." Ph.D. diss., West Virginia University, 1999.

Campbell, Paul McCormick. "Westmoreland Homesteads: A Planned Community for Destitute Bituminous Coal Miners and Low Income Industrial Workers." Master's thesis, University of Pittsburgh, 1940.

Cannadine, David. "Andrew Mellon: Making Money and Giving It Away." *Westmoreland History* 16, no. 2 (2011): 20.

Carriker, Robert M. *Urban Farming in the West: A New Deal Experiment in Subsistence Homesteads.* Tucson: University of Arizona Press, 2010.

Carter, Thomas, and Elizabeth Collins Cromley. *Invitation to Vernacular Architecture: A Guide to the Study of Ordinary Buildings and Landscapes.* Knoxville: University of Tennessee Press, 2005.

Cary, Michael, ed. "75 Years of Homesteading: A Tribute to Norvelt." Unpublished anniversary book in the possession of the authors, 2009.

Chafe, William. *The Rise and Fall of the American Century: The United States from 1890-2009.* New York: Oxford University Press, 2009.

Cohen, Adam. *Nothing to Fear: FDR's Inner Circle and the Hundred Days That Created Modern America.* New York: Penguin Press, 2009.

Cohen, Lizabeth. *Making a New Deal: Industrial Workers in Chicago, 1919–1939.* New York: Cambridge University Press, 1990.

Coleman, McAlister. *Men and Coal.* New York: Farrar and Rinehart, 1943.

Conkin, Paul K. *Tomorrow a New World: The New Deal Community Program.* Ithaca: Cornell University Press for the American Historical Association, 1959.

Cook, Blanche Wiesen. *Eleanor Roosevelt.* Vol. 1, *1884–1933.* New York: Viking, 1992. Vol. 2, *1933–1938.* New York: Viking, 1999.

Cooley, Jill. "John Hollis Bankhead II." *The Encyclopedia of Alabama.* http://www.encyclopediaofalabama.org/face/Article.jsp?id=h-1424.

Cowan, Ruth Schwartz. *More Work for Mothers: The Ironies of Household Technology from the Open Hearth to the Microwave.* New York: Basic Books, 1983.

Craig, John. *The Ku Klux Klan in Western Pennsylvania*, Bethlehem: Lehigh University Press, 2015.

Crawford, Margaret. *Building the Workingman's Paradise: The Design of American Company Towns.* New York: Verso Press, 1995.

Cromley, Elizabeth Collins. *The Food Axis: Cooking, Eating, and the Architecture of American Houses.* Charlottesville: University of Virginia Press, 2010.

Crouse, Joan M. *The Homeless Transient in the Great Depression: New York State, 1929–1941.* Albany: State University of New York Press, 1986.

Currell, Susan. *The March of Spare Time: The Problem and Promise of Leisure in the Great Depression.* Philadelphia: University of Pennsylvania Press, 2005.

Daniels, Roger. *Coming to America: A History of Immigration and Ethnicity in American Life.* New York: Perennial, 2002.

DellaVigna, Stephen, and Ethan Kaplan. "The Fox Media Effect: Media Bias and Voting." National Bureau of Economic Research Working Paper No. 12169, April 2006. http://www.nber.org/pa

pers/w12169. Accessed June 8, 2015.

"Depression Era: 1930s: 'Bloody Thursday' and Other Labor Strikes." *Picture This: California Perspectives on American History*. http://www.museumca.org/picturethis/timeline/depression-era-1930s/political-protest/info. Accessed July 21, 2014.

DiCiccio, Carmen. *Coal and Coke in Pennsylvania*. Harrisburg: Pennsylvania Historical and Museum Commission, 1996.

Dickstein, Morris. *Dancing in the Dark: A Cultural History of the Great Depression*. New York: W. W. Norton, 2009.

Dinnerstein, Leonard, Roger L. Nichols, and David M. Reimers. *Natives and Strangers: A History of Ethnic Americans*. Oxford: Oxford University Press, 2010.

Dolkart, Andrew Scott. *The Row House Reborn: Architecture and Neighborhoods in New York City, 1908–1929*. Baltimore: Johns Hopkins University Press, 2009.

Domhoff, G. William, and Michael J. Webber. *Class and Power in the New Deal: Corporate Moderates, Southern Democrats, and the Liberal-Labor Coalition*. Stanford: Stanford University Press, 2011.

Dougherty, James. "A Reference Guide on Coal-Mining and Involvement of African American Miners in the Central/Western Pennsylvania Region." *Indiana University of Pennsylvania Coal Culture*. http://digital.klnpa.org/cdm/ref/collection/mining/id/273.

Downey, Kirstin. *The Woman Behind the New Deal: The Life of Frances Perkins, FDR's Secretary of Labor and His Moral Conscience*. New York: Doubleday, 2009.

Dubofsky, Melvyn, and Foster Rhea Dulles. *Labor in America: A History*. 8th ed. Wheeling, Ill.: Harlan Davidson, 2010.

Dubofsky, Melvyn, and Warren Van Tine. *John L. Lewis: A Biography*. New York: Quadrangle Books, 1977.

Dunham, Arthur. "Pennsylvania and Unemployment Relief, 1929–34." *Social Service Review* 8, no. 2 (1934): 246–47.

Durham, Martin, and Margaret Power. "Transnational Conservatism: The New Right, Neoconservatism, and Cold War Anti-Communism." In *New Perspectives on the Transnational Right*, edited by Martin Durham and Margaret Power. New York: Palgrave Macmillan, 2010.

Edsall, Thomas Byrne, and Mary D. Edsall. *Chain Reaction: The Impact of Race, Rights, and Taxes on American Politics*. New York: W. W. Norton, 1992.

Edsforth, Ronald. *The New Deal: America's Response to the Great Depression*. Malden, Mass.: Blackwell, 2000.

Eisinger, Peter. *Toward an End to Hunger in America*. Washington, D.C.: Brookings Institution Press, 1998.

Enman, John Aubrey. "Connellsville Coke: Catalyst and Victim of Change." In Brestensky, *The Early Coke Worker*.

———. "The Relationship of Coal Mining and Coke Making to the Distribution of Population Agglomerations in the Connellsville (Pennsylvania) Beehive Coke Region." Ph.D. diss., University of Pittsburgh, 1962.

Fenster, Julie M. *FDR's Shadow: Louis Howe, the Force That Shaped*

Franklin and Eleanor Roosevelt. New York: Palgrave Macmillan, 2009.

Field, Alexander J. *A Great Leap Forward: 1930s Depression and U.S. Economic Growth.* New Haven: Yale University Press, 2011.

Fishback, Price. *Soft Coal, Hard Choices: The Economic Welfare of Bituminous Coal Miners, 1890–1930.* New York: Oxford University Press, 1992.

Fitch, John Andrew. "The Process of Making Steel." In *Work-Accidents and the Law*, by Crystal Eastman, 238–43, Pittsburgh Survey 2. New York: Charities Publication Committee, 1910.

Foner, Philip S., W. H. Sims, George H. Williams, Andrew McCormack, C. C. Mehurin, M. I. Mattox, and B. W. Scott. "Knights of Labor." *Journal of Negro History* 53, no. 1 (1968): 70–77.

Foster, William Z. *Pages from a Worker's Life.* New York: International Publishers, 1939.

Fowler, Mayhill. "Obama: No Surprise That Hard-Pressed Pennsylvanians Turn Bitter," *Huffington Post*, April 11, 2008. http://www.huffingtonpost.com/mayhill-fowler/obama-no-surprise-that-ha_b_96188.html.

Fox, Maier B. *United We Stand: The United Mine Workers of America, 1890–1990.* [Washington, D.C.]: United Mine Workers of America, 1990.

Fraser, Steve, and Gary Gerstle, eds. *The Rise and Fall of the New Deal Order.* Princeton: Princeton University Press, 1989.

Friedel, Frank. *FDR: Launching the New Deal.* Boston: Little, Brown, 1973.

Gantos, Jack. *Dead End in Norvelt.* New York: Farrar, Straus and Giroux, 2012.

Garner, James S. "Leclaire, Illinois: A Model Company Town (1890–1934)." *Journal of the Society of Architectural Historians* 30, no. 3 (1971): 219–27.

———. *The Model Company Town: Urban Design Through Private Enterprise in Nineteenth-Century New England.* Amherst: University of Massachusetts Press, 1982.

Garraty, John A. *Unemployment in History: Economic Thought and Public Policy.* New York: Harper and Row, 1978.

Garvey, Timothy J. "The Duluth Homesteads: A Successful Experiment in Community Housing." *Minnesota History* 46 (Spring 1978): 2–16.

Garvin, Alexander. *The American City: What Works, What Doesn't.* 2nd ed. New York: McGraw-Hill, 2002.

Ghirardo, Diane. *Building New Communities: New Deal America and Fascist Italy.* Princeton: Princeton University Press, 1989.

Gilens, Martin. "How the Poor Became Black: The Racialization of American Poverty in the Mass Media." In *Race and the Politics of Welfare Reform*, edited by Sanford F. Schram, Joe Soss, and Richard C. Fording, 101–30. Ann Arbor: University of Michigan Press, 2003.

———. *Why Americans Hate Welfare: Race, Media, and the Politics of Antipoverty Policy.* Chicago: University of Chicago Press, 1999.

Gilfillan, Lauren. *I Went to Pit College.* New York: Blue Ribbon Books, 1934.

Gillete, Howard, Jr. *Civitas by Design: Building Better Communities from the Garden City to the New Urbanism*. Philadelphia: University of Pennsylvania Press, 2010.

Gilliam, Franklin D., Jr. "The 'Welfare Queen' Experiment: Viewers React to Images of African-American Mothers on Welfare." *Nieman Reports*, Nieman Foundation for Journalism at Harvard University, 53, no. 2 (1999): 2.

Glassie, Henry. *Folk Housing in Middle Virginia: A Structural Analysis of Historic Artifacts*. Knoxville: University of Tennessee Press, 1975.

Golay, Michael. *America 1933: The Great Depression, Lorena Hickok, Eleanor Roosevelt, and the Shaping of the New Deal*. New York: Free Press, 2013.

Gottfried, Herbert, and Jan Jennings, *American Vernacular Architecture: Buildings and Interiors, 1870–1960*. New York: W. W. Norton, 2009.

Grattan, C. Hartley. "The Vine-Covered Factory Worker." *Harper's Magazine*, January 1946, 69.

Green, Hardy. *The Company Town: The Industrial Edens and Satanic Mills That Shaped the American Economy*. New York: Basic Books, 2010.

Gup, Ted. *A Secret Gift: How One Man's Kindness—and a Trove of Letters—Revealed the Hidden History of the Great Depression*. New York: Penguin Press, 2010.

Gwin, J. Blaine. "Subsistence Homesteads." *Social Forces* 12, no. 4 (1934): 522–25.

Haines, Michael. "Fertility, Marriage, and Occupation in the Pennsylvania Anthracite Region, 1850–1880." *Journal of Family History* 2 (1977): 28–55.

Harding, T. Swann. "The Record of the Subsistence Homesteads." *American Journal of Economics and Sociology* 4, no. 4 (1945): 499–504.

Hargis, Evelyn. *Crossville Chronicle*, June 2, 2009, as found at http://cumberlandhomesteads.org/history.html. Accessed June 7, 2012.

Harris, Howard, and Perry K. Blatz, eds. *Keystone of Democracy: A History of Pennsylvania Workers*. Harrisburg: Pennsylvania Historical and Museum Commission, 2001.

Harvey, George. *Henry Clay Frick, the Man*. New York: Charles Scribner's Sons, 1928.

Haywood, Harry. *Black Bolshevik: Autobiography of an Afro-American Communist*. Chicago: Liberator Press, 1978.

Heilbroner, Robert, and Aaron Singer. *The Economic Transformation of America: 1600 to the Present*. 4th ed. New York: Harcourt Brace, 1999.

Heineman, Kenneth. *A Catholic New Deal: Religion and Reform in Depression Pittsburgh*. University Park: Pennsylvania State University Press, 1999.

Hiltzik, Michael. *Colossus: Hoover Dam and the Making of the American Century*. New York: Free Press, 2010.

———. *The New Deal: A Modern History*. New York: Free Press, 2011.

Hoagland, Alison K. "Introducing the Bathroom: Space and Change in Working-Class Houses." *Buildings and Landscapes* 18, no. 2 (2011): 15–30.

———. *Mine Towns: Buildings for Workers in Michigan's Copper Country*. Minneapolis: University of Minnesota Press, 2010.

Hoagland, Alison K., and Margaret M. Mulrooney. *Norvelt and Penn-Craft, Pennsylvania: Subsistence-Homestead Communities of the 1930s.* Washington, D.C.: Historic American Buildings Survey / Historic American Engineering Record, National Park Service, U.S. Department of Interior, 1991.

———. "Norvelt: A Pioneer Planned Community." *Westmoreland History* 4, no. 2 (1999): 29–47.

Holt, John B. *An Analysis of Methods and Criteria Used in Selecting Families for Colonization Projects.* Social Research Report No. 1, U.S. Department of Agriculture, Farm Security Administration and the Bureau of Agricultural Economics, Washington, D.C., 1937.

Homestead Houses: A Collection of Plans and Perspectives Issued by the Division of Subsistence Homesteads of the United States Department of the Interior. [Washington, D.C.: Government Printing Office, 1934.]

Hornstein, Jeffrey M. *A Nation of Realtors: A Cultural History of the Twentieth-Century American Middle Class.* Durham: Duke University Press, 2005.

Hovanec, Evelyn A. *Common Lives of Uncommon Strength: The Women of the Coal and Coke Era of Southwestern Pennsylvania, 1880–1970.* Dunbar, Pa.: Patch/Work Voices, 2002.

———. "Southwestern Pennsylvania Coal and Coke's Legacy: Economics and Values." In Brestensky, *The Early Coke Worker.*

Howard, Ebenezer. *Garden Cities of To-Morrow.* Cambridge, Mass.: MIT Press, 1965.

Howard, Walter T. "The National Miners Union: Communists and Miners in the Pennsylvania Anthracite, 1928–1931." *Pennsylvania Magazine of History and Biography* 125, nos. 1/2 (2001): 91–124.

Hubka, Thomas C. *Big House, Little House, Back House, Barn: The Connected Farm Buildings of New England.* Hanover: University Press of New England, 1984.

Humphrey, Hubert H. *The Political Philosophy of the New Deal.* Baton Rouge: Louisiana State University Press, 1970.

Hyman, Louis. *Borrow: The American Way of Debt.* New York: Vintage Books, 2012.

Jackson, Kenneth T. *Crabgrass Frontier: The Suburbanization of the United States.* New York: Oxford University Press, 1985.

Jenkins, Philip. *Hoods and Shirts: The Extreme Right in Pennsylvania, 1925–1900.* Chapel Hill: University of North Carolina Press, 1997.

Johnson, Garrett. "Culture: Hunger on the March." *Bits of News*, February 25, 2008, http://www.bitsofnews.com/content/view/7336/. Accessed December 1, 2011.

Joseph, Miranda. *Against the Romance of Community.* Minneapolis: University of Minnesota Press, 2002.

Katz, Michael B. *The Undeserving Poor: From the War on Poverty to the War on Welfare.* New York: Pantheon Books, 1989.

Kennedy, David M. *Freedom from Fear: The American People in Depression and War, 1929–1945.* Oxford History of the United States 9. New York: Oxford University Press, 1999.

Kern, Paul J. "The Bankhead Experiment." *Law and Contemporary Problems* 1, no. 3 (1934): 362–72.

Kerr, Clark, and Abraham Siegel. "The Interindustry Propensity to Strike—An International Comparison." In *Industrial Conflict*, edited by Arthur Kornhauser, Robert Dunn, and Arthur M. Ross, 189-212. New York: McGraw-Hill, 1954.

Kessler, Sidney H. "The Organization of Negroes in the Knights of Labor." *Journal of Negro History* 37, no. 3 (1952): 248–76.

Kessler-Harris, Alice. *In Pursuit of Equality: Women, Men, and the Quest for Economic Citizenship in 20th-Century America*. New York: Oxford University Press, 2001.

Klehr, Harvey. *The Heyday of American Communism: The Depression Decade*. New York: Basic Books, 1984.

Knowles, Morris. *Industrial Housing: With Discussion of Accompanying Activities; Such as Town Planning—Street Systems—Development of Utility Services—and Related Engineering and Construction Features*. New York: McGraw-Hill, 1920.

Krugman, Paul. *Conscience of a Liberal*. New York: W. W. Norton, 2007.

Kyvig, David. *Daily Life in the United States, 1920–1940*. Chicago: Ivan R. Dee, 2002.

Lands, LeeAnn. "Be a Patriot, Buy a Home: Re-imagining Home Owners and Home Ownership in Early 20th Century Atlanta." *Journal of Social History* 41, no. 4 (2008): 943–65.

Lapsansky, Emma. "Building Democratic Communities, 1800–1850." In *Pennsylvania: A History of the Commonwealth*, edited by Randall M. Miller and William Pencak, 153–202. University Park: Pennsylvania State University Press, 2002.

Lash, Joseph P. *Eleanor and Franklin: The Story of Their Relationship Based on Eleanor Roosevelt's Private Papers*. New York: Signet, 1971.

Lauck, W. Jett. "The Bituminous Coal Miner and Coke Worker of Western Pennsylvania." *Survey* 26, no. 1 (1911): 41–53.

Lawson, Alan. *A Commonwealth of Hope: The New Deal Response to Crisis*. Baltimore: Johns Hopkins University Press, 2006.

Lawson, Laura J. *City Bountiful: A Century of Community Gardening in America*. Berkeley: University of California Press, 2005.

Ledbetter, James, and Daniel B. Roth, eds. *The Great Depression: A Diary*. New York: Public Affairs, 2009.

Leighninger, Robert D. *Long-Range Public Investment: The Forgotten Legacy of the New Deal*. Columbia: University of South Carolina Press, 2007.

Leiserson, William M. "Labor Conditions in the Mines of the Pittsburgh District." *Annals of the American Academy of Political and Social Science* 33, no. 2, Labor and Wages (1909): 92–101.

Leuchtenburg, William. *Franklin D. Roosevelt and the New Deal*. New York: Harper and Row, 1963.

Levenstein, Harvey. *Paradox of Plenty: A Social History of Eating in America*. New York: Oxford University Press, 1993.

Levine, Susan. *School Lunch Politics: The Surprising History of America's Favorite Welfare Program*.

Princeton: Princeton University Press, 2008.

Lewis, Ronald L. *Black Coal Miners in America: Race, Class, and Community Conflict, 1780–1980*. Lexington: University Press of Kentucky, 1987.

Ligutti, Luigi, and John C. Rawe. *Rural Roads to Security: America's Third Struggle for Freedom*. Milwaukee: Bruce, 1939.

Lind, Michael. *Land of Promise: An Economic History of the United States*. New York: Harper-Collins, 2012.

Loomis, Charles P. "Rebuilding American Community Life." *American Sociological Review* 5, no. 3 (1940): 311–24.

López, Ian Haney. *Dog Whistle Politics: How Coded Racial Appeals Have Reinvented Racism and Wrecked the Middle Class*. Oxford: Oxford University Press, 2014.

Lord, Russell, and Paul H. Johnstone, eds. *A Place on Earth: A Critical Appraisal of Subsistence Homesteads*. Washington, D.C.: U.S. Department of Agriculture, Bureau of Agricultural Economics, 1942.

Lowitt, Richard and Maurine Beasley, eds. *One Third of a Nation: Lorena Hickok Reports on the Great Depression*. Urbana: University of Illinois Press, 1981.

Lowndes, Joseph E. *From the New Deal to the New Right*. New Haven: Yale University Press, 2008.

Lubin, Isador. *Miners' Wages and the Cost of Coal: An Inquiry into the Wages System in the Bituminous Coal Industry and Its Effects on Coal Costs and Coal Conservation*. New York: McGraw-Hill, 1924.

Maclean, Annie Marion. "Life in the Pennsylvania Coal Fields with Particular Reference to Women." *American Journal of Sociology* 14, no. 3 (1908): 329–51.

Maloney, C. J. *Back to the Land: Arthurdale, FDR's New Deal, and the Costs of Economic Planning*. Hoboken, N.J.: John Wiley and Sons, 2011.

McAdam, Doug, and Karina Kloos. *Deeply Divided: Racial Politics and Social Movements in Postwar America*. New York: Oxford University Press, 2014.

McAlester, Virginia, and Lee McAlester. *A Field Guide to American Houses*. New York: Alfred A. Knopf, 1997.

McElvaine, Robert S. ed., *Down and Out in the Great Depression: Letters from the Forgotten Man*. Chapel Hill: University of North Carolina Press, 1983.

———. *The Great Depression: America, 1929–1941*. New York: Times Books, 1984.

Mechling, Jay. "Oral Evidence and the History of American Children's Lives." *Journal of American History* 74, no. 2 (1987): 79–86.

Metheny, Karen Bescherer. *From the Miners' Doublehouse: Archeology and Landscape in a Pennsylvania Coal Company Town*. Knoxville: University of Tennessee Press, 2007.

Miller, E. Willard. "Connellsville Beehive Coke Region: A Declining Mineral Economy." *Economic Geography* 29, no. 2 (1953): 144–58.

Mintz, Steven, and Susan Kellogg. *Domestic Revolutions: A Social History of American Family Life*. New York: Free Press, 1988.

Mock, Michelle. "The Modernization of the American Home Kitchen, 1900–1960." Ph.D. diss., Carnegie Mellon University, 2011.

Moley, Raymond. *After Seven Years*. New York: Harper and Brothers, 1939.

Montgomery, David. *Fall of the House of Labor*. Cambridge: Cambridge University Press, 1987.

Moore, Marat. *Women in the Mines: Stories of Life and Work*. New York: Twayne, 1996.

Morawska, Ewa. *For Bread with Butter: The Life-Worlds of East Central Europeans in Johnstown, Pennsylvania, 1890–1940*. Cambridge: Cambridge University Press, 1985.

Mosher, Anne E. *Capital's Utopia: Vandergrift, Pennsylvania, 1855–1916*. Baltimore: Johns Hopkins University Press, 2004.

Moynihan, Daniel Patrick. *The Negro Family: The Case for National Action*. Washington, D.C.: Office of Policy Planning and Research, U.S. Department of Labor, 1965.

Mulrooney, Margaret. *A Legacy of Coal: The Coal Company Towns of Southwestern Pennsylvania, Historic American Buildings Survey*. Washington, D.C.: National Park Service, 1989.

Nasaw, David. *Andrew Carnegie*. New York: Penguin Books, 2006.

"New Numbers of Just How Many Americans Are Living in Poverty." World News with Charles Gibson. blogs.abcnews.com.

Nyden, Linda. "Black Miners in Western Pennsylvania, 1925–1931: The National Miners Union and the United Mine Workers of America." *Science and Society* 41, no. 1 (1977): 69–101.

Nyden, Paul. "Miners for Democracy: Struggle in the Coal Fields." Ph.D. diss., Columbia University, 1974.

Nye, David E. *Electrifying America: Social Meanings of a New Technology*. Cambridge, Mass.: MIT Press, 1990.

O'Farrell, Brigid. *She Was One of Us: Eleanor Roosevelt and the American Worker*. Ithaca: Cornell University Press, 2010.

O'Hara, S. Paul. *Gary: The Most American of All American Cities*. Bloomington: Indiana University Press, 2011.

Osman, Suleiman. *The Invention of Brownstown Brooklyn: Gentrification and the Search for Authenticity in Postwar New York*. New York: Oxford University Press, 2011.

Ottanelli, Fraser. *The Communist Party of the United States from the Depression to World War II*. New Brunswick: Rutgers University Press, 1991.

Palmer, Walter, and Charles P. O'Neill. *Report on the Miners' Strike in Bituminous Coal Field in Westmoreland County, Pa., in 1910–11*. House document, U.S. House of Representatives, 62d Congress, 2d Sess. Washington, D.C.: [Government Printing Office], 1912.

Parrish, Michael E. *Anxious Decades: America in Prosperity and Depression, 1920–1941*. New York: W. W. Norton, 1992.

Peffley, Mark, Todd Shields, and Bruce Williams. "The Intersection of Race and Crime in Television News Stories: An Experimental Study." *Political Communication* 13, no. 3 (1996): 309–27.

Penix, Amanda Griffith. *Arthurdale: Images of America*. Charleston, S.C.: Arcadia, 2007.

Phillips, Sarah T. *This Land, This Nation: Conservation, Rural America, and the New Deal*. New York:

Cambridge University Press, 2007.

Pickett, Clarence E. *For More than Bread: An Autobiographical Account of Twenty-Two Years' Work with the American Friends Service Committee*. Boston: Little, Brown, 1953.

———. "The Social Significance of the Subsistence Homestead Movement." *Journal of Home Economics* 26 (1934): 477–79.

Piketty, Thomas, and Emmanuel Saez. "Income Inequality in the United States, 1913–1998." *Quarterly Journal of Economics* 118, no. 1 (2003): 118–39.

Powell, Jim. *FDR's Folly: How Roosevelt and His New Deal Prolonged the Great Depression*. New York: Three Rivers Press, 2003.

Purdy, Jedediah. "The Roberts Court v. America: How the Roberts Supreme Court is Using the First Amendment to Craft a Radical, Free-Market Jurisprudence." *Democracy* (Winter 2012): 47.

Rasmus, Jack. *Epic Recession: Prelude to Global Depression*. New York: Pluto Press, 2010.

Rauchway, Eric. *The Great Depression and the New Deal: A Very Short Introduction*. New York: Oxford University Press, 2008.

Raymond, Eleanor. *Early Domestic Architecture of Pennsylvania*. Atglen, Pa.: Schiffer, 2007.

Reed, Adolph. "Race and the New Deal Coalition. *Nation*, April 7, 2008.

Reibel, Daniel B. *Old Economy Village*. Mechanicsburg, Pa.: Stackpole Books, 2002.

Reinert, Stephanie L. "Historic Shoaf: Its Beehive Coking Industry and Patch Life." In Brestensky, *The Early Coke Worker*.

Renshaw, Patrick. *Franklin D. Roosevelt*. Profiles in Power. New York: Pearson Longman, 2004.

Reps, John W. *The Making of Urban America: A History of City Planning in the United States*. Princeton: Princeton University Press, 1965.

Rice, Millard Milburn. "Footnote on Arthurdale." *Harper's Magazine*, March 1940, 411–19.

Roediger, David R. *The Wages of Whiteness: Race and the Making of the American Working Class*. London: Verso Press, 1991.

Rohatyn, Felix. *Bold Endeavors: How Our Government Built America, and Why It Must Rebuild Now*. New York: Simon and Schuster, 2009.

Rollins, Alfred B., Jr. *Roosevelt and Howe*. New York: Alfred A. Knopf, 1962.

Roosevelt, Eleanor. *The Autobiography of Eleanor Roosevelt*. Cambridge, Mass.: Da Capo Press, 1992.

———. *This I Remember*. Garden City, N.Y.: Dolphin Books, 1961.

Roosevelt, Franklin. *Looking Forward*. New York: Touchstone Book, 2009.

Rosen, Elliot A. *Roosevelt, the Great Depression, and the Economics of Recovery*. Charlottesville: University of Virginia Press, 2005.

Roth, Leland. *American Architecture: A History*. Boulder, Col.: Westview Press, 2001.

Russo, David J. *American Towns: An Interpretive History*. Chicago: Ivan R. Dee, 2001.

Sandow, Robert M. "The Impact of Coking: A Case Study of West Overton Village, Westmoreland County, Pennsylvania." In Brestensky, *The Early Coke Worker*.

Schantz, John, Jr. *Historical Statistics of Pennsylvania's Mineral Industries, 1759–1955*. Bulletin of the Mineral

Industries Experiment Station, no. 69. University Park: College of Mineral Industries, Pennsylvania State University, 1957.

Scheler, Michael B. "Technological Unemployment." *Annals of the American Academy of Political and Social Science* 154, The Insecurity of Industry (March 1931): 17–27.

Schimizzi, Sandra Wolk. "Eleanor Roosevelt and the Creation of A Spirit in the New Deal Community of Norvelt." *Westmoreland History* 14, no. 2 (2009): 4-9.

Schimizzi, Sandra Wolk, and Valeria Sofranko Wolk. *Norvelt: A New Deal Subsistence Homestead*. Charleston, S.C.: Arcadia, 2010.

Schlesinger, Arthur M., Jr. *The Age of Roosevelt*. Vol. 1, *The Crisis of the Old Order, 1919–1933*. Boston: Houghton Mifflin, 1957. Vol. 2, *The Coming of the New Deal*. Boston: Houghton Mifflin, 1958.

Schrag, Peter. *Not Fit for Our Society: Immigration and Nativism in America*. Berkeley: University of California Press, 2010.

Sellers, Charles. *The Market Revolution: Jacksonian America, 1815–1846*. New York: Oxford University Press, 1991.

Shalloo, J. P. *Private Police, with Special Reference to Pennsylvania*. Philadelphia: American Academy of Political and Social Science, 1933.

Sheppard, Muriel Earley. *Cloud by Day: The Story of Coal and Coke and People*. Chapel Hill: University of North Carolina Press, 1947.

Shlaes, Amity. *The Forgotten Man: A New History of the Great Depression*. New York: Harper Perennial, 2007.

Shopes, Linda. "Oral History and the Study of Communities: Problems, Paradoxes, and Possibilities." *Journal of American History* 89, no. 2 (2002): 588–98.

Singer, Alan. "Communists and Coal Miners: Rank-and-File Organizing in the United Mine Workers of America During the 1920s." *Science and Society* 55, no. 2 (1991): 132–57.

Smiley, Gene. *Rethinking the Great Depression: A New View of Its Causes and Consequences*. Chicago: Ivan R. Dee, 2002.

Smith, Jason Scott. *Building New Deal Liberalism: The Political Economy of Public Works, 1933–1956*. New York: Cambridge University Press, 2006.

Smith, Jean Edward. *FDR*. New York: Random House Trade Paperbacks, 2007.

Smith, Page. *Redeeming the Time: A People's History of the 1920s and the New Deal*. New York: Penguin Books, 1987.

Spann, Edward K. *Hopedale: From Commune to Company Town, 1840-1920*. Columbus: Ohio State University Press, 1992.

Standiford, Les. *Meet You in Hell: Andrew Carnegie, Henry Clay Frick, and the Bitter Partnership That Transformed America*. New York: Crown, 2005.

Steeley, James V. "They Sang Their Way Out of Jail: Mother Jones and the Singing Miners' Wives." *Westmoreland History* 16, no. 1 (2011).

———. "Westmoreland Homesteads: A Little Touch of Heaven." *Westmoreland History* 7, no. 3 (2002): 2–12.

Steeley, James V., and Sandra Wolk Schimizzi. "A Place in Time: Richard Kenah's Norvelt Mural."

Westmoreland History 14, no. 2 (2009): 10–11.

Stein, Clarence S. *Toward New Towns for America*. Cambridge, Mass.: MIT Press, 1967.

Stephens-Davidowitz, Seth. "The Cost of Racial Animus on a Black Candidate: Evidence Using Google Search Data." *Journal of Public Economics* 118 (2014): 26-40.

Sternsher, Bernard, ed. *Hitting Home: The Great Depression in Town and Country.* Rev. ed. Chicago: Elephant Paperbacks, 1989.

Stiglitz, Joseph. "The Book of Jobs." *Vanity Fair*, January 2012.

Stott, William. *Documentary Expression and Thirties America*. New York: Oxford University Press, 1973.

Stuart, John. "Constructing Identity: Building and Place in New Deal South Florida." In Stuart and Stack, *The New Deal in South Florida*, 31–70.

Stuart, John A., and John F. Stack Jr., eds. *The New Deal in South Florida: Design, Policy, and Community Building, 1933–1940*. Gainesville: University Press of Florida, 2008.

Susman, Warren I. *Culture and Commitment, 1929–1945*. New York: George Braziller, 1973.

———. *Culture as History: The Transformation of American Society in the Twentieth Century*. New York: Pantheon Books, 1973.

Taylor, Nick. *American Made: The Enduring Legacy of the WPA; When FDR Put the Nation to Work.* New York: Bantam Books, 2008.

Taylor, Paul, and Norman Leon Gold. "San Francisco and the General Strike." *Survey Graphic* 25, no. 9 (1934): 405–11.

Terkel, Studs. *Hard Times: An Oral History of the Great Depression*. New York: Pantheon Books, 1970.

Thelen, David. "Memory and American History." *Journal of American History* 75, no. 4 (1989): 1117–29.

Thernstrom, Stephan, ed. *Harvard Encyclopedia of American Ethnic Groups*. Cambridge, Mass.: Harvard University Press, 1980.

Town of Norvelt (Westmoreland Homesteads), Norvelt, Westmoreland County, Pennsylvania: Photographs, Written and Historical Data. Historic American Buildings Survey, Department of the Interior, Washington, D.C. HAB No. PA-5921. Washington, D.C.: National Park Service, Department of the Interior, [1991]. http://cdn.loc.gov/master/pnp/habshaer/pa/pa2500/pa2599/data/pa2599data.pdf.

Tyler, Tom R. *Why People Cooperate: The Role of Social Motivations*. Princeton: Princeton University Press, 2011.

Upton, Dell, and John Michael Vlach, eds. *Common Places: Readings in American Vernacular Architecture*. Athens: University of Georgia Press, 1986.

U.S. Bureau of the Census. Census 1940, Statistical Abstract of the United States, 1940. http://1940census.archives.gov/.

———. Census 1950, table 38, General Characteristics of the Population, for Urban Places of 2,500 to 10,000: 1950. http://www2.census.gov/prod2/decennial/documents/23760756v2p38ch4.pdf.

———. Census 1960, General Population Characteristics: Pennsylvania. http://www2.census.gov/prod2

/decennial/documents /17216604v1p40ch03.pdf.

———. Census 1970, General Population Characteristics: Pennsylvania. http://www2.census.gov/prod2 /decennial/documents /00496492v1p40s1ch3.pdf.

———. Census 1990, Census of Population, General Characteristics: Pennsylvania. http://www.census .gov/prod/cen1990/cp1/cp-1-40-1 .pdf.

———. Census 2000, Profile of General Demographic Characteristics: 2000. http://factfinder2.census .gov/faces/tableservices/jsf /pages/productview.xhtml?pid =DEC_00_SF1_DP1&prod Type=table.

———. Census 2010, Profile of General Population and Housing Characteristics: 2010, 2010 Demographic Profile Data. http://factfinder2 .census.gov/faces/tableservices /jsf/pages/productview.xhtm l?pid=DEC_10_DP_DPDP1.

———. *Historical Statistics of the United States: Colonial Times to 1970s*. Bicentennial ed. Washington, D.C.: Government Printing Office, 1975. http://www2.census .gov/prod2/statcomp/documents /CT1970p1-01.pdf.

———. State and County Quick Facts: Westmoreland County, Pennsylvania. http://quickfacts.census .gov/qfd/states/42/42129.html.

U.S. Coal Commission. Press release. Washington, D.C., September 22, 1923.

U.S. Coal Mines Administration. *A Medical Survey of the Bituminous-Coal Industry*. Washington, D.C.: Government Printing Office, 1947.

Van Hise, Charles. *Concentration and Control: A Solution to the Trust Problem in the United States*. New York: Macmillan, 1912.

Wagner, Ann Prentice. *1934: A New Deal for Artists*. Washington, D.C.: Smithsonian American Art Museum, 2009.

Ward, Bryan, ed. *A New Deal for America: Proceedings from a National Conference on New Deal Communities*. Arthurdale, W.V.: Arthurdale Heritage, 1994.

Warren, Kenneth. *Wealth, Waste, and Alienation: Growth and Decline in the Connellsville Coke Industry*. Pittsburgh: University of Pittsburgh Press, 2001.

Watkins, T. H. *The Great Depression: America in the 1930s*. Boston: Back Bay Books, 1993.

———. *The Hungry Years: A Narrative History of the Great Depression in America*. New York: Henry Holt, 1999.

"We the People of the Homesteads Feel, Think and Say, as Recorded by The Wandering Reporter." *Pennsylvania in Review*, October 9, 2012, 6–8.

Williams, Bruce T. *Coal Dust in Their Blood: The Work and Lives of Underground Coal Miners*. New York: AMS Press, 1991.

Willis, Lillian Clark. "A Tribute to the Black Miners of Bovard." Bovard 75th Anniversary, 1910–1985. The Bovard 75th Anniversary Committee, 1985.

Wilson, M. L. "The Place of Subsistence Homesteads in Our National Economy." *Journal of Farm Economics* 16, no. 1 (1934): 73–84.

Wright, Gwendolyn. *Building the Dream: A Social History of Housing in America*. Cambridge, Mass.: MIT Press, 1981.

Wright, Richard R., Jr. *The Negro in Pennsylvania: A Study in Economic History*. New York: Arno Press, 1969.

Yankovich, Ed. "The Rise of the United Mine Workers in the 1930s." In Brestensky, *The Early Coke Worker*.

Youngs, J. William T. *Eleanor Roosevelt: A Personal and Public Life*. 2nd ed. New York: Longman, 2000.

INDEX